"*Stand Up, Stand Strong* is an extraordinary book. Sara Barratt clearly understands the appealing but deceptive cultural values that confuse and derail countless believers, who, apart from learning to think critically, will likely abandon their faith. Sara is immersed in a biblical worldview that permeates everything she says. She writes with rare wisdom and insight. Often I read books that don't quite live up to what they could have been. This one actually does. I highly recommend it for young people everywhere. Older believers could benefit just as much. This is a terrific book for families, groups, and churches to discuss together!"

Randy Alcorn, author of *Heaven*, *If God is Good*, and *Deception*

"*Stand Up, Stand Strong* is a clarion call for students today to live out the worldview of Jesus in a countercultural fashion. Sara offers a bold challenge to this generation, and she equips them with the tools to carry it out. I highly recommend it."

Sean McDowell, PhD, professor at Biola University, speaker, and author of *Chasing Love*

"In *Stand Up, Stand Strong*, clear and biblically grounded cultural analysis is joined with a compelling and Christ-centered call to action. While this moment is full of challenge, Christians are called to speak and act with conviction and compassion. Highly recommended!"

John Stonestreet, president of the Colson Center and coauthor of *A Practical Guide to Culture*

"In a time when many young adults feel paralyzed by anxiety and uncertainty, Sara Barratt shows the way to hope and courage. Gen Z is ready to rise, and *Stand Up, Stand Strong* shows them how to do it. Desperately needed and timely."

Jeff Myers, PhD, president of Summit Ministries

"Sara Barratt is a fresh and needed voice in the church. In *Stand Up, Stand Strong* she addresses issues critical to this generation with a calm, clear, and compassionate voice. If you've got young people in your life (whether Christians or not), get this incredibly timely resource!"

"In *Stand Up, Stand Strong* Sara offers vital answers to some of life's most critical issues. I value and appreciate Sara's grasp of the challenges young people face and the meticulous care she takes to equip them to know and live out God's truth. A must-read for any Christian struggling to communicate what they believe in a secularized and sexualized culture."

"In *Stand Up, Stand Strong* Sara Barratt thinks deeply through some of the toughest issues of our day. She offers her readers a biblical lens through which to view this cultural moment—a lens that is shaped not only by truth, but also by grace. Both reason and humility are on these pages. I love that Sara is willing to go here and would love to see more Christians do the same."

Praise for *Love Riot*

"Sara Barratt wants to start a riot. An uproar. A disturbance for Jesus. Unlike some teenagers who want to disrupt and destroy, she wants to bravely build. With *Love Riot*, she is calling apathetic bystanders around the church to become wholehearted followers of Christ. She is actively driving and motivating her generation to live with reckless abandon because of God's great love. Undoubtedly, when you read, you will be captivated by her unrestrained outburst of irresistible faith."

"God is at work among my generation. There's no denying that, especially after reading *Love Riot*. In this passionate plea to fellow teenagers, Sara calls us to join her in rebelling against spiritual apathy and choosing instead to wholeheartedly follow Jesus, no matter the cost. This book will challenge you, encourage you, and ignite your pursuit of Christ. I highly recommend it!"

Jaquelle Crowe Ferris, author of *This Changes Everything*

"Every teenager needs to read this book. *Love Riot* will challenge your idea of what it means to be a teen that truly follows Christ. Sara Barratt raises the bar and calls her peers to a higher standard. This book has the power to change lives!"

Kristen Clark and Bethany Beal, authors of *Sex, Purity, and the Longings of a Girl's Heart* and cofounders of Girl Defined Ministries

"*Love Riot* calls the teenagers of the world to step up and step out in their faith and cause a riot against the low expectations set for youth across the globe. It may be aimed at one generation, but *Love Riot* has the ability to cause the riot it's intending through the hearts of the young to the old."

Riley Banks-Snyder, author of *Riley Unlikely* and founder of Generation Next

stand
up,
stand
strong

stand up, stand strong

A CALL TO BOLD FAITH IN A CONFUSED CULTURE

SARA BARRATT

BakerBooks
a division of Baker Publishing Group
www.BakerBooks.com

Published by Baker Books
a division of Baker Publishing Group
PO Box 6287, Grand Rapids, MI 49516-6287
www.bakerbooks.com

Printed in the United States of America

Library of Congress Cataloging-in-Publication Data
Names: Barratt, Sara, 1999– author.
Title: Stand up, stand strong : a call to bold faith in a confused culture / Sara Barratt.
Description: Grand Rapids, MI : Baker Books, a division of Baker Publishing Group, 2022.
Identifiers: LCCN 2021036894 | ISBN 9780801094415 (paperback) | ISBN 9781540902085 (casebound) | ISBN 9781493434015 (ebook)
Subjects: LCSH: Christian teenagers—Religious life. | Christianity and culture.
Classification: LCC BV4531.3 .B3655 2022 | DDC 248.8/3—dc23
LC record available at https://lccn.loc.gov/2021036894

Published in association with The Steve Laube Agency.

Baker Publishing Group publications use paper produced from sustainable forestry practices and post-consumer waste whenever possible.

22 23 24 25 26 27 28   8 7 6 5 4 3 2

For the glory of my precious Savior, Jesus Christ.
While I was writing this book, You gave me a deeper passion for
Your Word, a stronger commitment to Your truth, and a greater
understanding of Your love. I'm humbled and thankful. Your truth is
not always safe, easy, or comfortable, but it is always good. I echo the
words of the apostle Peter: "Lord, to whom shall we go?
You have the words of eternal life" (John 6:68).

By Your grace. For Your glory. Always.

Contents

Contents

Part Three: Generation Change 101

Introduction

Standing Strong in a Crazy,
Upside-Down World

All around me, I see a world going crazy.

I look at the rapidly changing headlines, the online debates, the political unrest, the constant noise of everyone sharing their opinions, and it's easy to freak out. I see evil applauded as good and good depicted as evil. I squirm in my seat every time I sit in the movie theater while the previews play, and I have a hard time fathoming the lyrics of most hit songs. Gender and sexuality have become options you can choose and change, decided by emotions instead of biology. Conversations about abortion, racism, and politics grow more volatile and divisive every day. Issues of morality have gone from unthinkable to unquestionable, and the pressure to conform to societal demands continues to increase. The landscape of the culture is changing so fast it's hard to keep up. Even if you can keep up, it's difficult to process it all and know how to live in the middle of this crazy, upside-down world.

It's even harder being a teen in this culture. While I'm technically no longer a teenager, I can still relate to the experience of growing up in the middle of our messy society. Those of us in our teens and twenties are learning our foundational beliefs, riding the emotional roller coaster of entering adulthood, and figuring out how to handle everything coming at us from every side.

If it's hard being a teen, try navigating life as a *Christian teen.* How do we process the messages the world is screaming at us from our iPhones and TV screens? How do we determine which voices are worthy of our attention? How do we rationalize the gap between what the world tells us and what our churches, parents, and Bibles say? How do we stand strong under the pressure of the culture and our desire to fit in?

Deep in our hearts we may think, *I want to follow God . . . but I'm afraid of missing out.* Or, *I want to know what's true . . . but everything feels so confusing.*

I've seen this struggle in the lives of countless teens. I've seen it in my own life.

It's the quick burst of embarrassment we feel when everyone knows a popular song or joke and we don't. Or the hot rise of rebellion when our parents censor what we watch or tell us who we can and cannot hang out with. It's the desire to finally be accepted when we've always felt excluded and not-enough. It's the craving to experience everything the world has to offer and taste the pleasure it promises. It's the pressure to hook up and give in to our sexual desires or the confusion of same-sex attractions. It's not knowing what to say when a friend tells us they're gay. It's the tug-of-war between popularity and holiness, obedience to God and acceptance in the world.

Have you felt this pressure, or is it just me? I've often found myself asking questions like, "How can I know what's actually true when truth seems subjective? What does living for God in a turbulent culture really look like? Why are God's commands so different from the world's perspective on [such and such a hot-button topic]?" As I've searched God's Word for answers, I've learned He doesn't leave us to navigate our crazy world alone. He has clear answers to our most confusing questions, guidance for our most difficult decisions, and holy truth to lead us along the way. This truth has transformed my daily lifestyle, mindsets, and beliefs and led me to live with clarity and confidence.

God created us for this cultural moment and placed us in this time in history for a purpose. It's our responsibility to live well in the days we've been given. The challenges of our current moment do not alter our God-given purpose. Neither can they change what is true or steal the hope we have in God's sovereign goodness. Throughout history, Christians have always impacted the world when they made the conscious decision to run toward the brokenness armed with love and the power of Christ, instead of away. But in order to be ambassadors of God's love to a hurting world, we must be equipped with the truth and healing He extends.

Do you want to know how to navigate the opinions you face every time you scroll social media or sit in a classroom? Do you crave solid truths for your struggles with identity or sexuality? Do you long for something concrete to stand upon instead of being tossed back and forth by every headline and viral news story? If so, this book is for you. We're going to dig into today's hot-button topics and learn how to biblically navigate culture as we cut through the confusion to discover the clarity of God's Word.

You'll be hearing the word *culture* a lot in the upcoming pages. It might sound like an overused catchphrase or maybe an abstract force looming over the world, but it's actually as practical and personal as the smartphone in your pocket. It's the environment around us, the shared ideals of a collective group that have become so ingrained in our mindsets and lifestyles we call them normal. *Culture* is, as Merriam-Webster defines, "the characteristic features of everyday existence . . . shared by people in a place or time."[1] Culture itself isn't immoral or wrong. Instead, it's the ideas and perspectives held within a particular culture that make it either harmful or helpful, God-honoring or sin-glorifying.

The ingredients of every culture are decisions, mindsets, and beliefs that overflow into actions, laws, and inventions. If you have good ingredients—wise decisions, moral mindsets, and biblical beliefs—you'll end up with God-glorifying actions, laws that do good instead of evil and protect instead of harm, and incredible inventions and creations that help humanity thrive. But if the ingredients are toxic or corrupted—unwise decisions, immoral mindsets, and unbiblical beliefs—you'll end up with a culture flooded with dysfunctional ideas that is harmful to the weakest and most vulnerable members of society.

Sadly, many of the "ingredients" within our society directly contradict God's Word and go against a biblical framework of truth. The prevailing opinions often do not align with wisdom, morality, and biblical truth, and we're experiencing the results of the brokenness daily.

Culture matters because culture shapes us. We become what we're exposed to. But is it shaping us for good? Are we becoming all God wants us to be? These are questions we're going to ask, and in order to do so, we need to take a step back and rethink our normal.

Are you ready? This book is a journey through the minefields of the world around us. It won't be safe, and I can't promise it'll be easy, but I believe it's worth it. I invite you to join me on this journey as we learn how to stand up and stand strong in a culture of tremendous pressure—no matter the cost.

PART ONE

rethinking normal

1

One Man Flipped the World

*(Jesus Changed Everything . . . and Why
That Matters Today)*

Jesus turned the patterns of the world upside down.

From the beginning of Christ's life, He began impacting culture—as an ordinary yet extraordinary infant who made kings fear and wise men worship. This baby grew into a man who made the blind see, the lame walk, and the dead live again. Everywhere Jesus went, He created a stir and defied the normal order of people's lives and ideas. He pushed back against the status quo that shrugged and said, "This is how it's always been done" to initiate new and better standards defined by the culture of heaven. He made outlandish claims, saying He not only knew the truth but *was* the truth. Not only that He knew a way to God but was *Himself* the only way to God.

He was surrounded by followers and fans who later turned into mobs, bloodthirsty soldiers, and betrayers crying out with shouts of "Crucify Him!" and nailing Him to a cross. He breathed His last on that cross with the words "It is finished!" only to do the unthinkable, unimaginable, and incomprehensible three days later: come back to life.

Now, two millennia later, Jesus is still making waves.

The words and message of Christ have spanned the centuries and reached into our generation. Just like every prior generation, we have a decision to make.

We have to decide what to do with Jesus's words.

Some claim He was just a prophet or well-known teacher. If that were the case, we could take Him or leave Him.

But what if He is who He claimed to be? The very Son of God? The Savior of our souls? The way, the truth, and the life?

That would change everything. In fact, it *did* change everything. Ever since the empty tomb, the gospel has radically impacted individual lives and entire cultures. What impact does the gospel make on *our* culture? More to the point, what impact does the gospel make on the way we *live* in our culture?

As with the people who first experienced Christ's countercultural message, these gospel implications might rub us the wrong way. To have the boldness and grit to live according to His teaching, we need to fully understand the answers to two questions: First, are the words of Christ true? And second, do they have the authority to tell us how to live our lives?

Life Led by the Gospel

Most Christians would say they believe the gospel.

But not all Christians *live* like they believe the gospel.

Let's take a minute to define what I mean by "the gospel." The message of the gospel opens with a holy God and rebellious people in need of a Savior. When Adam and Eve sinned in the garden of Eden, humanity's relationship with God shattered and there wasn't anything we could do to fix it. Instead of leaving us to fend for ourselves, God mercifully set a plan in motion to restore our relationship with Him. When Jesus died on the cross, He took our punishment upon Himself and paid our debt with His own blood, building a bridge over the canyon of our sin. When He rose from the dead, He arose as conqueror over sin, Satan, and death. Because of Christ's death, but more importantly, because of Christ's resurrected life, we can have life in Him. His gift of salvation is freely given to all who repent of their sin and believe in Him. The way to relationship with God has been made, but there's only one way and that's Jesus.

This gospel—this *good news*—isn't like any other news in the world. This news is life changing. The gospel hits deep into the core of a person and flows through every part of life. It shows us the true condition of ourselves—sinners who deserve God's judgment—and provides the only way of salvation.

Most of us who are Christians will nod and skim past these words. We know the story. But here's the real question: *Do we actually believe it?* If we do, it will radically overhaul our lives and revolutionize how we engage the world. If we believe the gospel, it will become impossible for us to live like the rest of society—because our lives will be built on a drastically different foundation.

But too often Christians embrace a watered-down message. We're content to believe Christ's death means we can have eternal life—but it doesn't cross our minds that it should affect how we live here and now. We're thrilled Jesus loves us enough to save us, but the thought of Him also wanting to change us is uncomfortable. Yet we can't have it both ways. The truth of the gospel means that Christ's words *do* have authority to tell us how to live. That authority changes everything.

Believing the full, undiluted message of the gospel is the first step to living counterculturally. If our view of Christ's teaching is compromised, we'll crumble under the pressure to conform instead of standing strong. Shallow convictions lead to shallow living and shallow Christianity, but solid principles and convictions help us obey Christ's command, "Follow Me."

What does that look like?

The Gospel Changes Our Life Purpose

Christ's words are action filled.

"Go into all the world" (Mark 16:15).

"Take up your cross and follow Me" (see Mark 8:34).

The call to follow Christ is not simply a call to believe a set of facts but to live a drastically transformed life. When we accept Christ's gift of salvation, our life purpose alters, and that changes how we view and live in the culture.

The world defines life purpose mostly in terms of "getting" or "achieving." While most might view success through the lens of a job, bank account, or relationship status, Jesus tells us "treasures in heaven" (Matt. 6:20; see vv. 19–21) are worth far more. While popular opinion declares happiness is an emotion to be sought by whatever means in whatever way (through relationships, sex, possessions, position, pleasure, entertainment, etc.), Jesus shows us that building His kingdom is the path to true fulfillment.

The gospel changes our life purpose by giving us meaning beyond the transient things of this world. We live for Jesus, not ourselves.

The Gospel Designates a Source for Morality

The Bible shares a jarring declaration: "There is none righteous, no, not one" (Rom. 3:10). The basic idea of morality today says you're moral if you're a good person who doesn't harm others. The flaw with this idea, however, is that it suggests humans can determine what is and is not moral. If we look to ourselves or other people to determine morality, we'll find an ever-changing definition.

Going back to the Bible, we realize "all have sinned and fall short of the glory of God" (Rom. 3:23). A sinner can't be an authoritative source for morality. We need a source of morality outside ourselves. Morality is not a concept for *us* to determine. Jesus, the only sinless person, has already determined it.

The Gospel Defines Truth

How do you know how to live if you don't know what to believe? How do you know what to believe if you don't know what's true? This is the conundrum our culture finds itself in. Truth has been subjected to feelings, and no one knows what's true anymore.

One of Christ's most audacious claims was about truth. He didn't say He had it or He knew it. He said He *was* truth. "I am the way, the truth, and the life. No one comes to the Father except through Me" (John 14:6). We can have confidence that our Christian message is actually true. Not true because we believe it to be but true whether or not we believe it. Christianity tells the truth about all of reality and the world itself.

In a society that denies the authority of objective truth, we're called to live according to the gospel's definition of truth. Because the key player in the gospel—Jesus Christ—isn't just a bearer of truth, but truth Himself.

The Gospel Reorders Our Priorities

"No one can serve two masters" (Matt. 6:24). Enter again the radical words of Christ, leading us to a crossroads. Throughout the Gospels, the kingdom of God is portrayed as a prize above all else. To those who love possessions, Jesus tells to seek treasures in heaven (see Matt. 6:19–21). To those who crave comfort, He hands a cross (see Mark 8:34–37). To those who long for familiarity, He says, "Don't look back" (see Luke 9:62). We are to seek *first* the kingdom of God (Matt. 6:33).

Our daily lives reveal our priorities. Christ? Comfort? Wealth? Security? Success? We can't serve them all. The heartbeat of the gospel is that Christ died so "that those who live should live no longer for themselves, but for Him who died for them and rose again" (2 Cor. 5:15). The gospel reorders our priorities, placing Christ above all.

The Gospel Realigns Our Authorities

Whether we realize it or not, through the saturation of social media, we've given our favorite YouTubers, Instagram influencers, and TikTok stars authoritative voices in our lives. We can all admit to being swayed by the loudest and most prominent voices around us, simply through the permeation of their influence. The gospel realigns these authorities, distinguishing between voices worthy of our respect and those that shouldn't have influence. We filter all authority through Christ—our supreme authority. We don't turn to the voices of the world for guidance on how to live, but rather to the words of Scripture.

For authorities designated by God (such as political leaders and law enforcement), we humbly submit to their governance in areas that align with God's laws. In the words of Christ, we "render to Caesar the things that are Caesar's" (Mark 12:17). But if earthly authorities ask us to sin, like the apostles forbidden to preach the gospel, we turn to our ultimate authority, declaring we "obey God rather than men" (Acts 5:29). As the Manhattan Declaration proclaims, "We will fully and ungrudgingly render to Caesar what is Caesar's. But under no circumstances will we render to Caesar what is God's."[1]

The Gospel Infuses Our Hearts with Hope

Because of Christ's jaw-dropping redemptive work in our lives, we can have hope in the midst of chaos and uncertainty. "Let not let your heart be troubled," Jesus said in John 14:1 (NASB). In a world gone crazy, we have confidence in His words: "I have overcome the world" (John 16:33). And not only has He overcome this broken place we call earth, He has also secured an eternally perfect place in heaven for those who trust in Him. We have hope that this world is not all there is. One day, every sorrow will be turned to joy (John 16:22), every tear wiped from our eyes, and every broken thing made new (Rev. 21:4–5). No matter what happens in this earthly life, this promise is secure. When we understand this, it radically shifts how we live here and now. Fear and anxiety don't have to rule our lives, but rather we can live with confidence and hope—our eyes fixed on Jesus, our hearts set on the goal of drawing others to know the hope we have in Him (Heb. 12:1–2).

A World Turned Upside Down

What would happen if we lived a gospel-defined life? How would the world change? How would *we* change?

As we consider how the gospel affects our lives, we're presented with a difficult and costly decision. Every day, you and I make a choice between three options:

1. We can live in sync with the world. We can disregard the words of Christ, follow secular patterns wherever they lead, or blaze our own path according to personal preferences.
2. We can push the issues of the world to the back burner in our minds and retreat from 100 percent following Christ. We can hold biblical beliefs on topics that make us feel good and speak out when it's uncontroversial. We can settle for an easy

life defined by compromise and subtle complicity, believing God's Word when it's convenient and comfortable. We'll be "Christians" but won't live as followers of Christ.

3. We can boldly counter the culture and live according to God's truth no matter the cost or risk. We can believe the Bible is the inerrant Word of God, mold our lives to its standards, and seek God for strength to live according to His ways.

I don't know about you, but for me the greatest temptation is the second option—retreat. It's the easiest choice for those who want to be Christians but also want a comfortable and risk-free life. Retreat is the choice many believers have subconsciously made. We've sat back in apathy and comfort and turned our backs on the brokenness instead of engaging the world as Christ commissioned.

Yet each day, we are given the opportunity to make our choice again. So, which path will we choose? Will we sit on the sidelines or will we rise up? Will we let the voice of truth die out on our watch or will we be the ones to raise our voices and proclaim it?

This is our time, and it's *not* time to retreat. Yes, it will be hard. We won't be popular. We won't be politically correct or culturally accepted. But God is calling us to this work and searching out those who will rise up and live out His truth. He's calling us to be a church that neither succumbs nor retreats, but stands firm upon His truth and shines a light in the darkness of our world.

Two millennia ago, that's what Jesus did. He shone the greatest light humanity has ever seen into the blackness of a broken world and illuminated the dark. That light was His love, His shed blood, and His resurrected life.

Wherever the gospel goes, it makes waves. If you counter the culture with the gospel and live according to its precepts, you will too. Are you willing to take the risk? Because it will be a risk, make no mistake about it.

With a wooden beam, a few nails, an empty tomb, and perfect love personified, one man flipped the world. The world desperately needs to encounter the power of the gospel. Will they see it in us? Believe it or not, the first step in letting the world see Christ in us is evaluating how *we* see the world.

Going Deeper

1. What's the hardest part of being a young adult in the current culture for you?
2. Would you say you believe the gospel? Do you think you live like you believe the gospel?
3. Have you ever encountered or believed a compromised gospel? What does a compromised gospel look like?
4. Outside of the six ways listed above, how else should the gospel transform your life?
5. Which of the three options of how to live daily did you choose? Which have you chosen in the past?

Further Resources

- *Counter Culture: Following Christ in an Anti-Christian Age* by David Platt
- *This Changes Everything: How the Gospel Transforms the Teen Years* by Jaquelle Crowe Ferris

2

What on Earth Is Worldview?

(Looking at the World through a Filter)

All I wanted to do was sit back and relax.

I was hanging out at a friend's house about to watch a movie. I had my favorite cuppa, a yummy apple scone, and a blanket. I was completely prepared to zone out in front of the corniest chick flick we could find.

But I just couldn't do it.

As the story unfolded, red flags began rising. I set aside my mug of tea, grabbed a piece of paper, and began writing down the messages coming through the story line and dialogue: ideas about the purpose of life, the meaning of relationships, and what it means to be happy and fulfilled. I'd noticed these ideas before, of course, in other films or song lyrics or while scrolling Instagram, but that night, I couldn't brush them aside. By the time the credits rolled, I had two pages filled with my messy scrawl.

All I'd wanted to do was zone out and relax. But I couldn't turn off my worldview.

It's an exhausting way to watch a movie. But it's absolutely the right way to live.

What Is a Worldview?

Whether you realize it or not, your worldview impacts nearly every part of your life. From beliefs as big as how the world was created to questions as important as "What career should I pursue?" to decisions as daily as what to watch on Netflix tonight, your worldview affects the answer, and the answer affects how you live.

Simply put, your worldview is the way you view the world. (You didn't see that coming, did you?) According to *Making Sense of Your World: A Biblical Worldview*, a worldview is "the framework of basic beliefs we have, whether we realize it or not, that shapes our view *of* the world and *for* the world."[1] Like a filter on Instagram, your worldview colors the picture you hold of reality and adjusts your outlook and perspective.

Who is God? Who am I? Why am I here? Why is the world so broken? What determines right and wrong? Have you ever asked yourself these questions? If so, you've wrestled with the foundations of this concept called *worldview*. Your answers to these questions point to what kind of worldview you hold.

Worldview is your built-in bias. You don't *put on* a worldview the same way you *put on* a pair of sunglasses. Professor Phillip E. Johnson explains, "Understanding worldview is a bit like trying to see the lens of one's own eye. We do not ordinarily see our own worldview, but we see everything else by looking through it."[2]

For example, your worldview may be different from mine because of our different backgrounds. Someone living in a developing country holds vastly different perspectives than someone who's never set foot outside suburban America. It's been said worldviews are "caught more than taught": you don't wake up one day and decide to embrace a particular worldview. Neither do you go to "Worldview College" and browse through the options to decide how you're going to perceive the culture. Instead, the process entails a slow formation of ideas and beliefs that cement themselves in your heart and mind.

In their book *Understanding the Times: A Survey of Competing Worldviews*, Dr. Jeff Myers and David A. Noebel say, "We call a pattern of ideas a worldview. . . . We all develop ideas . . . and our ideas naturally give rise to a system of belief that becomes the basis for our decisions and actions. Our worldview is like a map. It helps us know where we are, where we need to go, and the best route to get there."[3]

Some worldviews are true. Some are false. The defining aspect is what foundation a worldview is built upon. What ideas does it hold? Where did those ideas come from? Everyone's worldview is a bit different, but each is rooted in bigger beliefs about the existence of God, the meaning of life, the definition of morality, and the answer to what's wrong with the world. Just like a culture is concocted through its ingredients, so also a worldview can be measured by the validity, credibility, and truthfulness of the ideas it holds.

These ideas aren't waiting for us to come find them either. Every time we pick up our phones or walk into a store, we're being bombarded with messages. Your favorite song has a worldview. The shows you scroll past on Netflix do too, as well as the one you just binge-watched. How often are story lines focused on finding satisfaction or fulfillment—whether in a relationship, career, or fun? How often do social media posts tell us, "This is the perfect life"? How often do commercials or YouTube ads sell us something with the promise that we'll be just as happy as the people in the commercial if we do this or buy that? The ideas blasted at us from every side are rooted in a bigger worldview. The question is "Will we buy these ideas?" and "Will we catch this worldview?" Either way, these ideas impact our lifestyles, mindsets, and decisions.

For example, people who hold opposing worldviews will have different beliefs on what gives life meaning. Someone who holds a belief system that claims God doesn't exist will think it's foolish to expend their life obeying a higher power that (according to their beliefs) isn't real. They'll look for meaning in other things. On the other hand, someone who holds a belief system in which an all-powerful God is central will conclude that nothing is more important than serving and obeying the God who created them and who holds their future eternity. These beliefs will affect the choices each individual makes. *What kind of career should I have? How should I spend my days? What should I do in my free time?* A person's beliefs about God determine how they answer those everyday questions.

If we don't examine our beliefs on these fundamental topics, they will color our lives and choices while we remain unaware of their influence. We can't simply assume we have the correct worldview. We have to be sure of it.

In order to be sure of it, we have to know the source of truth.

One True Worldview?

Four percent.

That's how many Gen Zers hold a biblical worldview.[4]

That means only 4 percent of Gen Zers hold a majority of biblical perspectives on topics like the origins of the world, morality, identity, and the meaning and purpose of life. Only 4 percent look to the Bible to determine moral and spiritual truth and to guide their daily lives. But since *everyone* has some sort of worldview, what do the remaining 96 percent believe?

That's harder to answer because of the myriad worldviews in, well, the world. Researchers have narrowed in on several main worldviews, however, to make sense of how people view life and answer life's big questions. While we don't have space to explore them all, let's address two of life's biggest questions and discuss how various perspectives answer them.

I want to handle these perspectives with respect, even as I affirm there is only one true worldview and religion—that of Christianity and Jesus Christ. I agree with evangelist Chuck Colson's assessment that "the Christian worldview is more consistent, morally rational, and more workable than any other belief system. It beats all other contenders in giving credible answers to the great questions any other worldview must answer."[5]

The Existence of God

The foundation of every worldview is one major idea: the existence of God. Is there a God? If so, what kind of God is He? How do we learn about Him? What relationship does He have with humanity?

The God of the Bible is *Yahweh*—the all-powerful, all-good God who created the world in six days by speaking it into existence. He lovingly and justly reigns over the world He made and oversees the workings of the universe and the lives of every individual. He is trinitarian (Father, Son, and Holy Spirit). He came to earth in the person of the Son, Jesus Christ, to live, die, and rise again to provide salvation from the consequences of humanity's universal sin of rebelling against Him. The way to a relationship with God was bought by Christ's death on the cross. Jesus is the one way to God, a way of forgiveness paved by grace for all who repent and believe.

Islam answers the question "Who is God?" in some ways that are similar to Christianity—but different in many critical ways. The Arabic word for "God" is *Allah*.[6] In Islam, Muhammad is Allah's prophet. Contrary to the message of grace in Christianity, the way to eternal life in Islam is found by being a good person. If your good deeds outweigh your bad, you can gain entrance to Allah's paradise. Allah's mercy is still central, however. Muhammad reportedly said, "None of you would get into Paradise because of his good deeds alone, and he would not be rescued from Fire, not even I, but because of the mercy of Allah."[7] Islam also claims to be the only way to God. The nature of the Islamic god is sharply different than the Christian God. He is not a personal god who created humankind in his image. Nor does he relate to his people through the forms of Son or Spirit in the Trinity. Muslims strongly reject the doctrine of the Trinity and deny Christ's deity, as well as the validity of His resurrection. Allah is not viewed as a loving father but as an exacting master; humans are considered slaves, not sons and daughters.

On the flip side, atheists and secularists believe humans are the center of reality and that there is no God. Myers and Noebel suggest secularists "disdain the influence of those who believe in ideas of gods, an afterlife, or anything beyond what we can sense."[8] While Islam and Christianity are marked by belief in an all-powerful God, secularism is marked by belief in nothing but physical material. There is no God to obey, no afterlife to strive for, no ultimate authority beyond humanity. "Man is the measure of all things" sums up their perspective.

The Nature of Humans

The next question is "Who are humans?" How did humans come to exist? Do humans have value and dignity? If so, what gives them value? Are humans chemical machines who respond to external stimuli? Or sophisticated animals with advanced DNA? Every worldview has an answer.

Starting with the Christian perspective, the God of the Bible distinctly reveals His relationship with humanity. He says we are made in His image. The Bible shares the story of God's creation of humanity, how He breathed flesh to life from the dust of the earth, crafted both genders to complement each other, gave humans responsibilities, and established a covenant relationship with His people. We're not simply physical beings but spiritual, possessing God-given souls that will live on after our physical deaths, either separated from God in hell or in communion with God in heaven. Christianity affirms three truths about humanity: First, humans are intentionally created, not accidental by-products of natural causes. Second, humans have worth and dignity because they are made in God's image. Third, humans are designed to have a personal relationship with the God who created them.

Secularists believe the theory of evolution explains who we are and how we came to exist. They claim the creation of every living thing, from the smallest insect to your beating heart, evolved first from bacteria-like microorganisms that were modified and differentiated over hundreds of millions of years. Natural selection or "survival of the fittest" was key in this evolutionary process. Secularists refute the idea of intelligent design or anything spiritual. We are soul-less bodies that function because of a random chance of DNA. There's no afterlife, because the death of our physical bodies spells the death of our human consciousness. Intrinsic value and dignity are foreign concepts in the secularist worldview. As secular philosopher Peter Singer once stated, "Why should we believe that the mere fact that a being is a member of the species Homo Sapiens endows its life with some unique, almost infinite value?"[9] Human value in this perspective is found in the eye of the beholder, or in the value we give ourselves, not as an immutable reality held by every individual.

New Age spirituality has a completely different view of humanity than Christianity or secularism. Instead of affirming that we're created by God or believing we came from nothing, New Age spirituality believes we are in fact . . . God. At least we're all a part of something divine. *Everything* is spiritual. We're a part of "all that is," individual "droplets of consciousness,"[10] not distinct and created individuals. These beliefs are also called *pantheism* (*pan* means "all" and *theos* means "God," which translates as "all is God"). In this perspective, connecting with our godlikeness is humanity's goal.

As you can see, these worldviews hold vastly different opinions about God, life, and purpose. And they can't all be right.

The Battle of Ideas

Did you recognize any of these ideas? While you may not have heard these labels before, I'm sure the mindsets are familiar to you. Maybe you've seen traces of secularism in your classroom or noticed threads of New Age spirituality in a show you watched.

While current relativistic thinking might encourage us to affirm perspectives outside our own or to believe "All roads lead to God" or "Every religion is basically the same," we should have no doubt of the sharp differences that exist in worldviews. We didn't even address topics such as morality, the various perspectives on the afterlife, or details of how the world was created. Not all roads lead to God. Not all paths even claim to. In the same way, not all worldviews lead to the same answers on how we should live and what constitutes a meaningful life. Not all worldviews lead to the same standard of morality, because each has a different moral code.

The most dangerous aspect of worldview beliefs is that *you don't have to embrace the whole to believe and be influenced by the part.* You don't have to become an atheist to hold beliefs rooted in secularism. You don't have to convert to Islam to have a distorted picture of God's nature or consider yourself a New Age spiritualist in order to be influenced by New Age beliefs on humanity and purpose. You don't have to fully reject the Christian message to hold a worldview riddled with unbiblical perspectives. It's possible to claim to be a

Christian but live with a confused, secular worldview. It's possible to believe in God without letting a Christian worldview impact your daily life.

The less aware we are of the innumerable ideas around us, the more susceptible we are to believe whatever we're told or whatever we absorb. Worldviews must be taken seriously, because they're a composite of ideas. Ideas must be taken seriously, because they affect not only our lives but also the lives of those around us, and yes, even the entire world.

Ideas live within each human heart, venture into the world, and leave consequences in their wake. But consequences can be positive or negative. The words of Christ and the power of the gospel—the ideas of the Word of God—can positively impact our world. What if we set Christianity free from the bonds of cultural captivity and let the Word of God boldly impact every aspect of our lives? Can you imagine the impact it would have on the world? Ideas have consequences. God's truth has life- and culture-changing impact.

What Does the Gospel Offer Culture?

Every belief system acknowledges that something is wrong with the world. That's right—Christians, Muslims, and atheists all share common ground in thinking the world has issues.

But every worldview *does not* agree on the solution. Each offers a proposed solution, but their methods vary. Islam, for instance, claims God's mercy is given if one's good deeds outweigh one's bad deeds, thus encouraging people to live in ways that will earn them mercy. New Age spirituality and other pantheistic religions believe in karma, the idea that people are in a cycle of reincarnation and their actions in a previous life affect this life and that their actions in this life will affect the next. Atheists don't believe in God, so they say humanity is its own best hope.

Do you see the pattern? Other belief systems place *us* in the role of savior. Instead of thinking humanity could be the problem, they make humanity the solution. But when it comes down to it, what do we get? More of ourselves.

More of the problem. Not a solution.

What does the gospel offer in contrast?

Apologist Abdu Murray describes it brilliantly in his book *Saving Truth: Finding Meaning and Clarity in a Post-Truth World*:

> Where atheism tells us that we are the measure of all things, the gospel tells us that God is the standard by which we are measured. Where pantheism tells us that our problem is that we have forgotten that we are God, the gospel tells us that our problem is that we wanted to *be* God rather than commune with God. Where Islam tells us that we can earn God's forgiveness, the gospel tells us that such a view is self-contradictory and only Jesus' payment for our sins solves the contradiction. . . . The gospel tells us we are the problem and so, quite logically, cannot be the solution.[11]

The gospel stands in stark distinction to every other worldview. It traces the story of humanity through the phases of our creation and subsequent fall, which resulted in a broken world of sin, then writes a chapter of redemption and offers us a Savior. Christianity places Jesus front and center as our redeemer and restorer. That's why the gospel is good news to a broken culture and broken people. It doesn't minimize or deny our brokenness, nor does it compromise the solution.

Humanity will never be able to save itself. Our sin and immorality are too deeply rooted. We need a Savior outside ourselves to pull us from the depths of our sin. Jesus alone holds that power.

The gospel is the hope every human heart craves. The gospel restores our dignity, while being honest about our sin. It frees us from the burden of being our own rescuer and directs us to the One who went on the ultimate rescue mission. The gospel reveals our purpose in Jesus Christ and points to our distinct and deliberate design. No other worldview or religion has the depth to take on our hardest questions, deepest fears, and darkest struggles. Therefore, no other worldview can offer humanity what Christianity does.

If we're going to live boldly for Christ in a secular culture, we need to rebuild our worldview on the foundation of God's Word.

Building a Biblical Worldview

When it comes to forming a worldview, *intentionality* is key. As I said earlier, most worldviews are caught instead of taught, so we need to be careful about what view we're catching. What sources do we look to? Do we turn to friends, social media, TV shows, and the general mindsets around us? Or do we intentionally take a step back and go on a deeper search for truth?

First, who do you believe is God? What perspective holds the truth about Him? I believe Christianity holds the truth about God and that Jesus Christ is the one true way, the ultimate source of truth, and the giver of all life. Maybe you believe that too, but the next question is just as important.

How much influence does God hold over your daily life? Every worldview begins with a foundation. For followers of Christ, our beliefs about God are our foundation. But too often, we believe God to be the source of our salvation and the foundation of our spiritual lives, but not the foundation of the *entirety* of our lives. Our worldview is split down the middle, one half molded by God, the other shaped by the world. That's why many self-proclaiming Christians don't live Christ-transformed lives. That's why only 17 percent of Christians' beliefs align with a biblical worldview.[12] We've separated our relationship with God from our daily lives and are living out the great disconnect with compromise and complacency.

We cannot segment our lives into areas marked "secular" and "sacred." Christ's work on the cross was comprehensive and complete and calls for radical abandonment to His love. It leads us to lay everything—our preferences, our passions, our choices, our loves—at His feet and take up His standard as our own.

How do we intentionally allow God to be Lord of our entire lives?

It begins with absolute surrender to His lordship. Accepting not just His salvation but His saving truth into every corner of our hearts and souls. Inviting Him to overtake and overhaul us from the inside out. Identifying and eliminating any thought process or belief that doesn't align with His standards.

This is an ongoing process as we learn more of God and His Word. It's the continual practice of Romans 12:2: "Do not be conformed to this world, but be transformed by the renewing of your mind, that you may prove what is that good and acceptable and perfect will of God." The Word of God is good mind-renewing material. It's "living and powerful, and sharper than any two-edged sword, piercing even to the division of soul and spirit, and of joints and marrow, and is a discerner of the thoughts and intents of the heart" (Heb. 4:12). The Word of God cuts deep into our soul and spirit, down to our deepest beliefs about life's biggest questions and the struggles we face in this world of confusion. There is no belief we hold that God does not know, no thought in our hearts the Word of God cannot pierce.

We need to close the gap between our beliefs and God's truth, allowing His words to utterly impact and influence us. No more disconnect, no more double standards, no more split worldviews.

Earlier I said a worldview was like a filter on Instagram. It colors our perspective and molds our idea of reality. It adds splashes of color or mutes ideas and thoughts into tones of gray. There are myriad worldviews, and each makes the picture of the world look different.

God has given us a filter and it's His Word. As we dig into its truth and absorb God's perspective, allowing it to change our hearts and mold our minds, our view of the world will change. We will think differently, act differently, see things differently.

But maybe, instead of simply coloring our perspective with another filter or distorting our view, these words of truth will strip the subpar filters from our eyes, and we'll be looking at the world the way it was meant to be viewed all along.

We'll be looking at the world in truth.

Going Deeper

1. Before reading this chapter, how familiar were you with the concept of worldview? Did you realize you had a worldview?

2. Did you recognize the ideas in the different perspectives discussed? Where and how have you encountered those ideas before?

3. Which worldview do you believe is true? Do you recognize ideas from any other worldviews in your life?

4. What do you believe is the solution to the world's problems?

5. How can you let God's truth transform your life? What would that look like?

Further Resources

- *Understanding the Times: A Study of Competing Worldviews* by Dr. Jeff Myers and David A. Noebel
- *Understanding the Culture: A Survey of Social Engagement* by Dr. Jeff Myers
- *A Student's Guide to Culture* by John Stonestreet and Brett Kunkle
- *The Secret Battle of Ideas about God: Overcoming the Outbreak of Five Fatal Worldviews* by Dr. Jeff Myers
- Colson Center for Christian Worldview (www.colsoncenter.org)
- Summit Ministries (www.summit.org)
- Worldview Checkup (www.summit.org/individual-worldview-checkup/)
- BreakPoint podcast (www.breakpoint.org)

3

The Battle Surrounding You

(There's a War for Your Heart)

The year—605 BC. The place—Babylon. After King Nebuchadnezzar invaded Jerusalem, many teens found themselves torn from their homes and transported to a kingdom as foreign as it was immoral. Four of them were named Daniel, Hananiah, Mishael, and Azariah.

Put yourself in their shoes. Can you imagine being kidnapped and taken to a foreign country? Can you feel the despair? The ache for those you love? The anger at being the victim of your enemy's victory?

What would you have done? Rebelled? Attempted escape? Broken down in tears?

That's not what we see Daniel and his friends doing. Instead of attempting to escape their new life in Babylon, we see them attempting to live a holy life *in* Babylon.

Nebuchadnezzar's plan was simple—brainwash the youth. Teach these smart young men to forget their God and indoctrinate them into the gods and customs of the Babylonian Empire. Nebuchadnezzar knew the power of this one truth: if you own the youth, you own the future.

Nebuchadnezzar spared no expense in accomplishing his goal. The young men brought from Jerusalem were given three years of intense training and a portion of the king's delicacies. This wasn't mere basic provision. This was lavish, over-the-top, the greatest of honors.

And here, far from home, battling extreme loss and change, these four young men took a radical stand for the God they served. They said no.

They refused the delicacies and the lavish life Nebuchadnezzar offered. Daniel 1:8 tells us, "But Daniel resolved not to defile himself with the royal food and wine, and he asked the chief official for permission not to defile himself this way" (NIV).

When I first read this, I wondered, *Why the big deal over something as simple as food?* Didn't they have greater worries? But it wasn't just about the food for Daniel and his friends. It was about making an intentional choice to not allow the culture of Babylon to infiltrate their lives. By eating the king's food, not only would they have violated the dietary restrictions outlined in the Old Testament, they also would have been associating with the false gods the food and drink were no doubt dedicated to and with the notoriously immoral culture of Babylon. That was a price they refused to pay. A line they refused to cross.

They couldn't help that they were *in* Babylon. But they refused to be *of* Babylon.

The Battle for Your Heart

This world is a battleground.

Good and evil, right and wrong, God's ways and the world's ways are engaged in a fierce fight. And we are not neutral territory.

Maybe you look at the world and think, *It doesn't seem like a battleground to me.* Or maybe all it takes is opening your favorite social media app to catch a glimpse of the competing ideas and volatile messages on display. Everywhere we turn, we're blasted with messages about sexuality, identity, and marriage and surrounded by opinions about politics, religious freedom, and gender. The ideas we hear today have the ability to share the worldview we hold tomorrow.

And here we are, trying to sort through the bombardment of ideas, figuring out what we believe and why we should believe it. What's true? What's false? Should we even care?

Like Daniel, Hananiah, Mishael, and Azariah, we're stuck in a culture of immorality. The goal is not to figure out how we can escape "Babylon," but rather, through the power of God, how we can live a holy life *in* Babylon. Jesus prayed that His followers would not be taken out of the world, but kept from the evil one, because "[we] are not of the world, just as [He is] not of the world" (John 17:16). I love how Philippians 2:15 states our goal: "that you may become blameless and harmless, children of God without fault in the midst of a crooked and perverse generation, among whom you shine as lights in the world."

This is "a crooked and perverse generation," no doubt about it. But we can still live as "children of God without fault." Let's discover five battlegrounds of our hearts and culture.

Battleground #1: Identity

The first thing Nebuchadnezzar targeted was *identity*. Changing the names of Daniel, Hananiah, Mishael, and Azariah to Belteshazzar, Shadrach, Meshach, and Abed-Nego was step one in the process of indoctrinating them.

Each of their Hebrew names had meanings connected to God. For example, Daniel means "God is my judge," and Hananiah means "*Yah* is gracious." Nebuchadnezzar knew this and changed their names to refer to Babylonian idols. Belteshazzar means "Bel protects his life," and Abed-Nego means "Servant of Nebo."[1] By changing their names, Nebuchadnezzar sought to rebrand their identity and shift the object of their worship from Yahweh to the idols of Babylon.

Our generation is experiencing an unprecedented identity crisis. We don't know who we are, why we're alive, or what our purpose is. The main message proclaimed from our T-shirts, Instagram stories, and coffee mugs is: "Be yourself." "Find your true self." "Be who you want to be." "Don't let anyone tell you who you are." *Be you.*

But what does that really mean? Countless resources encourage teens to engage in a process of self-discovery. We're encouraged to find out who we are and also told we can *select* our identity. We can identify with anything imaginable, and it will be affirmed that is indeed *who we are*. Our identity is not intrinsic but chosen.

You would think in this atmosphere that identity crises would be nonexistent. But they're not. Instead, we're floundering for objective truth about identity and purpose. Choosing our own identities is pressure we were never intended to carry, because God has already written the script that defines who we are.

Our identities aren't malleable to our preferences but secure in God's absolute truth. We have an intrinsic, God-given identity that is secured the moment we are conceived. Followers of Jesus also have a blood-bought identity that is secured the moment we are saved. Nothing the world says or does can alter these two truths.

Understanding our identity begins with a greater understanding of God. While culture places secure identity within a journey of self-discovery, that journey is a dead-end road. We don't need more self-discovery. We need more God-discovery.

Battleground #2: Loyalty

Daniel and his friends drew a line in the sand when they refused to eat the king's food. But fast-forward three chapters and suddenly the issue wasn't food anymore. Suddenly it was a life-or-death decision of loyalties.

Nebuchadnezzar made an image of gold, set it up, and demanded loyalty to him and him alone with the words "Bow down." With the order to bow came the consequence of refusal—immediate death in a fiery furnace. In this battle of culture, the stakes had just increased. What choice would Shadrach, Meshach, and Abed-Nego[2] make in the face of certain death?

They didn't falter or waver. Their loyalty remained with God no matter the consequences. They refused to bow.

Nebuchadnezzar raged, the furnace was heated, and three men stood strong with the words, "Our God whom we serve is able to deliver us from the burning fiery furnace, and He will deliver us from your hand, O king. But if not, let it be known to you, O king, that we do not serve your gods, nor will we worship the gold image which you have set up" (Dan. 3:17–18).

Culture always asks us to bow down. The question is—*to what?* And will we recognize the bend of our knees before we hit the ground? The battle for our loyalties is fierce and "gold images" abound.

Why is peer pressure strong? Why is it hard to say no? Why is it difficult to walk a different path? Because others have already bowed to the idols culture creates. The majority of the world has—consciously or subconsciously—cast their loyalties at the feet of an immoral culture's golden images. Our world worships sex, unrestrained self-expression, self-indulgence, pleasure, and unfettered autonomy. It chafes at restrictions, guidelines, and moral codes and rebels against the truth that there is a holy God who created us, desires our loyalty, and has the authority to direct our lives.

By rejecting these truths, many people believe they're living out the definition of freedom. But what they don't realize is they're actually casting their loyalty into the hands of a ruthless master, selling themselves for the price of "freedom." The apostle Paul says it best in Romans 6:16: "Don't you know that when you offer yourselves to someone as obedient slaves, you are slaves of the one you obey— whether you are slaves to sin, which leads to death, or to obedience, which leads to righteousness?" (NIV).

No matter an individual's beliefs about God, we are hardwired to worship. The idols of culture seek to be the objects of our worship. Like Shadrach, Meshach, and Abed-Nego faced with a golden statue and a command to bow, we have a choice. Will we submit to the idols culture sets up? Or will we make a conscious choice to serve God alone?

Battleground #3: Thoughts and Mindsets

Nebuchadnezzar's plan of brainwashing the young men from Jerusalem was initiated with three years' training to teach them "the language and literature of the Babylonians" (Dan. 1:4 NIV). These three years could more accurately be called retraining. Changing a person's thought patterns requires more time and effort than simply teaching them new information.

The way we think changes the way we live. When it comes to mindsets, the biggest problem is not that bad ideas exist. Bad ideas have always existed and will continue to exist while sin remains. The biggest problem is we have lost our ability to think. We think more frequently with our emotions instead of our intellect. *How does this make me feel?* is considered more important than *Is this true? Is it moral? Does it make logical sense?* We don't know how to dissect ideas without being influenced by them or entertain a thought without accepting it. We don't recognize the countless messages we process every day or those staring us in the face in every media outlet. Instead, the ideas permeating our culture have reached the point of simply becoming *normal.* Once an idea becomes normal, it becomes incredibly powerful.

We need to backpedal from our opinions on what constitutes normal and reactivate our brains to dig deep into concepts to evaluate them for truth. Our goal is not to be insulated from secular ideas but to intellectually and spiritually evaluate them and make a conscious decision to accept or reject them. Much of our society has an atrophied ability to reason, but God calls us to wise thinking and sound minds. The words of 2 Corinthians 10:5 give us our battle plan: "We demolish arguments and every pretension that sets itself up against the knowledge of God, and we take captive every thought to make it obedient to Christ" (NIV).

Battleground #4: Habits and Lifestyles

In the sixth chapter of the book of Daniel, we catch a glimpse of Daniel's habits. Three times a day, he knelt in his room and prayed and gave thanks to God. This habit was a bedrock of strength as he sought to remain faithful in a culture of opposition. But naturally, the opposition put up a fight.

We can't blame Nebuchadnezzar for this one, since another king—King Darius—was now reigning over Babylon. The government officials were upset by how much the king trusted Daniel and how he was rising in the ranks of the kingdom, so they began to plot a way to trap him. The only problem? Daniel was so faithful his only "weak link" was his devotion to God. So the government officials issued a decree: anyone praying to or petitioning any god or man except King Darius should be thrown into a den of lions. This decree struck a targeted blow to Daniel's habit of prayer.

But what's the next thing we see Daniel doing? Continuing to pray. They attacked his habit, but he didn't give in. Once secular culture has control of our lifestyle, its rule over us knows no end. Our habits are at the core of our lives and priorities. These habits aren't simply what we do every morning or how we spend our free time but extend into thought patterns and lifestyles. We have relationship habits that affect how we treat people and dating habits that affect our romantic relationships and views of sexuality. We have entertainment habits that impact what we spend our time watching, listening to, or reading. We have spiritual habits that impact the role we give God, church, and the Bible. Our lives are flooded with both internal and external habits, and understanding how culture impacts those habits is important.

Battleground #5: Spiritual Forces

Years after arriving in Babylon, Daniel came face-to-face with a spiritual battle raging around him. God began revealing information about future events to Daniel through dreams and visits from angels (Dan. 7–8). In the midst of receiving these prophecies, God led Daniel to fast and pray for three weeks. After the three weeks were over, he had another visit from an angel. This angel told Daniel that his prayers had been heard from day one, but an evil angel, "the prince of the kingdom of Persia," had fought against him (Dan. 10:13).

The angel spoke of invisible battles raging over countries and cultures. The Bible affirms the reality of these spiritual wars in Ephesians 6: "We do not wrestle against flesh and blood, but against principalities, against powers, against the rulers of the darkness of this age, against spiritual hosts of wickedness in the heavenly places" (v. 12).

We are ultimately in a spiritual battle. Satan and his demons are waging war over every country and culture, seeking to hinder the spread of the gospel, weaken God's people, and broaden the influence of evil. Far from being relegated to horror movies, demons and evil are alive and active in the world. We often live completely unaware of the spiritual battles around us, but the evidence is present at every turn. From movies, music, and books that glorify evil to people dabbling in witchcraft and the occult to the subtle ways we allow sin to grow in our lives, the devil is prowling about like a lion, wielding his weapons and "seeking whom he may devour" (1 Pet. 5:8).

We need to be aware of this battle for three reasons: First, we need to know how to fight. We're called to "be strong in the Lord" and "put on the whole armor of God, that [we] may be able to stand against the wiles of the devil" (Eph. 6:10, 11). Second, we cannot give evil entrance into our hearts and lives. Even the smallest doses we think we can "handle" open the door wider for greater demonic influence. We can't play with evil but must fight against it with the armor God has given us in His Word. And finally, we must remember that we don't wrestle against flesh and blood. People are not our true enemy. Neither are politics, media, or other secular systems, though Satan may use them to fulfill his agenda.

Like Daniel, we are participants in the battle. Daniel's prayers exactly covered the time the angel was wrestling with the prince of Persia, and his prayers had an impact on the invisible realm. Prayer, praise, and God's Word are powerful weapons. We have a complete set of spiritual armor described in Ephesians 6:

> Stand your ground, putting on the belt of truth and the body armor of God's righteousness. For shoes, put on the peace that comes from the Good News so that you will be fully prepared. In addition to all of these, hold up the shield of faith to stop the fiery arrows of the devil. Put on salvation as your helmet, and take the sword of the Spirit, which is the word of God. (vv. 14–17 NLT)

While spiritual battles may rage, we can approach the fight with confidence because Jesus already won the war. He broke the power of darkness with His resurrected life and one day He will return and bind all the powers of evil once and for all (Rev. 20:10).

Your Counterattack

Now that we've discussed five battlegrounds of culture, let's dive into four ways to stay strong.

1. Know Your Weapons

Every battle requires weapons, and God has powerfully equipped us. The Word of God is "living and active, and sharper than any two-edged sword" (Heb. 4:12 NASB). Not only do we have the written Word, we also have the incarnate Word—Jesus Christ.

In order for Daniel and his friends to stay strong in Babylon, they had to take a radical stand for God and be entirely convinced of what they believed and who they believed in. Apologetics professor Nancy Pearcey says, "We must begin by being utterly convinced that there *is* a biblical perspective on everything—not just on spiritual matters."[3] We must intentionally ground our hearts and minds in the truth of God and His Word and be saturated with Scripture if we desire to have the same strength of conviction as these four young men.

2. Stand Strong in Prayer

Whether we realize it or not, prayer has a powerful impact on the landscape of society. I sometimes wonder if one of the reasons we're witnessing such rapid moral shifts in our society is because Christians have neglected their responsibility to pray.

Paul ends his description of our spiritual armor in Ephesians with a call to pray "always with all prayer and supplication in the Spirit" (6:18). Prayer is the way we engage in spiritual battle and the very reason we're armed. Putting on the armor of God prepares us for battle; prayer is stepping onto the battlefield. It is some of the hardest culture-impacting work we can do, because we usually don't see the fruit of our labor with our own eyes. Yet our prayers *do* make a difference, and prayer strengthens our own walk with God. Writing to a church living in the midst of a dangerous environment, Peter encouraged them this way: "But the end of all things is at hand, therefore be serious and watchful in your prayers" (1 Pet. 4:7).

If we're serious about living boldly for God and engaging culture with the gospel, we must also be serious in our prayers.

3. Evaluate Messages

Evaluate the things you come across each day to determine the concepts they hold. A song, something a teacher or textbook says, a TV show, the magazines on display at the grocery store. Study the ideas they promote and ask yourself these questions:

- What is this saying?
- What source is saying this? Is this source trustworthy?
- What lifestyle is this idea promoting?
- What worldview is being promoted?
- What does the Bible have to say about this idea? Can it be backed up by Scripture?
- Is this idea influenced by evil?
- Have I ever believed this idea?
- If I believed this idea, how would it change the way I live?

The more you practice evaluating messages, the more quickly you can identify the answers to these questions and how those messages affect you and your beliefs about God, yourself, and the world.

4. Draw Your Line

We often think of "big things" when it comes to standing strong—fighting for a cause despite opposition or refusing to compromise even if it means losing a job, friend, or reputation. But if we're going to be faithful in those moments, we have to draw the line further back and be faithful in small areas, such as developing strong spiritual disciplines (like Bible study and prayer) or saying no to entertainment with unbiblical worldviews.

Daniel and his friends weren't immediately confronted with fiery furnaces and lions' dens when they arrived in Babylon. It would have been easy to look at the sumptuous spread of the king's food and blow it off as no big deal. But if they had, how prepared would they have been to face a wall of fire or a violent lion? Their faithfulness grew with their daily decisions, which prepared them for the battles to come. You don't get to the point of staring boldly at the face of death if you cower at the thought of discomfort, ridicule, or people's opinions. Draw your line and refuse to compromise. As Jesus said, "If you are faithful in little things, you will be faithful in large ones" (Luke 16:10 NLT).

Bold Faith in the Battle

We will never impact the world if we become like it. The beauty of Christ's love will never shine through if our hearts are clouded with secular messages.

Every time Daniel, Hananiah, Mishael, and Azariah took a stand for holiness and refused to compromise, God's glory was put on display. From fire that couldn't consume to lions with closed mouths, the greatest displays of God's power came after the greatest acts of obedience. By their faithfulness to God, these young men inspired ungodly kings to worship and declare the splendor of the God they served.

If we, like them, will have the courage to live boldly for Christ in the middle of our Babylon, our transformed lives of faithfulness can be a picture of the power of the God we serve: the One who walks with us through fire, shuts the mouths of lions, and redeems broken cultures for the glory of His name.

Going Deeper

1. How familiar were you with the story of Daniel and his friends? Do you notice any parallels between their story and your own life?

2. What messages about identity have you noticed within society?

3. What habits do you have that culture has impacted? Why are habits important?

4. Why is it important to recognize and evaluate the messages we encounter?

5. What lines have you had to draw *or* what lines do you need to draw? Why is daily faithfulness so vital?

Further Resources

- *The Screwtape Letters* by C. S. Lewis
- *The Invisible War: What Every Believer Needs to Know about Satan, Demons, and Spiritual Warfare* by Chip Ingram
- *Living Among Lions: How to Thrive like Daniel in Today's Babylon* by David and Jason Benham

4

Don't Buy the Lies

(Knowing Truth in a Post-Truth World)

"Everyone can believe anything they want so long as it doesn't hurt anyone," Abby said. "After all, it's impossible to know what's true, so we should each just live our own truths."

"Well, that may be true for you," Devin responded, "but it's not true for me. Truth is really just a matter of opinion."

"All religions are basically the same, anyway," Grace affirmed. "People just need to get over their differences and coexist."

These three statements are classic examples of a mindset infiltrating our society. This mindset is defined as *post-truth*.

Say Hello to a Post-Truth World

In 2016, the Oxford Dictionary named *post-truth* their word of the year. Oxford defines *post-truth* as "relating to or denoting circumstances in which objective facts are less influential in shaping public opinion than appeals to emotion and personal belief."[1]

A post-truth environment exists when people are directed by subjective feelings rather than objective facts. We're all susceptible to this. We innately stick with beliefs and ideas that make us feel good. While post-truth mindsets are becoming more evident culture-wide, these seeds of relativistic thinking grow in each of our hearts. A post-truth world is not one in which truth has ceased to *exist*, but one in which truth has ceased to *matter*. Truth becomes personal, all "truths" (aka opinions) are equally valid, and feelings have the upper hand. "What's true for you doesn't have to be true for me" is the mantra of the post-truth age.

This clash with truth occurs on a daily basis in ways big and small. Have you ever read a news story only to find out later it was slanted to the writer's agenda and didn't tell the full story? Or have you ever seen someone believe something (or held a belief yourself) just because it was posted on social media when a few moments of research would have quickly debunked the idea? Or had a conversation and listened to someone stubbornly hold to their perspective even if concrete facts supported another view?

Each of these examples points to a post-truth mindset. We want truth when it conforms to our own point of view and affirms what we already believe. Facts are willingly sacrificed to project an agenda or affirm one's own bias.

Post-truth thinking is able to thrive because people have become confused on what *truth* even means. What is truth, anyway? Is it possible to know truth? How can you be certain of what's true?

The answer to these questions comes when we understand the various forms of truth that exist. One form is *subjective truth*. "Country music is the best" is an example of subjective truth. That statement is 100 percent true in my opinion because I love country music, but the same statement is 100 percent false for someone who can't stand John Denver or Carrie Underwood. The statement is only true for people who enjoy country music—it's a subjective truth claim because it deals with preference and personal taste. In cases of subjective, personal inclinations, "True for you, but not for me" is, well, true.

On the other hand, there is *objective truth*. "Grass is green," "George Washington was the first president of the United States," and "Two plus two equals four" are all statements of objective truth. You can't argue with them and you can't disagree with them. They're simply statements of reality. In cases of objective actuality, "True for you, but not for me" is simply ludicrous.

Secular culture doesn't deny the existence of objective truth (you'll never find a politician arguing that grass really isn't green . . . I hope). But it does argue over what does and does not equal objective truth. Matters of religion, morality, and identity have all moved from the "objective" category into the "subjective." "Jesus is the Son of God," "Gender is fixed, not fluid," and "Marriage is meant to be between a man and a woman" are now considered statements more reflective of personal opinion than objective reality.

But that all depends on who gets to determine objective reality. According to culture, we are the ones who get to decide based on our preferences. According to God, He is the only One who has the authority to make that distinction. Moral absolutes do exist if a moral authority also exists. But because even the existence of God has become a subjective truth, everything else in our lives and society that really matters has also been relegated to the realm of the subjective. And post-truth is born the moment the objective is placed in the position of the subjective.

Post-truth thinking is deadly. If we don't know the truth, how will we know how to live? How will we define right and wrong? For Christians seeking the absolute truth of God, post-truth thinking is incredibly serious. Is it any wonder there's an attack on truth in our society when the enemy of our souls is the father of lies? Satan "does not stand in the truth, because there is no truth in him. When he speaks a lie, he speaks from his own resources, for he is a liar and the father of it" (John 8:44). Why wouldn't Satan target truth? Getting people to doubt truth and believe lies causes them to speak his native language.

God, however, is the opposite of post-truth. Every word God says is true. Every aspect of God is true. There are no hidden theories or shady agendas when it comes to God.

Truth matters to God. That's why truth should matter to us.

Meet the Culture of Confusion

Post-truth has been around for a while. It all began with a question. A subtle, slick indictment against God from the lips of Satan. "Has

God really said . . . ?" (Gen. 3:1 NASB). With this question, doubt was cast on the validity of God's words.

Satan promised life and clarity when he told Adam and Eve, "Your eyes will be opened, and you will be like God" (Gen. 3:5). They took the bait, but instead of clarity, all humanity has gained is a miry pit of confusion.

Abdu Murray calls this the "Culture of Confusion." In his book *Saving Truth*, he writes,

> Post-truth has now blossomed into a Culture of Confusion. Confusion is embraced as a virtue and clarity shunned as a sin. The answers to life's questions no longer need to correspond to reality. They need only cater to our desires. . . . When we look at our world today and see all the questions being asked amid a culture not truly committed to sound answers, it's hard to imagine a land more confusing.[2]

How could society be anything but confused when we've yanked the foundation of truth out from underneath us? When we attempt to respond to the most important questions of life with subjective answers based on personal preference, we don't receive satisfying answers and there's no bottom line to return to in the event of disagreement. There's no objective right or wrong. No black and white. We've muddied up the lucidity of truth and settled for a dingy color of gray called preference. Who has the final word? When there's no truth, the one who is simply the loudest or most obnoxious is heard. Not the one backed with unbiased facts or evidence. As theologian and philosopher Francis Schaeffer pointed out, "If there is no absolute beyond man's ideas, then there is no final appeal to judge between individuals and groups whose moral judgments conflict. We are merely left with conflicting opinions."[3]

But it's restrictive to say there's only one right perspective, some will say. Aren't all truths valid?

Consider this: Matt believes avocados are fruits. He's kind of a nerd, and he enjoys studying the science of plants. His study has shown him this fact about avocados. But Kara thinks avocados are a vegetable. After all, she doesn't put any other fruit on her burrito bowl—only vegetables. Who is right? Matt is guided by facts, Kara by personal opinion. Is it restrictive of Matt to tell Kara that her preferences are incorrect when it's a solid fact that avocados are *not* a vegetable? Can both their perspectives be true? Kara can, of course, continue to believe what she wants, but she would continue to be wrong. That's not restrictive. That's basic fact.

It *would* be restrictive of Matt to try to convince Kara that avocados are the best fruit there is. If Kara doesn't like avocados, Matt can't force her to change her mind. Her preference falls under her right to have an opinion. But her belief on what constitutes an avocado does not.

To take this argument further than our Gen Z love for avocado toast, the same logic can be applied to our beliefs about God, creation, and life. Is there a God? How was the world created? When does life begin? These questions can be answered with absolute truth. But not everyone will prefer those answers. Opinions will vary and disagreements arise, but will each opinion be objectively true or as equally valid? Of course not. Either there is a God or there isn't. Either the world was created by a Creator or it wasn't. Either life begins at fertilization or it doesn't. Everyone can't be right. That's not restrictive. That's basic fact.

This kind of clarity is shunned. It's a virtue to be "open-minded" and "tolerant." The prevailing opinion of our society considers placing these beliefs in the category of objective truth to be narrow-minded and restrictive. Feelings dictate the conversation, and with each argument, we look at the fruit of post-truth thinking with the question, "Has God really said . . . ?"

Too often, like Eve, we have taken and eaten of the fruit, and our eyes and minds have been blinded by confusion. We've bought the lies that say truth is personal and subjective and allowed even formerly clear-cut definitions to become cloudy and uncertain. Many words today have entirely different definitions than they once did. These definitions have been altered by feelings and preferences.

For example, tolerance no longer means *tolerating*. To *tolerate* is to disagree with or dislike but to put up with the person or thing anyway. True tolerance requires two steps. First, two individuals must hold different beliefs and convictions (in short, they need to disagree with each other). Then, despite their differences, they must choose to endure one another. They don't change their own views or claim that the other person's perspective is just as valid, but they make the decision to respect them. They *tolerate*—but they don't affirm.[4]

But in our cultural climate, tolerance has slipped from the realm of disagreement into acceptance and affirmation. It's not enough to peacefully allow someone to hold an opinion that varies from our own. We have to consider that opinion equally valid. Author and philosopher Dallas Willard brilliantly sums it up:

> Tolerance, because truth has been pulled away from it, has slipped over into the idea that everything is equally right. No longer is tolerance a matter of saying, "I disagree with you and I believe you're wrong, but I accept you and I extend to you the right to be wrong." That's not enough. We're now in a situation where everyone must be equally right, where you cannot say that people are wrong and still claim to love them.[5]

If you don't agree with or applaud certain actions (such as abortion or same-sex marriage), you're considered intolerant. But as pastor David Platt clarifies, "Toleration of beliefs does not require that we accept every idea as equally valid, as if a belief is true, right, or good simply because someone expresses it."[6] This is a true definition of tolerance, but the new definition requires the addition of affirmation, which eliminates the value of personal convictions and a foundation of absolute truth.

Another example of an altered definition is the word *marriage*. Merriam-Webster's dictionary currently defines marriage as, "The state of being united as spouses in a consensual and contractual relationship recognized by law."[7] When I simply googled the word *marriage*, the top search result from *Psychology Today* stated, "Marriage is the process by which two people make their relationship public, official, and permanent. It is the joining of two people in a bond that putatively lasts until death, but in practice is often cut short by separation or divorce."[8] These are the top definitions of marriage in our society, but go back to 1828 and the definition was drastically different. The 1828 version of the Webster dictionary defined marriage as "the act of uniting a man and woman for life."[9]

Do you notice the difference? The 1828 version brings decisive clarity on who marriage is between (a man and a woman) and what its purpose is (to unite them for life). Neither of our current definitions offer such clarity but instead dilute the entire concept of marriage to make it between any two people (regardless of gender). While *Psychology Today* acknowledges that marriage is supposed to be "public, official, and permanent," it also makes every allowance for that bond to be broken. How can we have clarity when a simple term like marriage has undergone such radical change and has such an ambiguous definition?

These two altered definitions give us a glimpse of the confusion we're experiencing. Throughout the centuries, definitions have been altered on topics such as justice, love, gender, the meaning of life, the sanctity of life, and, of course, truth itself. These altered definitions may not always be reflected in our dictionaries, but they make their mark on our mindsets. Some of these changes have been for the better and some are due to the simple evolving of society. But other definitions have been changed in an attempt to refute truth and replace it with personal opinions, as in the two instances above. It comes down to the fact that no one can claim a belief rooted in truth, because it will eventually clash with someone else's opinion. No one can disagree on the basis of truth because there's no source above human opinion that determines what's actually true. How confusing is that?

While this is our current version of post-truth, these perspectives are not unique to our day and age. Every generation since Adam and Eve has experienced forms of post-truth thinking, as humanity has attempted to rewrite the script of truth with their own opinions. As Proverbs says, "All the ways of a man are pure in his own eyes, but the LORD weighs the spirits" (16:2). We all want our ways to be right. But our ways are human and fallible. God's are not. God's truth is founded upon reality as much as "two plus two equals four." In fact, more so. Without God's truth, no other truth would exist, and we'd be floundering in a world where everything is subjective. God gave us the gift of truth so we could live with clarity, wisdom, and order. But to do so, we have to accept *His* standards above our own.

Truth is not a personal preference. Truth is a person, and that person is Christ.

Truth in a World of Fake News

It's hard to know who and what to believe anymore.

Is this true? Is this false? Does it matter?

Like the game two truths and a lie, sometimes the lies are buried beneath ideas that appear right on the surface but underneath are supported by nothing but fake news.

How can we stand for truth in this environment?

The first step is knowing the source of authoritative truth—God Himself. To begin our pursuit of truth any place other than a greater knowledge of God would be putting truth above the God who created it.

God gave us a tool to know His character and learn His truth—His Word. Minister and civil rights activist John M. Perkins writes, "What is the ultimate standard of truth? It is not our feelings. It is not popular opinion. It is not what presidents or politicians say. God's Word is the standard of truth."[10] Scripture is God's witness of Himself. Not only does God's Word reveal God Himself but it also speaks practical insight and guidance into our daily lives.

There are many sources of information in the world. Some people turn to social media. Others look to news anchors, politicians, or celebrities. Others seek out Christian sources like their pastor or favorite author or speaker. But what these sources have in common is that they're human. And humans are fallible. While we can and should learn from the sources available to us, they should never be our first source for truth. Test everything against the Word of God—including this book. Only one person and one book can hold claims of inerrancy, and that's Jesus Christ and the Word of God.

We need wise insight from others. But when we search for additional sources, we need to consider what source those individuals are looking to. If we're listening to someone who isn't led by God's truth, they're not a reliable source.

What sources do we turn to for our worldview? Are they solid and truth-filled? Do they seek out the facts and speak with accuracy, authenticity, and transparency? Do they hide details that matter or flaunt facts that make another side or person look bad? Are we always looking to only one person or one view? Are we acting out of a confirmation bias and seeking sources we know will affirm what we already think? Because of our commitment to God, Christians, of all people, should be the most dedicated to seeking out the truth of a matter, discontent with easy answers and trite responses.

The search for truth is uncomfortable and will not always align with our personal preferences. Our inbred, sinful nature chafes against truth and when we find it, it will often make us uncomfortable. That's what Jesus's words did to the people of His day, and that's what Jesus's words are still doing to genuine truth-seekers today. But comfort isn't what we need—truth is. Author and theologian C. S. Lewis wrote, "If you look for truth, you may find comfort in the end, but if you look for comfort, you will not get either comfort or truth—only soft soap and wishful thinking to begin with and, in the end, despair."[11]

When We Encounter Post-Truth

We encounter post-truth thinking every day. How should we respond when we're faced with these mindsets? There are three places where we need to be aware of the possibility for post-truth thinking—the world, the church, and ourselves.

1. The World

Post-truth thinking has overtaken much of our society and dominates social media feeds, news channels, and political arenas. Topics like identity, sexuality, and gender have been targeted and made issues of preference. Even subtly, we can sometimes allow the opinions of the world to influence our own perspectives, especially on topics where subjective preference has become "normal." When faced with ideas in secular culture, carefully evaluate them like we talked about in the last chapter by filtering them through a series of questions and holding them against Scripture.

2. The Church

Abdu Murray explains two ways the church has succumbed to post-truth thinking: "On one hand, Christians have compromised the clarity of Scripture for the sake of acceptance and to avoid conflict. On the other hand, Christians have indulged the cultural practice of vilifying those with whom they disagree."[12]

The first way—compromising Scripture—is becoming more common in our "politically correct" culture. The Bible is distorted to affirm popular views on hot-button topics like marriage, sexuality, or the value of life. If it's not distorted, it's ignored or diluted. We take the truths of Scripture and weaken them until they're simply ideas or opinions we can push around at will or leave behind altogether. Or we settle for a Christian version of post-truth that says because only God knows truth in its totality, we should keep an open mind and validate every perspective as a possible truth.

Each of these tactics—distortion, avoidance, or dilution—compromises the power of God's Word and turns Scripture into a pawn in a cultural game. We are not supposed to be the ones to dictate and change Scripture. Rather, Scripture is to dictate and change us. When we find the truth within God and His Word, we are to cling to it with holy stubbornness. While our understanding of the truth is limited by our humanity—we will never exhaustively comprehend the mind of God and will continue to be perfected as we grow in our knowledge of Him—He has still revealed His ways to us and enabled us to understand them. He has not hidden His truth from us but made it accessible to all who are willing to accept it.

The second way—vilifying those we disagree with—happens when we mistakenly draw battle lines and turn those who don't agree with us into enemies to be conquered instead of individuals to be loved. We lose sight of our common human brokenness, and in an attempt to level the field, we make the "other side" out to be as evil as possible. When we sacrifice truth, fudge details, or spread slanderous remarks about people we disagree with, we give in to a self-righteous form of post-truth that discredits the name of Jesus and gives Christianity a poor reputation. Our love grows cold, our churches become unwelcoming, and our witness is tarnished when we forefeit truth to make others look bad.

While both mindsets have at times found a place within the church, we can drive out post-truth mindsets by replacing them with Christ's teaching—words of absolute truth and countercultural love. Like Murray says,

> The church can recapture its positive cultural influence if it rekindles its passion for the principles that revolutionized the world so long ago. In sharp contrast to our current adversarial attitudes, Jesus told us to love our enemies and to pray for those who persecute us (Matt. 5:44). Christians are to be "the salt of the earth" and "the light of the world" (Matt. 5:13–14). . . . What we need is neither complacency nor indignation. What we need is wisdom.[13]

3. Ourselves

Genuine change starts with *us*. I'd like to think I'm above the lure of a post-truth mindset, but I know I'm not. It shows up when I ignore the truth because it makes me uncomfortable or when I'm tempted to color a story to make myself look better.

The seeds are planted every time we doubt God, spread a lie, or self-righteously elevate ourselves. When we look to other opinions before God's Word or judge someone for their different perspective on a secondary issue. *We* are not the standard of truth. Our opinions, thoughts, feelings, and preferences may be wrong. If we set *ourselves* up as the gold standard for what's true, we're in a dangerous place.

To embrace God's truth, we need to humble our hearts and recognize that if we want our world to come back to God's ways, first *we* must be committed to them.

Becoming Truth-Seekers

Culture desperately needs clarity. Deep down, the foundations of our society are crumbling without the groundwork of truth to sustain us.

Thankfully, we're not lost without a compass. We have true north, and that's Jesus Christ. In His own words, "If you abide in my word, you are truly my disciples, and you will know the truth, and the truth will set you free" (John 8:31–32 ESV).

It's time for us to know the truth and be set free from the culture of confusion. To become seekers of our truth-bearing, truth-filled God and abide in His words. In a world of shifting morality, endless definitions, confusing choices, and ever-changing ideals, there is One who is steady, never changing, and constant. His ways are sure. His truth is absolute.

Going Deeper

1. Had you heard the term *post-truth* before? In what context?
2. How have you encountered post-truth thinking?
3. Why is it dangerous and confusing to place emotions above truth?
4. What sources do you look to for your worldview? How do you know they're reliable sources?
5. What do you think of the phrase "Truth is a person, and that person is Christ"? How does that affect your idea of truth?

Further Resources

- *Saving Truth: Finding Meaning and Clarity in a Post-Truth World* by Abdu Murray
- *Total Truth: Liberating Christianity from Its Cultural Captivity* by Nancy Pearcey
- *True for You, But Not for Me: Overcoming Objections to Christian Faith* by Paul Copan
- *Live Not by Lies: A Manual for Christian Dissidents* by Rod Dreher

PART TWO

tackling the nitty-gritty

5

Identity

(Knowing Who You Are in a "Be Yourself" World)

I felt like a different person.

I sat on my bedroom floor, knees pulled up to my chest, tears falling down my face, my shoulders shaking. Less than twenty-four hours before, I'd said goodbye to the man I thought I'd one day marry. I never wanted a breakup to be part of my story, but there I was, both my relationship and my heart broken.

Four days prior, my family, boyfriend, and I had piled into my dad's Jeep to make the ten-hour drive to spend Thanksgiving with my boyfriend's family. I couldn't remember being happier. My future looked secure. I was happy, hopeful, and head over heels in love.

Over the next four days, everything collapsed. My dreams shattered around me. I made the drive home with my heart in pieces, a weight on my chest like I'd never experienced. When I walked through the front door, the realization hit me. I didn't feel like the girl who'd left four days earlier. I was returning to the same world a different person.

My identity was rocked. I felt like a different person, but fundamentally, I was still me. I'd lost my boyfriend, not my soul. But I still felt changed from the inside out, and I was scrambling to recover who I used to be.

Breakups, failures, changed relationships, confusing emotions, unfulfilled dreams, dashed hopes—these all impact our identity. When our world is rocked or we go through the natural phases of growing up, we find ourselves asking, *Who am I?* followed by *Am I enough?* Are we the sum of who others say we are? Are we who we choose to be or who our emotions proclaim us to be? Are we the filtered, edited version we project to the world? Or the messy, crying-on-the-floor, filled-with-self-doubt reality? Or is there a base-level truth that defines our identity no matter the ever-changing circumstances of our lives or fluctuations of our emotions? How can we truly know who we are in such a "be yourself" world?

Who Am I? The Big Question

Be yourself.
Follow your heart.
Live your truth.
You are what you feel.
Connect with your true self.

These phrases are a sampling of how our culture encourages us to view identity. We're invited to engage in processes of self-awareness and self-discovery. Knowing ourselves is considered the pinnacle of all goals, and being true to ourselves is the way to happiness, mental health, and a fulfilling life. Post-truth speaks up in the identity conversation, declaring that our emotions and personal preferences are the most important part of who we are. Do you see the post-truth ideas in the above phrases? Did you notice the disconnect from a higher standard of truth and instead an exaltation of "our truths" and, in short, ourselves?

Identity is an integral part of our worldview. How we view identity and how we view ourselves guides our thoughts, actions, and ideas about right and wrong. As John Stonestreet, president of the Colson Center, has said, "The moral challenges of our day are the fruit, not the root. They're the effect, not the cause. The moral shifts in our society are the result of a much deeper shift. It's a shift in *what we think it means to be human.*"[1] So many nitty-gritty topics go back to the foundation of identity. Sexuality and gender are issues of identity. So are the value of life, racism, and justice.

These are all identity issues because they ask several fundamental questions: What does it mean to be human? Who are we? What has the power to define us? Do we matter?

With post-truth mindsets infiltrating identity, we're floundering for authentic and lasting answers to these pivotal questions.

Just Be Yourself

We're all searching for truth about our identity. The very existence of the countless personality quizzes floating around online is proof of that. I mean, why are we so interested in finding out the answer to "Which fruit are you?" or "Which *Lord of the Rings* character are you?" Does it really add that much to our lives to know that we're a pineapple or Aragorn? (Apparently I'm Frodo, in case you're interested.) We're constantly searching for insight into who we are.

And not only *who* we are, but more importantly, *if we matter*. If we're unique and valuable. If we can measure up to the people around us. Humanity is always asking three questions: Am I loved? Am I significant? Do I have purpose?

If we can answer yes to these questions, our identity is secure. But everyone searches for answers in different places and in different ways. Many of the loudest voices in our culture tell us that love, significance, and purpose are found in embracing the current identity mantra: just be yourself. Yet the first thought many of us have when we hear "Just be yourself" is *Who am I?*

The phrase "just be yourself" is a double-edged sword. On the one hand, we *should* be ourselves because God made us unique. He created us to display different talents and gifts, enjoy different things, and simply be different people. Some people are athletic; some aren't. Some are talented artists; others can't draw a straight line. Some are outspoken; others are reserved. It's healthy to recognize and be aware of our differences. When it comes to our unique personalities, abilities, and interests, we should embrace "being ourselves" because these things are a part of how God wired us.

But on the other hand, the "just be yourself" narrative has been taken to a dangerous level. There are two pitfalls in how we often search for identity.

1. Looking for identity in people, possessions, or prestige (external).
2. Looking for identity in emotions and desires (internal).

Let's tackle the external first—looking for identity in people, possessions, or prestige. Have you ever been introduced to someone, and one of the first things you're told is their career? "Hi, meet Chris! He's a computer technician." Chris equals computer genius. But Chris is more than just a computer technician. Small talk aside, what if Chris looks to his career to answer his three questions? "Am I loved?" becomes "Do people approve of the things I do and think well of them?" "Am I significant?" turns into "Does the work I do matter in other people's lives?" And "Do I have purpose?" really means "Is my work giving me the fulfillment I crave?" If Chris turns to his work for answers, what will happen if he loses his job? He will suddenly feel unloved, insignificant, and purposeless. So Chris (who is no longer the computer technician) no longer knows who he really is.

What happens if someone who places their identity in a relationship suddenly goes through a breakup? What if someone who seeks their identity in popularity suddenly isn't popular? Or if someone who looks for purpose in sports suddenly can't compete?

Identity crisis after identity crisis. The security we found in that job, relationship, or ability is compromised, and we feel empty, insecure, and vulnerable. Any huge life change naturally leaves us reeling, but when our identity is wrapped up in it, it's more than devastating, it's debilitating.

Because externals can change in a moment, it's easy to see we can't derive our identity from them. Which leads to the second way we look for identity: within ourselves (emotions and desires). According to most of society, the path to our identity is a straight-shot, well-beaten road into the middle of our hearts and emotions. "The real you is who you are inside," we're told. If we don't obey our thoughts, feelings, and desires, we're being untrue to ourselves. This mindset can be boiled down into a few points:

1. Our truest self is our emotional self.
2. Following our emotions leads us to embrace our most authentic self.
3. Authenticity means displaying outwardly what we feel inwardly.
4. Emotions trump reality. Therefore, we're not defined by external realities, but by internal feelings.

This mindset shows up clearly in matters of sexuality. Sexual desires are considered the pinnacle of identity. With this thinking, our sexual attractions label us: Heterosexual? Homosexual? Bisexual? Asexual? It's no longer about *who we're attracted to*, but *who we are*. The same goes for gender: Cisgender? Transgender? Your gender isn't defined by your biology, but by your *feelings*. We're able to self-identify as whatever we want in the name of just being us. That's why, when someone comes out as gay or transgender, people say, "Finally, they can just be themselves." Our emotions are elevated above reality and become the key to knowing who we are.[2]

The tragic irony is that the more we look within ourselves, the emptier we discover ourselves to be. Despite every encouragement that we're enough, the deeper we dive into our hearts, the more we're met with a sneaking, nagging suspicion that we're actually *not enough*. When we look to our emotions as our source of identity, we believe ourselves to be the standard of truth, but it's an insufficient and unsatisfactory standard. Our thoughts and feelings become our source of truth instead of God and reality. In a sense, we make our emotions our god.

But emotions can lead us astray.

After all, emotions ebb and flow. Feelings are an inconsistent ruler, constantly demanding something from us but changing the demands all the time.

Culture says, "Trust yourself." But if you desire an identity that lasts beyond the shifts of your emotions, please don't trust yourself.

Scripture says, "The heart is deceitful above all things, and desperately wicked" (Jer. 17:9). Digging within my sinful heart to find my identity will only leave me empty and lead me far from God. I can't search within myself for identity because I am not the source of truth and goodness. God is. I can't look to my emotions to label and define me, because my emotions are only one part of the multidimensional person God has designed me to be. My emotions may change; God will not.

I can't answer the three questions pounding on the door of my heart—Am I loved? Am I significant? Do I have purpose?—by looking to myself or my accomplishments. I can't look within or without to find the truth of my identity. Instead, I need to look above.

Identity Rooted in Theology

Culture's worldview of identity is all about *us.*

You're confident. You're powerful. You're successful. Just look within your heart. Your truest self is deep within your soul. And always remember, you're enough.

Affirmations like these give us a quick boost of encouragement but fall flat when our identity is deeply tested. When I was crying on my bedroom floor after my breakup, I didn't want to hear about myself. If someone had sat beside me and said, "I know this hurts right now, but you're going to be okay because you're strong and confident. You're enough," I wouldn't have believed them. I didn't feel strong or confident. I felt beaten down, broken, and very *not enough*. In that moment, I couldn't look to my in-a-million-pieces heart or bleeding emotions. I didn't need to be reminded who I was. I needed to hear who God was.

I once heard a quote that said, "Knowing yourself is the beginning of all wisdom." That sounds good, doesn't it? It sounds like the kind of quote I'd see on an Instagram post or printed on a T-shirt. But Scripture has an entirely different take. Check this out: "*The fear of the* Lord *is the beginning of wisdom, and the knowledge of the Holy One is understanding*" (Prov. 9:10, emphasis added).

There is an intrinsic and God-spoken truth that can radically transform our view of identity and answer our deepest questions about what it means to be human. What is this truth? That we are made in the *imago Dei*. Translated from Latin, *imago Dei* means, "the image of God." In the beginning of creation, when God breathed life into the first human being, we see that people were distinct and set apart from the rest of creation. No other creation on earth can boast the privilege of being formed in the very likeness of our Creator. Not only does *imago Dei* imbue humanity with distinct value and dignity, it also reveals who we're meant to be and how we're called to live. It means we've been given responsibilities, endowed with a mind that can reason, free will that can choose, and a soul that can know God Himself. Our purpose and the reason for our existence is to glorify and exalt the God who created us and who daily sustains us. Our Creator's fingerprints are upon each of our unique lives, showing us that *imago Dei* doesn't mean we all popped out of one generic mold, but were individually and intentionally formed. Our distinctive traits show the creativity and goodness of God. Our identity and value are not human constructs, but a God-gifted reality. Our identity does not fluctuate like our emotions, cannot easily change like our circumstances, and cannot be taken away like people, possessions, or prestige. The stamp of God upon our lives is as intrinsic as the breath inside our lungs.

Yet the true beauty of *imago Dei* is found not only in the fact that we bear God's image but in the character of the God whose image we bear. Who is this God who would stamp His likeness upon His creation? To truly understand our identity, we must know the God in whose image we are made.

When you think of God, what do you imagine? Sometimes we have a false picture of God in our minds. This picture is formed by what we hear about God in our churches, from our families and friends, or in the world around us. It's also formed by life experiences. Someone who has experienced nothing but grief and rejection may have a hard time believing in God's love. Someone who has heard only about God's love may not believe in His justice or righteousness. God's description of Himself in Scripture is the only unbiased foundation that can answer the question "Who is God?" C. S. Lewis once wrote, "I need Christ, not something that resembles Him. . . . Not my idea of God, but God."[3]

We need Christ, not just our idea of Him. Is your perception of God rooted in Scripture? Do you understand His holiness, righteousness, and desire to make you more like Himself? When you hear that God loves you, do you believe it? When you're told that He created you with intention and a purpose to glorify Him, do you let that truth sink deep into your heart? It's only when we see God in truth that we can begin to see ourselves in truth. As God healed the deep layers of hurt from my breakup and other painful rejections in my life, He revealed areas where I had misperceived His character. For years, I had lived with the subconscious idea that God loved me only when I was perfect and put together (not that I ever really was). I assumed He would get tired of my brokenness and abandon me like my boyfriend and so many others had. My misconceptions of God distorted how I viewed myself.

Who is God? What is He like? What is His character?

He is a God of absolute love (1 John 4:7–19; Rom. 8:37–39) and complete justice: "For all His ways are justice, a God of truth and without injustice; righteous and upright is He" (Deut. 32:4). If you've struggled with projecting the hurt and rejections you've experienced from people upon God, thinking He's just like them, remember, "God is not a man, so he does not lie. He is not human, so he does not change his mind. Has he ever spoken and failed to act? Has he ever promised and not carried it through?" (Num. 23:19 NLT).

He is a God who cares so intensely about our emotions that He puts our tears in a bottle (Ps. 56:8), hears us when we call to Him (Ps. 55:17; 116:1–2), and suffers pain when we reject Him, crying out with groans of "How can I give you up?" (Hosea 11:8). He punishes evil but has mercy on the repentant (2 Thess. 1:8–9; 1 John 1:9). He is our Shepherd (Ps. 23:1), our strong tower (Ps. 61:3), and the only One who can save us from our sins (Acts 4:12). He is unchanging (Heb. 13:8). He created the heavens and the earth and breathed us to life from the dust of the ground (Gen. 1–2). He is omnipotent (Col. 1:16–17), omnipresent (Ps. 139:7–10), and all knowing (1 John 3:20; Rom. 11:33–35). He is God.

Until we know who God is, we will never understand who we are. Society says to follow our hearts to discover our identity. But we cannot find within ourselves what can only be found within the heart of God. This is what identity rooted in theology means. It means our identity is secure because God is unchanging. Our status as image bearers is set in stone and carved within every unique imprint of our fingertips.

Truth That Transforms Your Identity

A biblical worldview of identity renovates our view of ourselves and our purpose in the world. While "just be yourself" makes it all about us, identity rooted in theology makes it all about God. The question is not "How can I be true to myself?" but "How can I honor God?" When moments of uncertainty and doubt hit us and we question our place in the world, the solution isn't to simply look within to discover our purpose, but to consider how we can serve and glorify the One who created us. When our emotions spin out of control, we don't have to follow them wherever they lead, but we can look instead to what is true and real about God or His creation of us. When our answers to the questions of *Am I loved? Am I significant? Do I have purpose?* are challenged, we don't have to run to people, accomplishments, or accolades but instead seek our God who calls us beloved and commissioned us to live according to His purposes.

But this isn't easy. Questions of identity, worth, and purpose are tough.

In the months after my breakup, I struggled deeply with feeling unloved and rejected. I would be hit suddenly with a wave of painful memories. In a moment, I was back in a situation or conversation, feeling the confusion, rejection, and knife-sharp pain slicing into my heart. I felt less-than and unloved, like who I was hadn't been enough. Would never be enough. Thoughts kept coming, telling me, *You should have been more like this. You should have done less of that. Maybe if you'd been different, this wouldn't have happened.*

When failure comes, when confusion arises, when the breakup breaks your heart, when lies and criticism cut into your soul, when feelings of inadequacy attack and the pain seems too strong to bear, that is when you come to the end of yourself. Facing the uncomfortable questions of "Who am I?" and "Am I enough?" we reach a place where looking to ourselves is a dead-end road. But maybe that's when we'll stop looking to *us* and start looking to God. Theology professor Gerald Sittser writes,

> In coming to the end of ourselves, we have come to the beginning of our true and deepest selves. We have found the One whose love gives

shape to our being. . . . We need someone greater than ourselves to help us forge a new identity. God is able to guide us on this quest, to help us become persons whose worth is based on grace and not on performance, accomplishments, and power.[4]

God's love gives shape to our being. His words about us are absolute truth. He doesn't toss around easy platitudes that tell us we're enough or that we're perfect. He knows us too well. He knows how weightless fickle answers are against our deepest hurts and turbulent feelings. We need deeper answers rooted in an unchanging source—God Himself. His truths about who I am last longer than my ever-changing emotions. By looking to His words instead of my feelings, I don't have to be a slave to the lies that paint a distorted picture of myself.

If my only goal was to discover myself, I would be destined for pain and insecurity as I realized the depth of my inadequacy. Because I *am* inadequate. You are inadequate. God created us flawlessly, but sin shattered the perfect design—sin that leads to our identity crises and questions. Trying to free myself from my own inadequacy will keep me stuck in a cycle of inferiority. But understanding my inadequacy and looking to God's grace—*that* has the power to set me free. John 8:32 says, "And you shall know the truth, and the truth shall make you free."

Discovering myself can't set me free. Culture's view of identity can't give me hope. Only knowing God and experiencing His grace can truly free my heart from the lies and fears that bind it.

Who We Are: Children of God

God made us in His image. Knowing Him is the key to freedom from the burden of questions of identity. If we know God's character, when we struggle with insecurity, we can ask ourselves, "What kind of God made me? What kind of God is watching over my life?" Then we can point to the truth of Scripture and respond, "*This* kind."

I've wrestled with questions of worth and purpose. I've felt unloved and rejected. But these struggles and emotions yield to the truths I cling to in Christ. Because I know who my God is, I can trust the truths He says about me. The more I fill my eyes with the beauty of Christ, the less I see of myself and the less insecure I feel. I can trust I'm loved. I can believe I have purpose. How? Because I am loved with an everlasting love by a Savior who died to redeem me. I have purpose to live for Him and His glory.

First John 3:1 says, "Behold what manner of love the Father has bestowed on us, that we should be called children of God!"

That is the depth and true measure of our identity for those in Christ—*children of God*. We are secure because He calls us His children and because He is a good Father. That is a richer and truer identity than just "be yourself." That's an identity that can last.

Help! I Think I'm Having an Identity Crisis!

Are you wondering who you are? Wondering if you matter? Are you feeling purposeless? Inadequate? Unloved? We all walk through seasons when we ask these questions and experience these emotions. Here are five biblical steps to take when you feel like you're having an identity crisis.

1. Get Back to the Truth of God's Character

Study God's character in Scripture and confess any inaccurate perceptions of God that you believe. Does the image of God in your mind match the one described in Scripture? Have you studied who God is in His Word? Our hearts can never fully comprehend the immensity of God's grace and love, so pray for His help in realigning your heart to His truth. Dig into God's perfect character and fix your eyes on those unchanging truths.

2. Seek Truth over Emotions

Our emotions are always trying to tell us who we are. But often, our emotions lie. I've learned that my emotions are not truth; God's Word is truth.

When your emotions are trying to tell you a fact about yourself, don't automatically believe it's true. Whether it's about your body, value, gender, purpose, or future, acknowledge the emotion, but then look to what God says about it. If the two don't align, choose to trust God's Word over your feelings.

3. Trust That God Created You for a Purpose

God has a unique purpose for your life. We don't see the full span of our lives, but God does, and He knows His plans for us. Psalm 138:8 says, "The Lord will fulfill his purpose for me; your steadfast love, O Lord, endures forever" (ESV). If we know God's character and love, we can trust that He will fulfill His purpose for us. He will complete the work He began (Phil. 1:6) as we seek to obey Him. We can take comfort in the truth that God—not us—is in control of our lives.

God's ultimate vision is not to see us accomplish great things but to mold us into the image of Christ and know us intimately. Our number one purpose is to know, love, and serve Jesus Christ. In the book of Ecclesiastes, Solomon (who was having a serious identity crisis) brought our life goal to ground level when he wrote, "Let us hear the conclusion of the whole matter: Fear God and keep His commandments, for this is man's all" (12:13). No matter what changes, this purpose remains.

4. Ask God to Give You Clarity on His Will for Your Life

In moments of limbo—when we're past one season and not sure of the next—we often struggle with identity. These seasons are hard and discouraging, but they're unique opportunities to seek God. Use the waiting periods to draw nearer to God and strive for daily faithfulness. God doesn't reveal His entire plan, but He asks us to obediently follow Him one step at a time. The future is not ours to know, but His to hold. He will lead us as we're faithful to seek and obey Him.

5. Get Out of Yourself

Sometimes our biggest problem when we're struggling with identity is simply that we're too focused on ourselves. The more fixated we are on ourselves, the more insecure we are. Jesus calls us to serve and love and use our lives to share Him with others and meet the needs around us. If you're struggling with identity, get your mind off yourself and serve and love someone else.

Going Deeper

1. Have you ever experienced a situation (a loss, breakup, change, etc.) that rocked your identity?
2. In what ways have you encountered culture's ideas of identity? How does this chapter alter your perspective?
3. Why are we not a reliable source for truth?
4. Where do you look to answer your three questions: *Am I loved? Am I significant? Do I have purpose?*
5. How does knowing God change your identity? Why is finding identity in Christ important?

Further Resources

- *You're Not Enough (And That's Okay): Escaping the Toxic Culture of Self-Love* by Allie Beth Stuckey
- *Why You Matter: How Your Quest for Meaning Is Meaningless without God* by Michael Sherrard
- *The Image Restored: The Imago Dei and Creation* by Glenn Sunshine and Timothy D. Padgett

6

Sex, Purity, and Relationships

(Moving Past the Hookup Culture)

She looked about sixteen. Younger than me. Straight blond hair, skinny jeans, and Converse sneakers. She was in the grocery store with her mom, standing in front of the stocked shelves, about to make a selection.

I stood at the other end of the aisle, browsing the beauty care products. At first I didn't pick up on their conversation or what they were purchasing, but then something the mom said snagged my attention.

"Well, honey, if you're going to do it, I want you to be protected."

That's when it hit me.

This mom was helping her daughter pick out birth control options.

In our society, this is normal. It's perfectly acceptable for a sixteen-year-old to be sexually active. Provided with protection and her parents' awareness, this situation would even be considered healthy and appropriate.

Except it's anything but.

A Sexually Broken Society

My heart aches for this girl and millions like her who are buying into the world's perception of sexuality. I recently browsed the websites of several popular teen magazines and passed article headlines like these:

"Everything You Need to Know about Having Safe Sex"

"What Actually Counts as Sex?"

"The Best Hookup Apps to Download Right Now"

Our culture is sexually broken. Evidence of this brokenness is everywhere. Sex is something you can find by hooking up on an app or browsing the internet. Porn addictions are rampant. Heartbreaking stories of sexual abuse are common. We're living in a hypersexualized, sex-obsessed world.

The standards for sex promoted within our society through mass media, celebrities, and school classrooms set us up on a heartbreak cycle. Relationships aren't permanent. Sex isn't reserved for a husband and wife (or for any specific relationship or gender for that matter). Casual hookups are consequence free. *Teen Vogue* outlines a few of the most important factors to determine if you're ready for sex as knowing what makes you feel good, not feeling pressured, and choosing to have sex because *you* want to.[1] In a nutshell, it's the age of sexual autonomy.

These worldviews are sneaking into the church as well. According to a 2020 study by Pew Research, half of Christians say casual sex (defined as sex between adults not in a committed relationship) is sometimes or always acceptable.[2] In addition, cohabitation is becoming more common and accepted in Christian circles, as nearly half of evangelicals ages fifteen to twenty-two say it's probable they'll cohabit in the future.[3] Post-truth thinking places the emphasis on our emotions and desires and not on an objective moral standard. So long as sex is safe, legal, and consenting, it's a green light.

We're sexually liberated. But desperately broken.

There's so much more to sex than what the world tells us. Not only are there physical consequences such as unplanned pregnancy or sexually transmitted diseases to consider, but culture's narrative on sexuality misses the mark by a mile when it comes to understanding a truly fulfilling view of sexuality. We're told we can separate sex from the committed relationship of marriage and the selfless love required to sustain it. We're even told we can separate sex from dating, romance, and emotions altogether.

This mindset fails to provide what our hearts genuinely crave and to validate the full measure of our God-given sexuality. It's a dead-end road of heartbreak. Sexually active teens also have higher rates of depression and suicide than those who are not.[4] The chemical bonding that takes place during sex knits individuals together only for them to be torn apart because there's no intentional, lifelong commitment. Pornography usage leads to dissatisfaction and a demanding addiction for something more exciting. Porn can also lead to sexual abuse and toxic perspectives of body image as it objectifies individuals and distorts a healthy view of sexuality. Heartbreak, depression, insecurity, and countless other painful circumstances accompany the current perspective of sex.

What if this view of sexuality is not liberating but damaging? What if God's plan leads to greater intimacy not less? What if God designed our sexuality with a purpose and plan? What if following His design for sexuality results in a more lasting, joy-filled experience of sex and relationships?

God's Good Plan

"We have been sexually discipled by the world."[5]

Dr. Juli Slattery, a clinical psychologist, says this in her book *Rethinking Sexuality: God's Design and Why It Matters*. "We have been taught to see sexuality from the world's narrative. I find that most Christians are more familiar with how to view sexuality through a cultural lens than with a biblical perspective."[6]

We've all encountered questions about sexuality—and wondered about them ourselves. Why save sex for marriage when everyone else is hooking up? Is porn really that bad? Everyone else seems to watch it, why shouldn't we? Why are spouses unfaithful? What about masturbation? Is cohabiting okay if you plan to get married? Can we watch sexually explicit films and TV shows?

We have so many questions, but we often look to culture for answers. To live out a biblical worldview of sexuality, we need to be discipled by the God who created and designed it and gave us His road map for healthy sex and relationships.

Our perspective of God as the creator and designer of sexuality is the most important part of fostering a biblical worldview on sex. God is intentional and purposeful in His creation. When God created Adam and Eve, He designed them as sexual beings. When God breathed Adam to life from the dust of the earth, He crafted the first human to be uniquely male. Adam's maleness was a distinct aspect of God's design, from physical appearance and the male hormones running through him to the male mind and personality God gave him. And God called it good. Adam's sexual design was a perfect part of God's creation.

The only thing Adam lacked was someone to share his sexuality with. His physical design and relational capacity revealed he was designed *for* someone. But there was "no helper just right for him" (Gen. 2:20 NLT). So out of Adam's side, God formed another being, this one uniquely female. Eve's femininity was also a distinct aspect of God's design, from the beautiful physical attributes God gave woman and the female hormones running through her to the female mind and personality God gave her. Adam's and Eve's sexual design was corresponding and complementary. They were uniquely and distinctly different so they could come together and experience intimacy and connection. Their sexual differences were not social constructs but God's purposeful intention.

In the context of a sin-free world, this design was breathtaking and perfect. Adam rejoiced for the woman God created, exclaiming, "This is now bone of my bones and flesh of my flesh; she shall be called Woman, because she was taken out of Man" (Gen. 2:23). No other creation was more perfect for Adam than Eve. In God's masterful design, their sexuality allowed them the intimacy of becoming "one flesh" (v. 24). They had perfect unity and "were not ashamed" (v. 25).

This view of God as our Creator tells us several things:

1. God intentionally created our bodies and our sexuality.
2. God's design for our sexuality is good.
3. God knows how He intended sex to work. As the creator of sex, He has the authority to set guidelines in place for our good.

Our sex-saturated culture idolizes any and all forms of sexual expression. Because of culture's obsession, we tend to swing to the opposite extreme and miss an important point: *sex is good*. Our sexual longings are God-given. Our design is intentional. Sexual longings and sex itself are not dirty or shameful. In fact, both can be *holy*. When used as God originally intended, sex is a breathtaking picture of creation that God smiles upon. God still calls sex good.

Following God's Good Plan

The caveat comes in using sex as God originally intended. When God created us as sexual beings, He knew how sexuality was supposed to work—and He still does. He put clear guidelines in place because no good gift comes without instructions for proper use. The problem came when sin entered the world and all creation—including our bodies—became imperfect. Because we live in broken bodies in a broken world, we have broken sexuality. We disregard His plan and choose to write our own rules, and the effects of the brokenness continue to spread like cracks through glass—affecting every person and relationship. Dr. Slattery writes,

> Trusting God as the Creator means that we hold to His unchanging design for our sexuality. If God created our sexuality, His intentions as expressed in the Bible have not evolved over time. If God is *not* the Creator, then we are free to define our sexuality as we see fit. The problem is that many Christians want it both ways: to profess a faith in God but reject the design of His creation.[7]

God *is* our Creator, and He *does* have authority to define sex. He purposefully created our sexuality, wrote the longing for intimacy upon our hearts, and gave us a covenant relationship where that intimacy could flourish. That covenant relationship is marriage between one man and one woman.

No exceptions. No caveats. No compromises.

Culture may call it restrictive, but in truth, God's design for marriage and sex is brilliant. Humans are not created to live independent of each other. God designed us to be relational beings, and He designed marriage to be one of the most important and impactful relationships we hold. Marriage by God's design is permanent and exclusive. It's a promise shared and held between one man and one woman for life. It's within this commitment that God's design for sex can be fully discovered and celebrated.

The *Yada'* Factor

We all possess an innate craving for intimacy and commitment. We long to know and be known. Within marriage, sex is one of the most intimate forms of knowing another. In fact, the Hebrew word often used for sex in Scripture is *yada'*.[8] It means to be deeply known in every way, not just informationally, but personally. We see this word translated in the context of God knowing us, us knowing God, and in the intimacy of sexual knowing. Think about *that* the next time you hear someone say "yada, yada, yada"!

Hookup culture tells us sex means nothing. The words "existentially meaningless"[9] were used by a drummer in Austin, Texas, to describe this intimate act. "[It's] a piece of body touching another piece of body,"[10] he said. If this were true, any restrictions against sex would be unfounded. Why limit something that means nothing? But does that sound like *yada'*? God's design for sex isn't a mere physical act. It's to deeply know, serve, and love another. God created us to bond sexually, but culture says it's perfectly acceptable to use a person's body, no strings (emotions, commitment, relationship) attached. Instead of placing a higher value on sex, culture devalues it, because those who buy these lies have a lower view of its worth.

Sex or any form of sexual expression outside marriage falls short of God's perfect plan. It uses one of the most powerful methods of bonding two souls without any exclusive commitment. Sex is like "relationship superglue." Physical intimacy releases the hormone oxytocin, which can cause increased levels of trust, fidelity, and emotional bonding.[11] Sex is literally designed to knit two people together on multiple levels—physically, emotionally, and relationally. It's a part of God's brilliant design to bond a man and woman together. But without the commitment of marriage, the power of the "glue" is more harmful than helpful and causes more pain because you're bonding yourself to someone you're not committed to in a one-flesh union. When marriage and sex are separated, the plan backfires, resulting in heartache and brokenness.

Sex outside God's original context is not only a sin against God but a sin against yourself. Paul wrote to the church in the hypersexualized city of Corinth and challenged them to "flee sexual immorality. Every sin that a man does is outside the body, but he who commits sexual immorality sins against his own body" (1 Cor. 6:18). In other words, sexual sin may look and sound appealing, but run from it, because if you give in, you're causing self-inflicted pain. Your body is "the temple of the Holy Spirit who is in you, whom you have from God, and you are not your own. . . . For you were bought at a price; therefore glorify God in your body and in your spirit, which are God's" (1 Cor. 6:19–20).

Our bodies matter to God. Because of this, what we do with our bodies matters to God. As Paul says, "Now the body is not for sexual immorality but for the Lord, and the Lord for the body" (1 Cor. 6:13). Our bodies were created for a higher purpose—to glorify God. We glorify God by following His design, and as we do so, we realize God is not against our bodies but rather *for* them. Every part of His plan for sex is intentionally designed to help us flourish and prosper.

God's plans are always multifaceted, but practically speaking, God has two main purposes for sex. The first is procreation. Yep, there's the answer to every five-year-old's question, "Where do babies come from?" John Stonestreet, president of the Colson Center for Christian Worldview, and Brett Kunkle, founder of MAVEN, write,

> God's first command to Adam and Eve was to "be fruitful and multiply and fill the earth." Therefore, sex must not be completely severed from

reproduction. Why? Because our creator fashioned family in such a way that the permanent commitment between husband and wife is the proper and ideal environment for childbearing and child rearing and, thus, filling the earth.[12]

The second purpose of sex is for marital intimacy and oneness. Sex between a husband and wife is a powerful bond that can strengthen and sustain their relationship. Along with oxytocin, it's scientifically proven that one of the neurochemicals released during sex is dopamine, which is, in a sense, a "craving chemical." Dannah Gresh, popular Christian speaker on sexuality and purity, talks about this in her book *What Are You Waiting For?: The One Thing No One Ever Tells You About Sex*:

> Can you see how this is part of God's plan for sex within marriage? He put it in black and white when He inspired these words: "The two shall become one flesh" (Eph. 5:31). While a man and woman's "oneness" extends beyond the physical, the evidence suggests that God designed our emotional headquarters to be made "one" through the physical act of sex. . . . God designed our emotional system for one lifelong, mutually monogamous relationship.[13]

When the Good Plan Got Broken

Sin has sown brokenness and pain within our sexual design. Whether you've never had sex, have too many regrets to count, battle a pornography addiction, struggle with same-sex attraction, find your mind to be a constant war zone, or have been sexually sinned against, you are not alone. We all experience the brokenness of living in a sexually fallen world.

We have an enemy who takes God's gifts and twists them into something perverted. What God designed to be self-giving has become self-serving in the hands of Satan. Scripture says husbands and wives are to serve and love one another through sexual intimacy (see 1 Cor. 7:3). But most people view sex as a way to satisfy themselves. Hookups are not for the good of another, but to satisfy lust. Porn objectifies others to fulfill a craving and addiction. Making the choice to have sex outside of marriage doesn't take into consideration the potentially long-term effects such as pregnancy or STDs, but thinks only about how it feels in the moment. Sexual abusers violate innocent individuals to fulfill their own lust. The goodness of God's plan is distorted beyond belief when the focus is turned toward self.

Every battle with pornography, every body abused by lust, every marriage rocked by unfaithfulness, every heart broken by no-strings-attached sex, every lustful thought and act stem from the selfishness and sin that's ravaged our world. It may look hopeless, but no situation is past God's repair. We're sexually broken, but we have a Savior who died to redeem us and cover our sins with His grace.

The most devastating results of the lust permeating our culture are victims of sexual abuse. If you have been sexually abused, I am deeply sorry and my heart hurts for you. I want you to know that the abuse does not reflect you or your ultimate value. You have been greatly sinned against, but your priceless and precious worth from God remains intact.

I'll never forget a conversation I had with a sweet young woman who had been sexually abused by her uncle. For years, she had been too afraid to tell anyone and had grown up carrying this heavy weight. This abuse is the opposite of God's plan. Sexual distortions like this are one of the darkest corruptions of our enemy and can leave the most painful and wounding scars. If you have been abused or are currently experiencing sexual abuse, *please* reach out and tell someone you can trust. Your safety is the most important thing to consider right now, and you need people to help you walk through your pain and begin the process of healing. Please don't ignore or hide the abuse; be brave enough to share it even if it happened in the past. And please know that God's heart is broken for the pain and injustice you've experienced. He longs to heal the wounds others have inflicted upon you. Your worth and value are not determined by what others have done to you, but secured and made whole in the unconditional, tender love of Jesus.

While our bodies are broken, there is One whose perfect body was broken to heal our shattered pieces and make us whole again. On the cross, Jesus gave *His body* to restore our bodies and redeem our pain. For the sexually abused, healing is found in Jesus. For the sexually addicted, freedom is found in the bondage-breaking power of His shed blood. For the sexually confused, truth is found within His words. For all our regrets, brokenness, shame, and pain, Jesus is the answer and the antidote.

Letting God's Truth Illuminate the Nitty-Gritty

"Just save sex for marriage" is often the sole encouragement offered in conversations about sex and purity, but there are many other more specific struggles in this area. Countless teens battle pornography addictions, wrestle with masturbation or erotica, or deal with lustful thoughts. Introduce these topics and the conversation about purity gets more complicated. How do we biblically handle these struggles?

Thankfully, Jesus offers more insight than "just save sex for marriage" because He understands the real-life battles we face in this area and how desperately we need clarity and direction. Jesus took the conversation of sexual morality to another level: "You have heard that it was said to those of old, 'You shall not commit adultery.' But I say to you that whoever looks at a woman to lust for her has already committed adultery with her in his heart" (Matt. 5:27–28).

Lust is at the root of every sexual struggle. Porn, masturbation, erotica, out of control thoughts—lust fuels them all. So, with Jesus's words on lust, He covers the whole gamut of our struggles. The overarching call within His words is to a higher standard of purity and a greater definition of love.

Let's consider pornography. Porn is an epidemic of massive proportions. Forty million Americans say they regularly visit porn sites, and 65 percent of men ages eighteen to twenty-four view porn at least once a month.[14] And it's not just a guy's problem either. One out of every three visitors to porn sites is a woman.[15] Porn is becoming acceptable to the point that only 43 percent of teens believe it's bad for society.[16]

Pornography distorts God's plan for sex and intimacy and turns countless individuals into objects to be lusted after instead of souls to be cherished. Kristen Clark and Bethany Beal, founders of Girl Defined Ministries, explain, "Sex wasn't created for *viewing*; it was created for *experiencing*. It was created for *relationship*. That's why

God made sex to be a covenant celebration between a husband and wife within marriage. . . . Porn is devoid of everything true intimacy was designed to be."[17] Comparing porn with Jesus's words, we see that looking lustfully (the point of porn) is no different than the sexual action. Porn is destructive to healthy relationships, true intimacy, and a God-glorifying vision of sex and sexuality. It also creates a cycle of addiction that's hard to break.

The same goes for masturbation. The cultural conversation about masturbating is that it's totally normal and "the safest sex there is."[18] Sexual desires are strong, and satisfying them through masturbation seems like a harmless substitute for sex. But masturbation, too, goes against every aspect of God's design for sex. He created sex to be relational, intimate, and selfless, but masturbation turns the focus inward and is isolated, superficial, and self-centered. It's fueled by lust and fantasizing, which, again, Jesus places even our sexual fantasies and imaginations on the same level as the acts themselves. It also often goes hand in hand with porn. Young adult pastor Jonathan Pokluda describes it like this: "According to God's stated standards, these things are still a form of sex outside of marriage: lust is sex with someone else in your heart, and masturbation is sex with yourself."[19]

Masturbation is done in isolation and lacks the objective of God-defined sex—relational intimacy within marriage. Clark and Beal also write, "Masturbation fails again and again to be an authentic form of sexual intimacy. . . . In the end, masturbation is nothing more than a counterfeit version of sex."[20]

If you struggle with porn or masturbation (or other forms of lust), please don't brush this aside. While breaking free from any addiction is a journey, no addiction is impossible to break. I encourage you to take several practical but intentional steps: First, run to people who can help. Share your struggle with a trusted friend or family member and ask them to check in on you regularly. While sharing deeply personal struggles is difficult, please don't let feelings of shame hold you back. Satan wants you to hide your sins because they can rule you in the dark. Bringing them into the light is the first step toward loosening their power over you (see John 3:19–21). You need people in your life to help you along this journey. Freedom from shame is found in uncovering the secret.

Second, identify points of temptation and remove access. For example, if you typically look at porn on your phone, cut off access on your phone, whether by locking apps, setting limits on when you can use your phone, or even ditching the smartphone and getting a simple flip phone instead. This may sound extreme, but is it worth it to hold on to something that causes you to sin? Jesus challenged us that it's better to get rid of things that cause us to sin—even if it means radical decisions—than to remain bound by the sin (Matt. 5:29–30). You can also install internet filters on your devices that block questionable content and give other trustworthy people full access to your devices. Whatever it takes, remove access to the temptation.

Third, set manageable goals. Relapse is probable if you simply decide today to never look at porn or masturbate again without having a solid plan in place. With the help of someone to keep you accountable, create a treatment plan and set goals, such as abstaining for one week or one month. As you successfully complete each marker, continue to lengthen and extend your goals with the help of an accountability partner.

Fourth, seek intentional healing for your mind and your perceptions of sexuality. Consider reaching out to a wise Christian counselor or someone who can mentor you on both the mental and spiritual effects of porn. Since porn, masturbation, and other addictive forms of lust can alter and affect the brain, you may need outside help to heal, as well as someone to help teach a better, more God-glorifying perspective of sex and to share practical strategies to fight lust and walk in sexual purity.

Lastly, pray for help and seek God's strength. This is the most important step. We can't fight these battles alone. We need His help. The good news is that through the power of His Holy Spirit, we *can* break free from addictions. Seek God for strength to guard your eyes, thoughts, and actions. You are not powerless to fight sin. You have the power of Christ's shed blood on your side. If you are in Christ, "the Spirit of life in Christ Jesus has made [you] free from the law of sin and death" (Rom. 8:2).

These struggles are real. They're hard. They're not just a guy struggle or a girl struggle but a human problem. But God's truth illuminates even these nitty-gritty areas. God's design for sex goes way beyond simply saving sex for marriage and extends to our heart attitude, lifestyle, thought life, and the way we use our bodies to glorify God.

If you're reading this and thinking, *I'm too far gone, too messed up, too dirty. There's no way I can change, and no way God would forgive me*, I want to encourage you that your sin is not greater than Christ's sacrifice. Forgiveness of and freedom from all sins is available in Jesus. No one is sexually sinless, and we all need Christ's forgiveness and redemption. There is no condemnation for those who come to Jesus with a repentant heart asking for strength to obey Him and follow His design. He comes alongside us in our struggle, forgiving us, strengthening us, and freeing us from the pain of our past and the bondage of our current struggles. Christ's blood and forgiveness cover and heal our sexual brokenness. You're *not* too far gone, and you *can* change.

Fighting for a More Beautiful View

We can't fight for sexual purity in a sexually immoral culture on our own. We could follow dozens of self-created rules and still not grasp God's good design for sex. What we need is heart transformation—a radical paradigm shift in our view of sexuality as we look to God's guidance for our bodies and relationships. If our hearts aren't changed, our actions won't stand a chance, no matter how many guidelines we put in place. God has given us more than a rule book. He has given us a masterpiece to study and live out, and that masterpiece is His design.

God doesn't put guidelines in place because He's a killjoy out to ruin our fun, but to protect His sacred creation. He has a higher purpose for our sexuality and cares for us too much not to protect us. His guidelines are guardrails to keep us from plummeting down a cliff of heartache and disaster.

Here's the truth—your sexuality is sacred, because *you* are sacred. You are made in God's image, created to glorify God and be a living, breathing temple of the Holy Spirit. There is a bigger purpose for your sexuality. A breathtaking story is unfurling behind the scenes. Our relationships are a reflection of a greater relationship, a more holy romance: that of Christ and the church.

Paul writes, "'For this reason a man shall leave his father and mother and be joined to his wife, and the two shall become one flesh.' This is a great mystery, but I speak concerning Christ and the church" (Eph. 5:31–32).

Scripture tells the greatest love story of all time. It's God's pursuit of His wayward people, drawing them to Himself with His *agape*—unconditional love. On the cross, Christ demonstrated agape by sacrificing His life so we could have a relationship with Him. Now, the church—aka us—can have a restored covenant relationship with God. It's the mind-blowing truth of the gospel. But the crazy part is that we get to tell the story of the gospel through our relationships. God designed marriage to be a reflection—a representation—of His agape love for us, an interwoven mystery between Christ and the church and between a husband and a wife (see Eph. 5:22–33).

When sex and relationships are abused and treated casually, we distort the picture of Christ and the church that those relationships are meant to represent. Marriage and sexuality are a canvas on which the portrait of the gospel can be painted and displayed to a watching world.

That's why sexuality is a battleground. That's why walking in purity and living according to our God-defined purpose is a struggle. We have an enemy seeking to destroy that canvas and the powerful witness it can be.

Our sexuality can be a holy thing when we choose to let God, not culture, define it. No matter your past, no matter what hurts you hold or regrets you have, God can redeem and heal those shattered pieces and give you strength to walk in the freedom of God-defined sexuality.

Yes, culture may be sexually broken. But God makes the broken whole again.

Going Deeper

1. What messages have you encountered about sex?
2. What is your perspective of sex? Does it look more like culture's perspective or God's?

3. How does the fact that God created sex change the way you view it? Do you believe God's plan is good? Why or why not?

4. We're all sexually broken. What sexual struggles have you experienced? How can God's design for sex set you free from those struggles? If you're currently struggling, what is one practical step you can take toward freedom today?

5. "Marriage and sexuality are a canvas on which the portrait of the gospel can be painted and displayed to a watching world." What do you think this means? How does this change your view of sex?

Further Resources

- *Rethinking Sexuality: God's Design and Why It Matters* by Dr. Juli Slattery
- *Why Does God Care Who I Sleep With?* by Sam Allberry
- *Outdated: Find Love That Lasts When Dating Has Changed* by Jonathan "JP" Pokluda
- *Holy Sexuality and the Gospel: Sex, Desire, and Relationships Shaped by God's Grand Story* by Christopher Yuan
- *Sex, Purity, and the Longings of a Girl's Heart: Discovering the Beauty and Freedom of God-Defined Sexuality* by Kristen Clark and Bethany Beal

Resources on Porn Addictions

- *Eyes of Honor: Training for Purity and Righteousness* by Jonathan Welton
- Covenant Eyes (www.covenanteyes.com)
- Fight the New Drug (www.fightthenewdrug.org)
- *Pornography: Fighting for Purity* by Deepak Reju

Resources on Masturbation

- *It's All about Me: The Problem with Masturbation* by Winston T. Smith
- "God's Truth on Your Secret Sexual Sin" by Tim Challies (https://www.reviveourhearts.com/articles/gods-truth-your -secret-sexual-sin/)

Resources on Sexual Abuse

- *Sexual Abuse: Beauty for Ashes* by Robert W. Kelleman
- *Rid of My Disgrace: Hope and Healing for Victims of Sexual Assault* by Justin Holcomb and Lindsey Holcomb
- *Making All Things New: Restoring Joy to the Sexually Broken* by David Powlison
- *Is It Abuse? A Biblical Guide to Identifying Domestic Abuse and Helping Victims* by Darby A. Strickland
- National Domestic Violence Hotline (www.thehotline.org)

7

Sexual Orientation

(God's Design in a Broken World)

"I'm fourteen years old. When I was six, I was exposed to lesbian pornography. I've watched it ever since. I'm struggling
with lesbian lust. I need help. No one understands how hard
this is for me. Sometimes I don't even think God does."

"I'm seventeen years old, and I consider myself part of the
LGBTQ+ community. I've stopped saying I have any kind of
religion, because I don't want to be grouped with 'Christians'
who say and do terrible things to homosexuals."

"My brother recently told my family he's gay. He doesn't act the
same anymore. I feel like I've lost my big brother. I just don't
know how to process this."

Three teens. Three different stories. One similar struggle. These
are real teens who shared their experiences with sexual orientation
and same-sex attraction with me. These topics reflect an internal
battle, a mind full of questions, or a changed relationship. While
there are many different experiences across the LGBTQ+ spectrum

and more options of sexual orientation being added all the time, in this chapter we're going to focus solely on same-sex attraction—homosexuality and bisexuality (attraction to both the same and the opposite sex). For simplicity, I'll be using the terms *homosexuality* and *same-sex attraction* most frequently. If you can relate to these three teens and their emotions and experiences, or if you want to better understand sexual orientation from a biblical perspective, my prayer is that this chapter will speak both biblical truth and compassionate love.

How Should We Think about Homosexuality?

How should each of these three teens think about homosexuality? The teen knee-deep in the struggle? The teen now identifying as gay? The teen witnessing a family member or friend's experience? What about the teen who finds themself consistently encountering expressions of homosexuality and isn't quite sure how to respond?

Culture has one answer; Scripture has another. No matter how we've personally encountered questions about sexual orientation, our viewpoints have been molded by one or the other.

The world's view on homosexuality is hard to miss. According to a recent Gallup poll, one out of six Gen Zers identify as LGBTQ+.[1] The LGBTQ+ narrative surrounds us as we see gay and lesbian couples in popular entertainment, social media feeds, and our day-to-day lives. Homosexuality is natural. Homosexuality is normal. That's what the cultural perspective proclaims. As the LGBTQ+ narrative seeps deeper into our minds and the agenda surrounds our subconscious, it becomes harder to sort through and distinguish our own convictions from the noise of the world.

When friends and family members come out as gay, we wonder how to respond. When our teachers and classmates promote the LGBTQ+ message and celebrate Gay Pride, we wonder if we should promote and celebrate it too. When we look into our own hearts and attractions, some may wonder, *Am I supposed to feel like this? Am I gay?* Others may question, *Why shouldn't people who love each other be together—even if they're the same sex? Why do some people*

95

experience same-sex attraction while others don't? Can someone be a Christian and identify with the LGBTQ+ community?

These are hard and important questions. And culture is waiting with answers. While these answers greet us on a regular basis, we have to intentionally search for God's answers and truth. However, the sad part is even God's answers have at times been distorted. Understanding what God's Word says about LGBTQ+ issues begins with clearing the fog of misperceptions.

It's a sad truth: many people believe Christians hate homosexuals. Research and communications experts David Kinnaman and Gabe Lyons say in their book *unChristian*: "When you introduce yourself as a Christian to a friend, neighbor, or business associate . . . you might as well have it tattooed on your arm: antihomosexual, gay-hater, homophobic."[2] According to their research with the Barna Group, out of twenty attributes associated with Christianity, the perception of Christians being anti-homosexual was at the top of the list.[3]

The pendulum of a Christian view on homosexuality tends to swing toward extremes. Some fuel the "gay-hating" perception with condemning attitudes and disdainful actions toward homosexuals. Many Christians have heard only one argument about homosexuality, a view that's been called the "argument of ickyness"[4]—a simple perspective that says homosexuality is gross and homosexuals are the worst kind of sinners. Others swing to the other extreme, fully supporting homosexuality and believing that loving the same-sex attracted means wholeheartedly affirming their attractions and lifestyle.

Neither approach is biblical or reflects God's heart. To understand a biblical view of homosexuality and same-sex attraction, we need to view them through the lens of the gospel, letting God's Word answer our questions, clear our confusion, and bring hope to our struggles.

From Genesis to Jesus—What the Bible Has to Say

Let's start by asking two questions: Who defines marriage? And who determines sexual morality?

With the Supreme Court's 2015 decision that made same-sex marriage legal, most point to a court of law to define marriage. When it comes to determining morality, most look within themselves. But it was never *our* job to define marriage and morality. Both have already been established by the One who created us. As David Platt says, "Ultimately, we do not look to any court or government to define marriage. God has already done that, and his definition cannot be eradicated by a vote of legislators or the opinions of Supreme Court justices. The Supreme Judge of creation has already defined this term once and for all."[5] The same goes for morality. The moral Creator of the universe is the One who holds the authority to set a moral standard.

It's upon this truth of God's supreme authority that we can build a biblical understanding of homosexuality. Let's start with God's design for marriage. A clear definition of marriage matters because, as we learned in the last chapter, God designed sexual activity to be reserved for marriage. If marriage is the only environment where sexual activity can occur, we need to know *who* can get married. Can marriage be between anyone? Or is it solely between one man and one woman? Let's take a look.

When God created Adam and Eve as sexual and gendered beings, He also created the marriage relationship for them to come together and be joined as one flesh. God designed Eve's femininity to complement Adam's masculinity. She was created to be "a helper comparable to him" because it wasn't good "that man should be alone" and because *no other* creation on earth was a suitable helper for Adam. Only God's design of woman could fill that role (Gen. 2:18–20). With the creation of Eve came the invention of marriage. The very concept of marriage is based on gender. Without gender differences, marriage would have no reason to exist. In calling Adam and Eve to enter this covenant relationship and become one flesh, God set the standard for marriage. The words "therefore a man shall leave his father and mother and be joined to his wife, and they shall become one flesh" (Gen. 2:24) aren't just about Adam and Eve, but about *all* marriages. Sam Allberry, a pastor and apologist, notes, "Their story is true for all of humankind. It sets up a pattern that we see repeated in every generation. . . . The account is not just about their union but every marriage union."[6]

Jesus affirmed these truths when He pointed back to the beginning of creation in Matthew 19: "Have you not read that he who created them from the beginning made them male and female, and said, 'Therefore a man shall leave his father and his mother and hold fast to his wife, and the two shall become one flesh'? So they are no longer two but one flesh" (vv. 4–6 ESV). By going back to the creation account, Jesus underlined the truths about marriage, sex, and gender found in the story of Adam and Eve and reiterated that God's plan of a covenant between one man and one woman still stands.

But what about homosexuality? What does this mean for the same-sex attracted? Has God changed the script to allow for same-sex sexual relationships?

Throughout the Bible, from Genesis to the words of Jesus to Paul's letters, two truths are affirmed: First, marriage and sexual relations are meant to be between only a man and a woman. Second, homosexual activity goes against God's design for sex and is a sin in His eyes. Nowhere does God allow for *any other* form of sexual activity, but speaks against all sexual sins, from homosexuality to adultery to lust (see Rom. 1:26–27; 1 Tim. 1:9–10; and 1 Cor. 6:9–10).

The brokenness of sin results in broken sexual desires. Sin distorts sexuality in countless ways, same-sex attraction being only one. We all have broken bodies and rebellious, sin-bent hearts that cause us to experience desires that may feel natural but are contrary to God's will. Our temptations and desires may differ, but whether it's a desire for someone of the same sex or lust for a member of the opposite sex, both are inconsistent with God's design, are consequences of a sin-riddled world, and spring forth from hearts rebelling against God and His ways.

These are tough words, I know. Same-sex attraction is deeply intense and personal for those who experience it. Telling someone that the strongest desires in their hearts go against God's standards for their sexuality feels cruel. Because of this, some try to find a loophole in Scripture that allows for same-sex sexual relationships. I've heard a gamut of arguments, from "The Old Testament laws don't apply to us" to "Jesus never actually spoke about homosexuality" to "Scripture is referring to sexual abuse, not consensual love." These arguments undercut the authority of the Bible and undermine the truth God has clearly laid forth in His Word. The Bible is not a book that offers truths buffet-style, where we select what we want and leave the rest behind. Instead, it contains total truth that never contradicts itself. Yet when God's truth conflicts with our feelings, we question it. We doubt God's goodness when our emotions get caught in the fray.

Our perspective on the goodness and authority of God directly impacts our view of sexuality and same-sex attraction. In a culture that encourages us to fulfill our desires in whatever way feels good or natural, we're called to submit our desires to God and trust in His plan for our bodies and sexuality. To discover the wellspring of life, hope, and forgiveness God extends to us in our brokenness, we have to take the leap of faith and first choose to believe that all His words are true and good—even those that go against the deepest desires of our hearts.

Four Biblical Truths about Sexuality and Same-Sex Attraction

Same-sex attraction is a layered and complex issue with much more to understand than what we can cover in this chapter. But to lay the foundation, let's dig into four biblical truths to bring clarity to the conversation.

1. All Are Sinners, All Sin Is Serious, and All Require Repentance

All sin is serious to our holy God. And we are all born with sinful hearts that rebel against God. While our individual sins are different, we all need the same Savior. Those on the LGBTQ+ spectrum are not more broken or more in need of Jesus than those who are not.

First Corinthians 6:9–11 says,

> Do you not know that the unrighteous will not inherit the kingdom of God? Do not be deceived. Neither fornicators, nor idolaters, nor adulterers, nor homosexuals, nor sodomites, nor thieves, nor covetous, nor drunkards, nor revilers, nor extortioners will inherit the kingdom of God. And such were some of you. But you were washed, but you were sanctified, but you were justified in the name of the Lord Jesus and by the Spirit of our God.

This passage clarifies that we are all sinners incapable of inheriting the kingdom of God without Christ. There are few of us who could look at this list and not recognize ourselves, especially considering Jesus's words in Matthew 5 that equate lust with adultery and hatred with murder. The most important message same-sex attracted individuals need to hear is not that homosexuality is a sin but that they are sinners in need of Christ's forgiveness—the exact same message every person needs to hear, regardless of their sexual attractions. Our specific sins are serious and must be repented of, but our biggest problem is not our individual actions but the overarching truth those actions point to—we are born with sinful hearts that must be redeemed and made new through Jesus Christ.

Poet Jackie Hill Perry shares a story in her book *Gay Girl, Good God: The Story of Who I Was, and Who God Has Always Been* of a young woman who was offended by Jackie's personal testimony of coming to Christ and rejecting her former lesbian lifestyle.

> After a few personal attacks and curse words, I asked her this question, "Let's just say homosexuality wasn't even an issue for you. Would God still be pleased with your life as a whole?" To which she responded, mildly caught off guard by the angle of my question, "Nah. Nah, He wouldn't." I asked her that question, specifically, because I needed her to see that God had more than her sexual actions in mind when He commanded her (and us) to repent and believe the gospel of Jesus Christ.[7]

No one, no matter their sexual attractions, can achieve holiness without Christ. Hope is written within the words, "And such were some of you"—but no longer, because the washing, sanctifying, and justifying power of Jesus Christ delivers us from our past identity of sin as we turn from sin in repentance. Those who experience same-sex attraction can find hope in this truth by knowing all sin can be forgiven and overcome through the blood of Jesus. Those who don't experience same-sex attraction can embrace a compassionate rather than condemning attitude because of the knowledge of their own deep sin, brokenness, and need of Christ's grace.

2. Our Identity Is More than Our Sexuality

"I identify . . ."

These two words define and dominate the sexual conversation. *I identify as gay . . . lesbian . . . bisexual . . . asexual. . .*

Sexuality has now been equated with identity. Sex is no longer simply an activity—something people *do*. Instead, it's an identity—something people *are*. Because sex has become a source of identity in our society, any restrictions on sex are considered coercive and oppressive. These restrictions are no longer considered to just be limiting activities but limiting identities. They're considered as not just targeting actions but targeting personalities.

I've recently seen several friends come out on social media as LGBTQ+. Their posts grieve my heart, not because of what they're experiencing but because even though they've grown up in the church, they've been searching for an identity and community that the church has not provided. The closest thing they've found is a community that validates their emotions and promises inclusivity and acceptance. But it's still a counterfeit. I long for them to know and grasp the truth that God has a richer, fuller identity to offer. God has given us our sexuality and made it a part of who we are, but stamped upon our hearts is a more fixed, unchanging identity—*imago Dei*. We are made for God, not sex. We are created to glorify our Creator, not live for sexual fulfillment. Our sexuality is a *part* of who we are, but not the defining attribute of our identity. Labeling ourselves by our sexual attractions is deeply sad. It's a small worldview, but God offers a better truth. We are so much more than our sexual attractions. To live according to God's truth, we must strip away our false identities and clothe ourselves with our God-given identity.

Nancy Pearcey writes,

> Why place sexual feelings at the center of our identity? The Bible offers a more compelling script that defines our identity in terms of the image of God, created to reflect his character. We are loved and redeemed children of God. When we center our lives on these truths, then our identity is secure no matter what our sexual feelings are—and whether they change or don't change.[8]

While our struggles may remain, they never have to define. Jackie Hill Perry encourages believers who struggle with same-sex attractions not to refer to themselves as "Gay Christians" but rather says,

> I don't believe it is wise or truthful to the power of the gospel to identify oneself by the sins of one's past or the temptations of one's present but rather to only be defined by the Christ who's overcome both for those He calls His own. All men and women, including myself, that are well acquainted with sexual temptation are ultimately not what our temptation says of us. We are what Christ had done for us; therefore, our ultimate identity is very simple: We are Christians.[9]

In a post-truth world that prioritizes emotions, placing our identity in Christ above our sexuality means trusting God's Word more than our feelings. Believing His creation of two different genders is good. Believing His design for marriage is perfect. Believing that His Word is truth, no matter our emotions. Because we live in a fallen world of sin, our feelings will not always align with God's reality. But our feelings must be subject to God's truth. As Perry wrestled with the contradiction between her emotions and God's Word, God spoke this truth to her heart: "'Jackie, you have to believe that my word is true even if it contradicts how you feel. . . .' Either I trust in his word or I trust my own feelings. Either I look to him for the pleasure my soul craves or I search for it in lesser things. Either I walk in obedience to what he says or I reject his truth as if it were a lie."[10]

This is a choice we each have to make. Will we look to God to define our identity, or will we identify ourselves according to our sexual longings? Looking to God doesn't mean our feelings change. God *is* powerful enough to transform someone's sexual attractions, but that's not a guarantee in Scripture. God's grace has the power to deliver us from every temptation (see 1 Cor. 10:13), but until heaven the battle against our sinful flesh continues. What is guaranteed is that we can be saved, sanctified, and made whole in Jesus Christ and that He is enough. *That* is our identity.

3. We're Called to Holy Sexuality

Homosexuality is a symptom of a bigger issue—the issue of sin. The main goal of Christians is not heterosexuality (which also has the great potential for sin) but to live a life of holiness before God. As Dr. Christopher Yuan, professor at Moody Bible Institute, clarifies, "I had always thought that the opposite of homosexuality was heterosexuality. But actually the opposite of homosexuality is holiness."[11]

However, we often miss this. For a long time, teenager Matt Moore did. Since the age of seven, he'd experienced same-sex attraction—but he also knew homosexuality was a sin. He said,

> [I knew that] not only did the Bible paint people like me in the light of all that is grotesque, but so did the people around me. Family, friends, football coaches. Everyone. To be gay was to be gross. To be gay was to be wicked. To be gay was to be scum. So I prayed. Oh. How. I. Prayed. *"God, make me normal." "God, make me straight." "God, make me like everyone else."* But God didn't answer those prayers.[12]

For years, Matt wrestled with his attractions, wondering why God wouldn't take them away. Then he realized something.

> I had no real interest in God *Himself.* I wasn't praying for God to do this because I loved Him or wanted to live my life for Him. I was actually pretty unconcerned about Him, to be honest. I wanted God to take away my same-sex desires for *my* own benefit—so that I could fit in, be normal, be one of the guys, and even so that I could just have sex with girls like all of my friends were. So I obviously wasn't worried about being sexually moral. *I just wanted to be sexually normal.*[13]

That's when Matt's focus changed. His attractions didn't go away, but he understood that same-sex feelings weren't the biggest issue in his life. "Yes, it's true that God hates homosexuality," Matt wrote. "But more than that, He hates that our hearts are opposed to Him. . . . God's foremost desire is that we would come to Him through Christ to receive new hearts that love and adore Him."[14]

Matt's right. Christ followers may struggle with same-sex attraction the same way Christ followers may fight for purity against heterosexual lust. Simply experiencing temptations is not sin. Acting upon them is. We're all bent toward temptation, but we can choose whether we live out our temptation. It's 100 percent possible for a Christian to live a life of holiness while battling same-sex attraction. But it's also 100 percent impossible for a Christian to live a life of holiness while acting on their same-sex attraction.

Christ sets us apart from the world and calls us to live holy lives through the power of the Holy Spirit. "Old things have passed away; behold, all things have become new" (2 Cor. 5:17). But Scripture still challenges us to "put off . . . the old man which grows corrupt according to the deceitful lusts, and be renewed in the spirit of your mind, and [to] put on the new man which was created according to God, in true righteousness and holiness" (Eph. 4:22–24).

This life of holiness has practical implications. Living in holiness means fighting the temptations that fill our hearts and resisting the urge to embrace our emotions that contradict God's Word. Following Christ means picking up our cross and denying ourselves (Luke 9:23). The cross individuals who experience same-sex attraction are called to carry is a heavy one of self-denial—denying the desire to fulfill their attractions. For some it will mean a life of celibacy, as singleness is the only holy option besides heterosexual marriage. For all of us it means a daily battle with our rebellious hearts as we bring our lives under God's control with the help of the Holy Spirit.

"Am I now straight?" Matt asks. "Am I now normal? Am I now free from same sex desires and attracted solely to women? No, no and no. My heart was changed instantaneously when I trusted in Christ and began to follow Him, but my mind was not. I now have a heart that genuinely loves God and desires to worship Him, but at the same time, I'm still utterly messed up and damaged by sin. . . . I might not be 'straight' or 'normal,' but I have a new heart, I have Jesus, and I have the Father. And that's all I really need."[15]

4. Sexual Design Is a God-Defined Reality

"Was I just born this way?"

People who experience same-sex attraction may ask this question. Lady Gaga says yes as she belts out, "Baby, I was born this way!" But those who wrestle with same-sex attraction often find this question deeply troubling and confusing, especially if they believe in God's design for sexuality. *Why do I feel like this?* they wonder.

Post-truth thinking encourages complete sexual autonomy—meaning we can choose our sexual orientation based on our feelings. But Scripture affirms we are born with a God-defined sexual design not dependent upon our emotions. Let's unpack this statement.

First, we know God designed two genders—male and female—and He designed those genders to be sexually compatible. This is God's plan for sex and He hasn't altered this design.

Second, Scripture shows God is active and present in the development of every life. Psalm 139 paints a stunning picture:

> I praise you because I am fearfully and wonderfully made;
> your works are wonderful,
> I know that full well.
> My frame was not hidden from you
> when I was made in the secret place,
> when I was woven together in the depths of the earth.
> Your eyes saw my unformed body;
> all the days ordained for me were written in your book
> before one of them came to be. (vv. 14–16 NIV)

God wove us together, knitting us into fully formed humans. Our gender is an intrinsic part of that formation and an immutable reality.

If our gender is an unchangeable component and if God's design for how those genders relate to each other sexually is unaltered, then our sexual design is also a God-defined, God-assigned reality. While our emotions may not always align with this reality, they don't alter the truths behind it.

This doesn't minimize that feelings of same-sex attraction are real. They're just as real and strong as opposite-sex attractions. Researchers have tried to determine why some people experience same-sex attraction and have laid out reasons like environment, prenatal development, upbringing, genetics, hormonal changes, and so on. However, it's still uncertain what exactly leads to same-sex attraction, though as Christians, we know it is a result of a fallen world. A proven "gay gene" has never been discovered. After a recent study on homosexual genetics, ScienceMag.org said, "Even all the markers taken together, however, cannot predict whether a person is gay, bisexual, or straight. Instead, hundreds or thousands of genes, each with small effects, apparently influence sexual behavior."[16]

The results of this study and others have found that genetics can explain only 8–25 percent of same-sex attraction. Other variables such as hormonal changes or lifestyle offer additional explanations, but there's still no clear-cut answer. This makes the question "Why am I feeling this way?" more confusing, because you can't point to a decisive answer. But it also shows we are not the sum of our desires and emotions. We're not powerless victims of genetic predeterminations that can define our deepest identity.

Post-truth culture tells us our sexual attractions decide our sexual orientation. "This is who I'm attracted to" becomes "This is who I am." But God tells us our sexual design is not fluid or based on our feelings or attractions, but fixed according to His plan.

What Do We Do Now?

In the real-life struggles of battling same-sex attraction, realizing that family members or friends are gay, and living in a sex-obsessed society, how do we apply these truths and live with biblical conviction?

Those who experience same-sex attraction and those who don't each have different, but valuable, stories and struggles, so I want to address each individually.

A Note to Those Who Experience Same-Sex Attraction

First, thank you for reading this chapter. I'm sure much of it was difficult and painful. While I have never experienced same-sex attraction and can only imagine the struggles and confusion you have faced, I know someone who has walked through great temptation and who is understanding and empathetic to your experiences. His name is Jesus Christ. Maybe you've encountered shame or condemnation from Christians because of your attractions. If so, I am deeply sorry. Please know that Christ's response to you is not one of condemnation or shame, but rather an invitation to come and be transformed by His love and mercy. He knows how it feels to wrestle with emotions and temptations. We do not have a High Priest who cannot sympathize with our weaknesses, but one who was "in all points tempted as we are, yet without sin" (Heb. 4:15). His life shows us we can struggle without sinning and be tempted without giving in. Through the gospel Jesus invites us to come to Him in our brokenness and is committed to walking beside us and giving us the strength and help we need, freeing us from the burden of sin (Ps. 46:1; Rom. 8).

God's design for marriage and sexuality may feel cruel when you hold it against the emotions you experience. Accepting God's truth when it goes against your feelings is not easy. But He did not plan His design for sexuality simply to frustrate or deny you; He created all things for your ultimate good and protection—even if it feels the opposite. I encourage you to seek Him for strength and endurance to stand upon His truth and to believe His words over your emotions. Jackie Hill Perry offers this encouragement:

> Being a Christian and having to deny SSA is difficult (difficult is an understatement), but just as the Father sent an angel to strengthen the Son, He has sent us someone way better: the Holy Spirit. It is when we are led by the Spirit, as we look to Jesus and not discouragement (or lies or condemnation) that we are able to do what pleases the Father. Being strengthened to endure and being given the power to obey doesn't make obedience easy, but it does make it possible.[17]

It's possible to live in holiness and obedience to God even in your deepest struggles. It's a huge step to choose to live by God's truth, deny yourself, repent of any lifestyles of sin, and possibly be ostracized by those who don't understand your choices. I pray you take that step, but I don't pretend it won't be hard. It's okay to wrestle with it. Please don't isolate yourself but reach out and share your struggles with someone you can trust. You need community and support, and I pray God provides people who will be caring and compassionate to help you along your journey.

I encourage you to stop defining yourself by the labels of the world: "gay," "lesbian," "homosexual"—these labels do not have to define you. Instead, choose to be defined by the truth God speaks. You are made in His image and loved beyond measure. If you haven't accepted His grace and forgiveness and surrendered your life to Him, you are able to through the power of Christ's death on the cross: "Whoever calls on the name of the Lord shall be saved" (Rom. 10:13). And not only saved but welcomed as His child and given a new heart.

If you're already a believer, you are not condemned for your struggles. Be honest with Him about your emotions, even your emotions of anger, confusion, or grief over why you experience these attractions and what His Word says about them. He won't be angry if you bring your emotions to Him. Instead, He is able to help you and to give your heart peace. While you may believe following your heart will lead to peace and that "Jesus would want you to be yourself," the truth is that God calls us all, as it says in Ephesians, to "be imitators of God" (5:1) instead of followers of our hearts. He calls us to seek Him, to walk in holiness, to obey Him, and to surrender our longings and emotions to Him (see 1 Thess. 4:7 and 1 Pet. 1:14–16). While walking in obedience often means taking the harder road, it's also the only one that can lead to authentic peace and abundant life.

Because, yes, following Jesus will be a hard road. God doesn't guarantee your attractions will change. He's powerful enough to do that, but it's not promised in His Word. What *is* promised is that He is constant, faithful, and strong enough to carry you through every trial and give you the endurance you need to press on. He will not leave you alone but will be faithful to walk with you until the day when every desire is fulfilled, every struggle put to rest, every sin overcome, and every heartache eased by the perfect love of Jesus in eternity. Your pain is not permanent. Your struggle will not last forever. Both will be eclipsed in heaven and will be distant memories from the past. So "do not cast away your confidence, which has great reward. For you have need of endurance, so that after you have done the will of God, you may receive the promise" (Heb. 10:35–36).

A Note to Those Who Don't Experience Same-Sex Attraction

When you don't wrestle with something personally, it's easy to brush aside the pain of others. However, God calls His children to a deeper level of compassion. This compassion should inform your attitude toward those who struggle but not alter your theology and convictions. For imperfect and sinful people, this is a delicate balance to achieve but one I'm confident God can give those who seek His wisdom.

Society will attempt to undermine the authority of God's Word and biblical convictions on marriage and sexual morality. You must be prepared for the backlash you will receive and equipped with the truth so you don't waver when the heat is turned up. Many today say biblical views on marriage and sexuality are bigoted and offensive. You may be ostracized, mocked, or called a bigot or heterosexist. But this isn't an issue to compromise on, because it's one that affects people for all eternity. "In the case of homosexual practice, the gospel is very much at stake," writes Sam Allberry. "Some forms of tolerance are sinful."[18]

My first question to you is, Will you believe and proclaim God's truth, even if it's unpopular, uncomfortable, and difficult? Or will you give your emotions and culture's voice more authority?

This leads to a second question, Will you choose to love as Christ loves?

When it comes to the swinging pendulum of opinions on same-sex attraction, we tend to think we need to choose between love and truth. Christ never called you to make a choice between those options; instead, He beautifully merged the two. He set the standard as He never once lowered the bar on morality, even as He ate with sinners and welcomed the outcast and hurting. And He calls His followers to do the same.

Those who struggle with same-sex attraction often feel shunned by the church or beaten over the head with loveless theology. For believers battling their attractions, relating to other Christians can be incredibly painful as they become isolated from the very support and community they desperately need. Sadly, because of the rejection and isolation they often receive from Christians, they turn to the community that welcomes them with open arms—nonjudgmental unbelievers and other individuals on the LGBTQ+ spectrum. LGBTQ+ unbelievers often assume the only thing Christians care about is their sexuality and that Christians have only a message of condemnation to offer.

This is not what God desires for the church. How can the church speak against homosexuality, then leave those wrestling with same-sex attraction to struggle alone? Christians and the church must set a different standard for how to relate to same-sex-attracted individuals. The response will vary based on whether the individual is a Christian or not and whether they're living out their attractions or fighting against them, but one thread should be present throughout each situation: love rooted in gospel truth.

Let's consider a good response if a friend confesses they're experiencing homosexual attractions. First, thank them for sharing. Likely, it was incredibly hard and vulnerable to do so. Second, ask questions like, "How have your attractions been hard for you? Who else have you told? How have these attractions impacted your life and relationships?" Then listen to their answers, showing that you genuinely care about their story and experiences. If they haven't shared with a trustworthy pastor or mentor, encourage them to do so. Honestly tell them what God's Word says about homosexuality and encourage them to turn from any sinful lifestyles. But make sure to affirm your love for them as an individual. Make sure they know you don't believe they're defined by their feelings—so neither will your relationship with them be defined by them. Encourage them to look to Jesus and seek His help and strength. If they're believers who choose to embrace God's truth over their emotions, be willing to walk with them through the challenges and pain their attractions may bring them, but don't dangle a promise of changed attractions. If they choose a life of singleness, be a support and community to them.

Remain steadfastly faithful to biblical conviction while letting love define the conversation. Sometimes it's possible to get caught up in seeing just the sin and not the soul. Only the lifestyle and not the life. But always remember that every person who experiences same-sex attraction is created in the image of God and is of inestimable worth.

That's why the gospel—the truth of Christ's great grace and love—needs to be the focus in your interactions with your nonbelieving friends who experience same-sex attraction, to show them the grace available through Christ. That's why the gospel needs to be the focus with your believing friends who experience same-sex attraction, to show them the power they have through Christ who hung and bled and died so they might have freedom from all sin. May you not brush aside the experiences of others but enter into them with the love and compassion of Jesus and the transformative power of the gospel.

We Can Trust God with Our Sexuality

As our Creator, God knows us better than we know ourselves. His Word holds incredible truth about our bodies and sexuality. His heart is for us, His compassion immeasurable, His help available, and His love greater than we can fathom. We can trust Him with our sexuality.

As we live in a world that applauds homosexuality, may we seek God for grace to love well. May we grow in compassion and become heartfelt listeners and genuine friends. May we remain uncompromisingly rooted to the Word of God and its teaching on marriage, sexuality, and gender. May we remain faithful to His design no matter the difficulties, opposition, or emotional pain. May we proclaim the good news of the gospel to a world sinking deeper into sexual sin and shine brightly the light of hope Jesus offers to all who are broken.

Going Deeper

1. Do you struggle with same-sex attraction, or do you know someone who does? What are your overall thoughts on sexual orientation?

2. What current mindsets and perspectives from culture have you heard on LGBTQ+ issues?

3. Why did God design marriage and sex to be between one man and one woman? Why is His design for our good?

111

4. "The opposite of homosexuality is holiness." Do you think this statement is true? How does it change your perspective on sexual attractions?

5. What's the hardest part about believing God's design for sexuality? How can you look to God's truth for that struggle?

Further Resources

- *Is God Anti-Gay? And Other Questions about Homosexuality, the Bible, and Same-Sex Attraction* by Sam Allberry
- *Gay Girl, Good God: The Story of Who I Was, and Who God Has Always Been* by Jackie Hill Perry
- *Same-Sex Marriage: A Thoughtful Approach to God's Design for Marriage* by Sean McDowell and John Stonestreet
- *Out of a Far Country: A Gay Son's Journey to God. A Broken Mother's Search for Hope* by Christopher Yuan and Angela Yuan
- *Homosexuality and the Christian: A Guide for Parents, Pastors, and Friends* by Mark A. Yarhouse
- *A Change of Affection: A Gay Man's Incredible Story of Redemption* by Becket Cook

8

Gender

(Clear Definitions in a Fluid Society)

When it comes to gender, we're living in a culture of confusion.

What is male? What is female?

The answers to these questions used to be simple. Now? Not so much.

In 2016, Joseph Backholm, former director of the Family Policy Institute of Washington, interviewed a handful of students on campus at the University of Washington. The video of his conversations went viral.[1] He began by asking them, "If I told you that I was a woman, what would your response be?"

"Good for you!" a curly-headed brunette responded.

"I don't have a problem with it," another girl replied.

Then the questions got a little more complicated. "If I told you I was Chinese, what would your response be?" he asked.

The students laughed and squirmed a bit, but didn't deny his claim. "Yeah, be who you are!"

The questions continued, getting more absurd each time. "If I told you I was seven years old, what would your response be?" "If I told you I was six foot five, what would your response be?"

Though taken aback, they refused to point out the obvious reality that stood before them and agreed to affirm that Joseph Backholm—a 5'9" white man—was a 6'5" Chinese woman.

Why? What would cause bright college students to affirm statements that are not only ridiculous, but obviously false? Their willingness to deny reality was rooted in post-truth beliefs that call someone's emotions more valid than their physical reality. To highlight the illogicality of this perspective, Joseph Backholm began with the now-accepted view of gender fluidity and then proceeded to apply the same logic to height, ethnicity, and age. Because the students fully supported gender fluidity, when backed into a corner by questions with obvious answers, they realized the only intellectually consistent reply would be to throw reality out the window and affirm Joseph Backholm's preferred "identity" to the point of absurdity.

These students' views aren't rare. In fact, they are opinions culture applauds. Most people don't take their logic that far, but many wholeheartedly believe that anyone who identifies as male, female, or nonbinary is exactly what they claim regardless of their biological sex. Their logic argues that how the person *feels* matters most. But let's be serious: no matter how much Joseph Backholm argues that he feels Chinese, eight inches taller than he is, or seven years old, reality tells us his feelings are simply not true. Why does that same logic not apply to gender?

Individuals whose emotions don't match their biological sex are encouraged to embrace their feelings and disregard their body. In fact, it's become the only acceptable response and all dissenting opinions are silenced and called bigoted or intolerant.[2] In a post-truth culture willing to disregard reality, how do we come back to real truth and discover real answers? What does Jesus have to say to individuals who are wrestling with their gender? How do followers of Jesus offer lasting hope to those struggling as we restore truth to the conversation?

Gender according to Culture

To bring clarity, we need to understand the current point of view. Gender theorists have created three categories to determine gender.

1. *Assigned sex.* This refers to the gender you were classified as when you were born, based on your physical anatomy. According to gender theorists, when you were born and the doctor said, "It's a girl!" or, "It's a boy!" the doctor "assigned" you a gender, instead of just stating the obvious. In other words, the sex assigned doesn't have to be the gender you choose to embrace because it could be wrong, even though it matches the biological and physical attributes of your gender, such as chromosomes and reproductive organs.

2. *Gender identity.* Gender identity refers to the gender you feel you are. The gender that aligns with our emotions is, according to gender theorists, the most reliable indicator of our true gender. Do you feel like a boy? A girl? Both? Neither? This view claims that gender is a state of mind, and it's entirely fluid. You could feel like a boy today and a girl tomorrow and both would be true. The body is entirely disregarded and has no bearing upon your gender identity. As a young woman who identifies as nonbinary said in a video with the BBC, "Gender is in the brain. . . . It doesn't matter what living, meat skeleton you've been born in; it's what you feel that defines you."[3] The term *transgender* refers to people whose gender identity is different from their assigned sex. *Cisgender* refers to people whose gender identity matches their assigned sex.

3. *Gender expression.* Gender expression is the third component. It's how people publicly manifest their internal feelings of gender. Gender expression refers to the clothes people choose to wear, their personality attributes, the activities they enjoy, and so on. Gender expression, like gender identity, may not match one's assigned sex. For example, a man who feels like a woman may wear women's clothing to express his gender identity and vice versa.

Instead of dividing the human race into male and female based on biological anatomy, gender theorists believe these three categories define gender. Your sex is not acknowledged, it's assigned. Your gender is not fixed, it's fluid; it's not physical, it's emotional. These beliefs have led to incredible confusion. The physical body has been severed from gender, and gender has become something you can choose and change.

Decades ago, the general consensus was you were a man if you had male anatomy and a woman if you had female anatomy. It's now believed that the differences between male and female don't matter, and our entire concept of gender as biologically determined is a social construct—meaning that because the world has operated under the labels *male* and *female* for so long, it's become a bias in our thinking that isn't actually rooted in reality. It's considered an outdated human idea, not an objective fact.

The attack on gender also targets language. The classic pronouns *him/her, he/she, his/hers* are considered too narrow because they exclude other gender identities. A whole host of other pronouns have been introduced like *zi, sie,* or *ve* (substituting for *he/she*). Sticking with gender-neutral words like *they/them* is also an option. Lately I've heard more people introducing themselves with their "preferred pronouns" or being asked for their preferred pronouns. Recently, I saw a children's book about the different pronouns kids could use, how to pick which was right for them, and why it was okay to not identify as their biological sex.

These mindsets infiltrate our lives and are now "normal," but they're dangerous ideology. Theories like these are a denial of basic biology and objective reality. These ideas are no longer hovering on the fringes of society. Instead, they're becoming fundamental education in classrooms across the country. The Sexuality Information and Education Council of the United States (SIECUS) put out a report in 2019, urging Texas to change their sex education curriculum. Their recommendations for sexual orientation and gender identity proposed that students in kindergarten through second grade should be able to "explain that some people's gender matches what their body looks like on the outside and others' do not."[4] As the grades progressed, the recommended "education" did too. Students in third through fifth grades should be able to "define gender identity, cisgender, transgender, and gender non-binary and explain that gender, gender roles, and gender expression exist along a spectrum."[5]

This proposal wasn't a radical concept, but SIECUS's idea of fundamental sex education. Five-year-olds are now expected to be taught and to believe that boys don't have to be boys and girls may not really be girls. How can children believe anything is rooted in truth and facts when they're being taught to doubt their own gender at the same time they're learning two plus two equals four? This ideology is being rooted in the minds of children and ingrained throughout every facet of society.

Transgender activists are seeking to degenderize society and rewrite reality about sex and gender. But God's design isn't easily rewritten. Gender matters. Bodily design and biology matter. God's creation of male and female matters.

Male and Female in God's Design

To navigate these opinions, we need a better understanding of both the *theology* and *biology* of gender.

When God created the world and breathed humanity into existence, He brought order out of chaos. Every part of God's design was intentional, especially His creation of humans. Genesis 1:27 says, "So God created man in His own image; in the image of God He created him; male and female He created them."

The phrase "male and female He created them" doesn't infer we're all a little bit male and a little bit female. It also doesn't mean there's a gender spectrum we slide down and wherever we land decides our gender identity. This passage features two distinct individuals. One male. One female. Their gender was not a social construction, but God's deliberate intention. He purposefully created each gender to be separate, distinct, and unique from the other.

In the perfect world of the garden of Eden, this design was flawless. But when sin entered the scene, gender, like everything else, experienced the devastating consequences. Romans 8:20–21 points back to the curse upon the earth detailed in Genesis 3: "For the creation was subjected to futility, not willingly, but because of him who subjected it, in hope that the creation itself will be set free from its bondage to corruption and obtain the freedom of the glory of the children of God" (ESV).

Creation was subjected to futility. It's messed up and broken—and so are our bodies. Whether that brokenness shows up in forms of physical illness or symptoms of gender dysphoria, our brokenness points to the biblical truth that we're living in a fallen world. This makes gender dysphoria a genuine struggle. Those who experience feelings of being trapped in the wrong body or having the wrong gender often don't choose their emotions. They don't understand the way they feel, and it's deeply painful. They are, like all of us, victims of a sin-soaked world.

Sin came with deep-seated rebellion against God. The first rebellion brought brokenness to the design. The continued rebellion glorifies the brokenness. The opinions promoted in our culture are open defiance to God as Creator and Lord. However, it's important to clarify that those who experience genuine gender dysphoria outside their control are not experiencing it because of *personal* defiance to God. It's not punishment for personal sin but evidence of universal sin. It's also important to distinguish between transgender activists, those who have been influenced by the transgender message, and those who experience gender dysphoria as a psychological condition.

God's ingenious design of gender is too intricate to be easily replaced by the post-truth transgender message. The biology of gender reveals that it's impossible to change a person's sex and that gender is not just an idea in our heads but reality throughout our bodies. We are gendered to the core. As cardiologist Paula Johnson said in her popular TED talk, "Every cell has a sex—and what that means is that men and women are different down to the cellular and molecular level. It means that we're different across all of our organs, from our brains to our hearts, our lungs, our joints."[6] Our sexual differences display themselves in external characteristics, like our reproductive system and physical features. It's possible to cause someone to *look* like a member of the opposite gender through cosmetic surgeries, but the individual's actual gender never changes.

Psychologist Dr. Leonard Sax has done extensive research on the variations between genders and, through multiple studies, says "research suggests that female brain tissue is 'intrinsically different' from male brain tissue."[7] These differences are genetically programmed and present at birth and have dozens of implications on how male and female brains function. For instance, these studies show that girls and boys feel pain differently,[8] girls tend to have more sensitive hearing than boys,[9] and even that eyesight variations exist.[10]

Our chromosomes (female chromosomes are XX, male are XY) distinguish our sex and affect not only our reproductive systems but every cell in our bodies. The differences between men and women are not only distinct but intricate.

God designed these differences purposefully. But somehow society has come to believe that *male* and *female* are interchangeable, like the heads of a screwdriver. The very idea is a direct insult to the intricacies of gender, not to mention blind to the obvious differences. You can't swap genders back and forth because gender goes too deep. No amount of surgery, hormone treatment, or alterations in appearance can change what's already been determined at the cellular level within our bodies—*and* determined at the divine level by the very hand of God, who ordained our gender through His wisdom and sovereignty. Walt Heyer, a well-known former transsexual who underwent surgery to live as a woman but transitioned back after he became a Christian eight years later, said, "The biological fact is that no one can change from one gender to another except in appearance. . . . I came to accept that gender surgery didn't change me into a woman. I was born a man, and I was still a man; my gender never changed."[11]

That's why sex-change surgeries often fail to bring the fulfillment and happiness people hope for. Transitioning is held out as the best option for people suffering from gender dysphoria. They're told that by removing healthy body parts or having hormone treatment they will finally feel at home in their body and their mental health will improve.

But in fact, the opposite has been found. A 2015 study in Boston of 180 transsexual youths who underwent surgery found "these youth had a twofold to threefold increased risk of psychiatric disorders, including depression, anxiety disorder, suicidal ideation, suicide attempt, self-harm without lethal intent, and both inpatient and outpatient mental health treatment."[12] One of the most thorough follow-up studies of individuals who transitioned took place in Sweden over the course of thirty years. The conclusion of this study was that "persons with transsexualism, after sex reassignment, have considerably higher risks for mortality, suicidal behaviour, and psychiatric morbidity than the general population."[13] This conclusion is in spite of the fact that Sweden is strongly supportive of transgenderism. As a recent analysis concluded, "A pattern begins to emerge as we survey some of the best and longest outcome studies on gender transition: the longer the studies and the better the methods, the more negative the results."[14]

Transitioning is offered as a false hope to suffering people, but no amount of external changes can cure mental struggles or alter biological realities. It's also disturbing that psychiatric evaluation and therapy is rarely offered and underlying mental health struggles are rarely addressed when an individual comes seeking sex reassignment surgery. Mental struggles such as depression, anxiety, or suicidal thoughts often accompany gender dysphoria, but these issues are rarely treated. Instead, society is facing its own self-made mental health crisis by attempting to fix mental struggles with physical surgery or altered hormones. Paul McHugh, former psychiatrist in chief of Johns Hopkins Hospital, wrote about teens seeking relief from underlying psychological issues through sex reassignment surgery. "The grim fact is that most of these youngsters do not find therapists willing to assess and guide them in ways that permit them to work out their conflicts and correct their assumptions. Rather, they and their families find only 'gender counselors' who encourage them in their sexual misassumptions."[15] After surgery, the original mental struggles remain and are often increased. Many individuals regret their surgeries.

For those struggling with gender dysphoria, the problem is not that they're living in the wrong body, but that their mind is at war with their body. In other cases of mental and physical incongruence, the mind, not the body, is treated. For example, someone with anorexia struggles with viewing their body as overweight, when in reality it's not. Doctors don't affirm these feelings and let the individual starve themselves, but instead focus on treating the underlying mental cause. Gender is the only instance where a mind/body incongruence is "fixed" through the body.

My heart breaks for those struggling through these cultural lies and confusing emotions. I think of Savannah—a girl I know who has battled depression and gender dysphoria for years. She recently came out as nonbinary and changed her name. She's now undergoing hormone treatment and is scheduled for surgery. She's open about her intense depression but keeps forging ahead because she believes "the next thing"—the next surgery, the next treatment—will finally bring the peace she's looking for. But why is she trying to treat her mental struggles with physical changes? She's bought the cultural lie that her body doesn't matter and her perceived gender is more important than her physical reality.

The truth is that her body is a relevant component of her overall identity and altering her flesh will not lead to emotional peace. We can't change what God has hardwired into our DNA. As Nancy Pearcey says, "Feelings can change. The body is an observable fact that does not change. It makes sense to treat it as a reliable marker of gender identity."[16] But in our post-truth environment, we give emotions more authority than facts.

These facts are not restrictive. They're what make us human. Separated by rebellion from the God who created us, we have lost the truth of what it means to be human and have forsaken the value of human life. If we don't know what it means to be human, we don't know what it means to be male and female either.

Bringing Hope Back to the Design

The truth of who we are can be restored only through the knowledge of God and the saving grace of Jesus Christ. If you're struggling with confusing emotions about your gender, first, let me validate how real and hard your feelings are. I can only imagine how deeply dark, painful, and confusing it is to experience this disconnect between your body and mind. I encourage you to openly share your struggles with your parents, pastor, counselor, or someone you trust. Hidden struggles fester under the surface, but sharing them can lift a weight off our hearts. While most of the voices you hear, both within your mind and from others around you, may tell you embracing your feelings over your body will lead to mental and emotional peace, let me gently point you to God's truth: your body and every aspect of its physical gender and sexual design are valuable, intentional, and a good gift from God. Your body is *not* a mistake. While your emotions may not align with your physical design, following your emotions will not lead to peace.

I don't pretend that choosing to believe your physical reality over your feelings will be easy or will heal your confusing emotions immediately, but I can encourage you that God's design is not intended to harm or frustrate you, but to lead you to fullness of life. The transgender message devalues the priceless worth of your body, but God's Word reveals your value and dignity. God is *for* your body because He created you with care and intention. Please reach out for help from others, and most importantly, turn to God with your pain and confusion and let Him help you wrestle through these emotions and questions.

Because the brokenness in our bodies came through the brokenness of sin, only the wholeness of Jesus Christ can restore us. Surgeries can't fix us. Only Jesus can. Sin jolted us out of the harmony between body and soul God first intended, but God's redemptive plan through Jesus offers hope that harmony will one day be restored. This doesn't mean becoming a Christian immediately solves gender struggles, but it does point us to a greater hope. Turning from sin and submitting ourselves to God's design, as well as seeking help from God and others, sets us on the path toward healing. As Sam Allberry encourages,

> Bodily brokenness of any kind, if we have eyes to see, can point us to the broken body of Christ—and through that brokenness, to the eventual restoration and healing that comes through him. Embracing Christ doesn't guarantee resolution in this life to the bodily brokenness we experience. But it does give us a sure and confident hope that we will have a perfect relationship with our body in the world to come.[17]

The identity God offers is deeper, rooted in His truths over our feelings. As followers of God, may we show compassion to the struggling but also boldly expose the dangerous lies purported by transgender activists. Once again, ideas have consequences. Bad ideas have victims. Gender ideology is a prime example of a bad idea crushing victims under the wheels of its lies. It's more loving to point people to a truth that contradicts their feelings than confirm a lie that coincides with their emotions.

Isn't That Discrimination?

A dangerous idea that comes piggybacked with gender ideology is the idea that anyone who doesn't affirm secular gender theory is guilty of discrimination. While many LGBTQ+ individuals have suffered injustice at the hands of uncompassionate and hate-filled individuals, I believe it's possible to disagree with LGBTQ+ opinions while still showing love and respect. Here are two reasons why.

- **It's not discrimination to affirm truth.** Christians are called to be truth-tellers, even if the truth is unpopular. Gender theory denies truth and reality in favor of preference and emotions. As we've already seen, the truth is that it's impossible to change gender. That's a matter not of bigotry but of biology. If we know the truth, the truth demands we yield to a higher opinion than our preferences. Affirming truth by pointing out lies does not equal discrimination.

- **Unconditional love does not equal unconditional affirmation.** Today's view of love means unconditional affirmation and approval. "If you love me, you'll accept me," some might say. But that's not actual love. Real love seeks the person's best, even if it goes against their desires. We see this in parents' goals to raise their kids well and protect them, even if it means telling them they can't play in the road, have to eat their vegetables, and need to do their schoolwork. The child may not like it, but it's an act of love that's for their good. Likewise, it's not loving to lie about something as important as someone's gender and sexuality and encourage them to deny reality. It's possible to tell hard truths in deep love and understanding. Doing so is not hateful. Loving someone enough to tell them the truth affirms their dignity and inherent value more than staying silent.

Discrimination exists, but denying reality is not the way to root it out. Truth is our tool, love is our method. As culture continues to promote gender theory, we can expect labels of discrimination and intolerance to increase. We must be committed to truth, despite the opposition, and prepared to stand strong through the long haul. Here are three practical steps.

1. Practically Affirm Truth

Gender-neutral bathrooms. Men playing on women's sports teams. Women playing on men's sports teams. Friends and family dealing with confusion over the ideology or battling personal gender struggles. Situations like these are becoming more common and lead to uncomfortable choices. One common question that often comes up is, Should I use someone's preferred pronouns? Is doing so affirming their choices and identity? Or is it showing them respect as an individual? It's a hot topic among Christians, and there are many different opinions.

In this question, *context* and *clarity* are key. I encourage everyone facing a situation like this to consider their response based on the context of the relationship. Is this person a professing Christian or not? Are they someone with whom you've had a prior relationship? Is your use or refusal something you can talk about with the individual? (See 1 Corinthians 5:9–13 for insight on responding to sexual sin in the world versus within the church.)

Our goal here is clarity. We serve a God of truth, and therefore, we cannot affirm lies. In no instance should we go against our conscience and affirm unbiblical views about someone's gender or identity. Our love for the individual as a person made in God's image must coincide with our firm stance on His truth. However, there may be specific and limited instances where a Christian may feel that using a preferred pronoun would allow for them to more effectively share God's truth with the individual than a blank refusal would allow for. I encourage you to prayerfully seek God, study Scripture, and evaluate each instance with careful deliberation. In any instance, God's truth must be made known and God's leading must be made clear. Here are two basic potential responses:

Response #1: "I understand your reasoning behind asking me to use these pronouns. I want you to know that I respect you as a person and I believe you are highly valuable and loved by God, but because of my convictions based on the Bible and my belief about God's design for gender, I cannot call you by your preferred pronouns. For me to do so would violate my convictions and conscience. I hope you can understand this. I would love to talk more about this, so I can better understand what has led you to this decision and so you can better understand my convictions."

Response #2: "I am choosing to call you by your preferred pronouns to show respect to you; however, I want to be clear that, according to my convictions based on the Bible and my belief about God's design for gender, I believe that we cannot change our gender. I will respect your request that I use these pronouns, but my using them does not equal my agreement with your choices or my affirmation that _____ is your actual gender. I would love to talk more about this, so I can better understand what has led you to this decision and so you can better understand my convictions."

Pray and seek God's wisdom as you consider these potential responses and how God would lead you to act. Either way, you must be committed to sharing the truth first and foremost and to act as God leads you—not how society may coerce you.[18]

As the pressure to conform increases, we have to be prepared to affirm truth through our actions as well as our words. Churches, ministries, businesses, faith-based schools and sports teams, teachers and students, Christian doctors, counselors, and Christians in roles of leadership will be pressured to violate their consciences and conform to the demands. A college student in Pennsylvania was kicked out of class for speaking up and saying there are only two biological genders after watching a TED talk from a transgender woman.[19] He used this opportunity in class to share his beliefs but suffered the consequences.

As the saturation of the ideology increases, so will these circumstances and decisions. People have been fired from their jobs, demoted, accused of hate speech, and taken to court over transgender issues, and consequences will only increase as free speech is limited and opposition is labeled discrimination. We must be prepared and equipped with our convictions and ready to stand strong despite the consequences.

2. Lovingly Care for Those Struggling

I know people struggling with gender dysphoria, and I'm sure you do too. The mental and emotional pain is excruciating for many. Some have been born with these struggles; others are victims of the transgender revolution. As followers of a loving and compassionate Savior, Christians have a greater love and hope to offer hurting individuals. Every person battling gender dysphoria is made in the image of God and is of inestimable value. I love how Abdu Murray puts it:

> All of us are fractured in *every way*, including *but not limited* to our sexuality. Every person—whether same-sex attracted or not, whether conflicted about his or her gender or completely sure of it—has veered from our originally intended purpose. We're broken in different ways, but we are broken together. Together we need restoration.[20]

It's from this place of mutual brokenness with a Savior big enough to carry our pain that we can reach out to the hurting with unconditional love. We speak truth with grace and compassion. We listen to their stories and take time to seek to understand. We pack up our hypocrisy that points a finger, lay down our condemnation, and instead show how Jesus makes the broken whole again. We affirm the value of their physical body and gender and encourage them to seek help in bringing their mind into alignment with their body. We must allow the church to be a place of truth and compassion, not condemnation or exile, where we open our doors to the hurting and confused so they can hear and understand God's design for their body and the good news of Jesus.

As we share Christ's love with those struggling with gender dysphoria, we must also point to lasting help and healing. The only option presented today is the diagnosis of transgenderism and a treatment of surgery or hormone therapy. But we can share a better option. We can help bring understanding to the incongruence between mind and body and help address any underlying mental struggles. We can offer godly counsel, support, and love as individuals wrestle with their emotions. Showing love doesn't mean hiding the truth. It means sharing the truth and walking with the hurting as they journey down the hard road of healing. It's not immediate. It takes time, compassion, and sacrifice. But it's part of being the hands and feet of Jesus.

3. Live Out and Affirm Biblical Masculinity and Femininity

When Bruce Jenner announced he was transitioning and would be adopting the name Caitlyn, the news was broadcast to the world through his idea of what it meant to be a woman—"sultry poses, thick mascara and the prospect of regular 'girls' nights to banter about hair and makeup." In other words, cultural stereotypes: "the kind of nonsense that was used to repress women for centuries,"[21] as a *New York Times* article put it.

The transgender message is heavily reliant upon gender stereotypes. After all, if you don't define gender by biology, what do you have left? Just external actions and internal feelings—both of which can be rooted in stereotypical ideas of how girls and boys are "supposed" to act or feel. Little girls like pink. Little boys play with trucks. Teen girls are emotional and like talking about feelings with friends. Teen guys avoid emotions and prefer to appear tough and strong. Even the terms *biblical masculinity* and *biblical femininity* can conjure pictures of stereotypical ideas that are not rooted in biblical truth. To fully live out God's design for masculinity and femininity, we have to reevaluate both secular stereotypes and those often promoted in the church and rediscover what God's Word actually says about the roles and design of men and women.

For decades, many have fought against the stereotypes in both healthy and unhealthy ways, but the transgender message sends society regressing back into them. These stereotypes have led people—especially kids and young adults—to question their gender. Those who don't fit the stereotypical molds of girly girls and tough boys feel out of place in the girl or boy world and are vulnerable to the transgender message. They're what many would call *gender noncon-forming*, and transgender activists argue that their nonconforming personalities mean they are transgender.

However, personality doesn't determine gender. What a person enjoys doing or their emotional nature doesn't establish whether they are male or female. These attributes are nonsexual, but the trans-gender revolution is turning the nonconforming into pawns in their game. Nancy Pearcey quotes a girl who struggled with cross-gender feelings and said, "American society is in danger of sexualizing what are really just character traits—putting people in a sexual box based on non-sexual traits and behaviors."[22] Temperament is different from sexuality, and God's design for male and female is big enough to encompass individuals who don't fit cultural stereotypes.

Our gender is first and foremost defined by the body God gave us. Living in that body well and living out biblical masculinity and femi-ninity means embracing both the body and the personality given by God and submitting ourselves to Him. At the core, biblical masculin-ity and femininity have more to do with our attitude toward God and our relationship with Him and obedience to His Word. Both men and women are called to seek God to live well in the body, circumstances, and roles He has given them.

To show truth to a confused world, it's important we live out bib-lical masculinity and femininity by letting God guide what it means to be male and female. Those who don't align with secular gender stereotypes can be encouraged that God didn't make a mistake when He created them but designed both their gender and personality on purpose. Pearcey suggests that

> nonconforming children . . . need support and empathy as they work through their painful feelings of alienation. Churches should encour-age them to value their unique temperament and to resist pressure to interpret it as evidence they must be transgender or homosex-ual. . . . In the body of Christ, we should celebrate a wide diversity of God-given personality types, even if they do not fit the current stereotypes.[23]

Counterculturally Male and Female

Living out these truths and navigating a gender-confused society isn't easy, but through God's power, it's possible. In a culture that calls gender fluid, we can live with clarity. In a world that denies the differences between men and women, we can take a countercultural stance and embrace the beauty of God's design for gender.

Both men and women hold equal value to God. Our differences don't add or detract from our worth but affirm our value in God's sight. It's good to be a man. It's good to be a woman. It's good to embrace the God-given gender we were born with. It's good because God called it good and because the unique and intricate differences between men and women are a part of His stunning design for humanity.

Going Deeper

1. Have you struggled with gender confusion in the past or are you currently struggling? Do you know someone who is? How does this chapter bring clarity to that struggle?

2. What do you believe determines gender?

3. Why are physical bodies more reliable indicators of gender than emotions?

4. What's the difference between unconditional love and unconditional affirmation? Why is it more loving to affirm truth than emotions?

5. How can you practically love those around you who struggle with issues of gender?

Further Resources

- *Love Thy Body: Answering Hard Questions about Life and Sexuality* by Nancy R. Pearcey

- *Gender Ideology: What Do Christians Need to Know?* by Sharon James
- *Understanding Gender Dysphoria: Navigating Transgender Issues in a Changing Culture* by Mark A. Yarhouse
- *When Harry Became Sally: Responding to the Transgender Moment* by Ryan T. Anderson
- *Why? Understanding Homosexuality and Gender Development in Males* and *Why? Understanding Homosexuality and Gender Development in Females* (DVD series: https://www.livehope.org/product/why-dvd-set-men-and-women/)
- *Let Me Be a Woman: Notes to My Daughter on the Meaning of Womanhood* by Elisabeth Elliot
- *The Mark of a Man: Following Christ's Example of Masculinity* by Elisabeth Elliot

9

Life

(There's a War on Life)

The building looked so ordinary.

That was my first thought as we walked up. Plain brown wood siding. The paint peeling just a bit. Bricks lining the front. I could've driven by and not given it a second glance. Not even the sign next to the door that read WOMEN'S HEALTH CENTER would have tipped me off if I wasn't paying attention.

But sometimes the most ordinary buildings hold the darkest stories.

The bored-looking security guard standing outside straightened his stance as my mom and I approached the grassy area by the side of the road. He gave us a once-over, then went back to consulting his clipboard.

We took our places in the designated spot. It was mid-October, right in the middle of the annual 40 Days for Life campaign.[1] Around the country, prayer vigils were being held outside abortion clinics, as individuals gathered together to pray for the saving of lives and an end to abortion. Today it was our turn.

For a few minutes, I just stood there, staring at the building. I was supposed to be praying, but all I could think was, *How many lives have ended here?* My throat tightened, tears pressing hot behind my eyes. How many women pulled into this parking lot, life growing safe within them, only to leave a priceless soul behind? How many drove away with a pill in hand that could end an unfolding life? Somehow standing in front of the building made it feel more real. Its very presence was a sobering witness to the fact that we're living in a culture of death.

In every "my body, my choice" abortion; in every depression-filled, hopelessness-induced suicide; in every "compassionate" medically assisted death is the lie telling us that life is cheap. Disposable. Somewhere along the way, we've forgotten three truths that counter the lie that says life doesn't matter: First, life is precious. Second, life is worth protecting. Third, life is worth living.

A View from the Front Lines—Abortion, Infanticide, and Embryology Research

Since *Roe v. Wade* in 1973, approximately sixty-two million unborn lives have been murdered in the womb. If counted, abortion would be the leading cause of death in the United States.

Stop and imagine that.

Sixty-two million children the world lost the privilege of knowing. Sixty-two million unique lives who would have altered and added to our society in untold ways. These are lives the world should mourn.

Instead, the push for more abortion continues. With the inauguration of one of the most proabortion presidential teams in 2021, these are dark days for unborn babies. The abortion industry continues to expand, and proabortion legislation is becoming more ingrained in the laws of the land. The government has become more interested in killing unborn children than in protecting them.

As I write this in late 2021, tension is thick on the political scene regarding abortion. But through all the supposed setbacks or assumed victories, I've become more convinced that the true battle of abortion does not happen in the arena of *politics*, but the arena of *mindsets*. Laws matter greatly and can either protect or endanger life, but laws alone cannot change hearts and minds. Even if laws change, perspectives remain. And it's perspectives and ideas that are the biggest danger to the unborn—and born. What we're witnessing is a battle of ideas. Sadly, death masqueraded as autonomy and choice is the narrative loudest in today's culture. And where mindsets go, laws will soon follow.

Proabortion ideology is celebrated and promoted by celebrities, politicians, and social media influencers in an attempt to dehumanize the unborn and normalize abortion's attack on life. In 2021, a Texas high school valedictorian's speech went viral when she explained how she needs access to abortion to fulfill her dreams. Limiting abortion access is, in her words, "dehumanizing . . . to have the autonomy over your own body taken from you."[2] Her point overtly ignores that there is something distinctly more dehumanizing than removing one's autonomy—killing another human being. Life has become devalued to the point that women are encouraged to "shout their abortions" and to know "abortion is normal."[3] Killing unborn children is not only okay, it's applauded.

The war against these precious and vulnerable lives is expanding to outside the womb. In Belgium, 94 percent of doctors support infanticide, or as they call it, "after-birth abortion," if the infant is disabled or unwanted. Infanticide is acceptable, because in their words, newborn babies are not "actual persons."[4] It's justified because "neither [a fetus or infant] is a 'person' in the sense of 'subject of a moral right to life.' We take 'person' to mean an individual who is capable of attributing to her own existence some (at least) basic value such that being deprived of this existence represents a loss to her."[5] In short, because a baby can't express that its own life has value, its life is worthless. "Parents should be given the choice to end the lives of their newborn babies shortly after they are born because they are 'morally irrelevant' and have 'no moral right to life.'"[6] Is there any deeper level of demented darkness? I don't think so.

Backpedal from infanticide to embryology research and you see another way life is devalued as millions of human embryos are discarded, harvested for stem cells (as are body parts from aborted fetuses), or used for unethical scientific research and genetic experimentation. Most people don't think of embryos as human beings, but as Dr.

Jeff Myers states, "We may treat the destruction of human embryos as no big deal, but in the process we forfeit the very idea of what it means to be human."[7]

No matter which way you look at it, from the destruction of embryos to early-term or midterm abortion to late-term abortion or infanticide, they all devalue and take human life. The concept of abortion hinges on the dehumanization of the unborn—saying a fetus is simply "pregnancy tissue," embryos are simply "clumps of cells," or that a full-term baby isn't an "actual person" or is only a "potential person." But the truth is that there is no fundamental difference between an embryo, a fetus, and a fully formed child in regard to their humanity, worth, and status as a unique, valuable person. Size, level of development, environment, and degree of dependency make no difference to someone's status as a human being and, most importantly, to their intrinsic value in the eyes of the God who created them and who knit their every cell together into the living, breathing, image-bearing individual they're designed to be.

Not only does abortion take human life, it also deeply affects the living. The scars and wounds of those who have had abortions go deep. While "shouting your abortion" may be encouraged, many women experience deep trauma after their abortions and try to bury their pain. I want to be sensitive to the pain of those who have had abortions, displaying clearly not only how God views abortion but also how deeply God loves each woman—no matter their past decisions or present pain. If you carry this weight, please know this chapter was not written to condemn you. Instead, let me point you to the fullness of God's grace and forgiveness in Jesus. Through Christ, your past can be forgiven, your present redeemed, and your pain healed. There is no condemnation or shame for those who are forgiven in Christ.

A View from the Front Lines—Euthanasia and Suicide

Taking innocent lives doesn't begin and end with the unborn. The war on life rages after birth with the rise of medically assisted suicide and other forms of euthanasia. Since June 2016, all Canadians over the age of eighteen have had the right to medically assisted death,[8] and at the time of this writing, assisted suicide is legal in nine US states. In 2020, the number of deaths by assisted suicide in the state of Oregon rose by 28 percent.[9] It's referred to as "dying with dignity" or "the most compassionate option," but as John Stonestreet explains, with the option of assisted suicide on the table, the "right to die" often turns into a "duty to die."[10] Consider the woman with cancer who was denied insurance coverage for chemotherapy treatments, but was told it would cost her only $1.20 for suicide pills.[11] Or the many elderly or terminally ill individuals who feel like a burden on their caretakers. When choosing to die becomes a viable option for the suffering, that option has the potential for serious abuse. Patients will be pressured to choose it because it's easier, cheaper, or a quick way out of pain.

These mindsets saturate the general culture and are trickling into our entertainment. Have you ever watched a movie glorifying death? Abortion is normalized in movies like *Unpregnant*, and assisted suicide is glamorized in films and books like *Me Before You*. While *Me Before You* is supposed to be a romantic drama, it takes a disturbing turn as one of the main characters, a paralyzed young man, chooses to end his own life because he doesn't consider his life worth living. "You only get one life," he says. "It's actually your duty to live it as fully as possible."[12] But despite his words, he decides to end his life through assisted suicide.[13]

These messages are eerily similar to a propaganda film produced in Nazi Germany called *Ich klage an* (English title: *I Accuse*), where a young woman diagnosed with multiple sclerosis pleads with doctors to kill her so she doesn't have to suffer. In the end, her own husband, a doctor, administers a lethal overdose, ending her life.

Media has the power to impact our worldview and normalize that which is ethically wrong. When *I Accuse* was released in 1941, it was a card played by propaganda minister Joseph Goebbels to raise public support of Germany's *Aktion T4* euthanasia program. The program's intention was to kill the terminally ill, elderly, emotionally unstable, or disabled—anyone whom the Nazis deemed "life unworthy of life."[14] Those who fell into those categories were called "burdensome lives" or "useless eaters," and thousands were murdered by starvation, lethal injection, or poisonous gas.

We may not have a nationwide euthanasia program, but the worldview that allowed for such atrocities is not as far out of reach as we might imagine. The perspectives that allow for assisted suicide call death a choice or a "compassionate option," but it's a slippery slope as soon as that option is on the table. Once the line is crossed that says it's permissible to intentionally end a life with certain caveats in place (such as a request for death or in cases of terminal illness), those caveats can be corrupted, and before you know it, people are being killed with or without consent. Which is what occurs during every abortion: an innocent, usually healthy human life is taken. The argument "My body, my choice" is often used to justify abortion, but that statement overlooks the other body involved—a body that doesn't have a choice.

Is it any wonder, with these mindsets, that suicide rates are at an all-time high?[15] In 2018, suicide was the second leading cause of death for those age ten to thirty-four.[16] That is a heartbreaking statistic. Too many of our youth are choosing death over life. There are many factors influencing why a person chooses suicide, but the overall demeaning of life cannot be overlooked as one of them.

When the Netflix show *13 Reasons Why* debuted in March 2017, suicide rates for those age ten to seventeen rose 28.9 percent.[17] The show depicted and glamorized the story of a girl who committed suicide and left behind audiotapes sharing why she chose to die. *13 Reasons Why* shared dangerous ideas and had countless victims.

Here we can practically see the impact of worldviews. The secularist worldview permeating our culture is one of hopelessness. There's no foundation beyond ourselves that measures human value or points to a future hope and no reason to press on if this life is all there is. The church has often stayed silent on the topics of suicide and euthanasia, but how can we afford to remain quiet when so many lives are ending without the hope of the gospel?

Through abortion, medically assisted death, and suicide, the value of human life has been annihilated by the voices of culture. If you destroy the value of life, you destroy the foundation of what it means to live. More than ever, we're struggling with knowing *how* to live. Depression, anxiety, hopelessness, and other mental health struggles contribute to many of these tragedies.

People need help living, not help dying. We need to know life is valuable, not dispensable. Death is not a choice to be selected. It's a reality we all face, but until that day, we need to know life is worth living. For ourselves, for our unborn children, for our terminally ill relatives and friends, for our dying elderly—each life is worthy to be fought for and protected. Life is too precious to be discarded in an abortion clinic, extinguished by a "merciful" prescription, or taken by one's own hand. Life is a priceless gift from our Creator God.

Unalterable Value

There is a higher standard of human worth and it's found in the *imago Dei*: the truth that we're all made in God's image. God, who formed and shaped us and knew us before we took our first breath, doesn't exclude any soul. Every life holds invaluable worth. This worth is not bestowed by parents, family members, friends, health, or personal opinion, but by the hand of God.

And all means *all*—from the tiniest embryo to the terminally ill cancer patient; from the newborn baby to your ninety-year-old grandma; from the child conceived through rape to the baby long prayed for; from the woman struggling with infertility to the one with the burden of a past abortion on her heart. Every human being has intrinsic value from the moment of their conception. Nothing—not size, shape, ability, gender, environment, or any other varying factor—can alter this truth. There are no caveats or exceptions when you view humanity through the lens of *imago Dei*.

The first words spoken about humanity in Scripture set us apart from the rest of creation. "Then God said, 'Let Us make man in Our image, according to Our likeness, . . . So God created man in His own image" (Gen. 1:26–27). God breathed the first human to life with His own breath and "man became a living being" (2:7). Only humans were created with the purpose of bearing God's image and endowed with the unalterable dignity that stems from this truth. If God gives His creation value, who is anyone else to deem it worthless?

Humans have always been bent toward the devaluation of life. When our hearts are hard toward God, our hearts naturally harden toward the creation that most reflects Him. Seeking to dethrone God inevitably leads to devaluing people. Every act that devalues life, whether abortion or medically assisted suicide, is, at its core, an attempt to *be* God, to determine which lives matter and claim others do not. But God alone holds the power to define our worth because God alone created us.

How can we embrace this mindset in a culture that cheapens life while helping others embrace it too?

1. Become Educated on the Value of Life

"Abortion is necessary because women should be allowed to have a choice."

What would you say? Would you be prepared to defend the unborn child with sound arguments to refute that view? What if the conversation turned toward a different topic and someone said, "Assisted suicide is sometimes the most compassionate option because it allows an end to excruciating physical or mental pain"? How would you respond?

At first glance, these arguments look convincing. But not only are there biblical truths to back up the pro-life stance, there's also scientific research and facts.

Suppose someone claims it's not our place to force pro-life views on others ("If you don't like abortion, don't have one"). Within that argument is the assumption that the only person affected is the woman having the abortion. They're assuming the unborn are not fully human. They wouldn't use the same argument against killing toddlers ("If you don't like to see toddlers murdered, don't kill them yourself"). That argument is ludicrous because everyone knows toddlers are human beings, and it's wrong to kill human beings. Pro-life activist Scott Klusendorf once said in a debate,

> The issue that divides us is just one question: What is the unborn? . . .
> If the unborn is a human being, killing him or her to benefit others is
> a serious moral wrong. . . . Conversely, if the unborn are not human,
> killing them through elective abortion requires no more justification
> than having your tooth pulled.[18]

To be prepared in our conversations and grounded in our own convictions, we have to be educated on the facts. Study Scripture to discover what God says about the value of life. Study the science of embryology and learn when life begins and why an embryo at the point of fertilization is fundamentally no different from a baby at full term. Discover mind-blowing facts like how at the moment of fertilization, all the necessary DNA for a new life is present, and around three weeks later, the baby's heart begins to beat. Become educated on fetal development and view the stunning 3D ultrasound images of priceless babies in the womb. Learn the incredible value of life so you'll be prepared to affirm its worth.

And don't forget the compelling power of story. Facts can be blown off and ignored, but personal stories often linger and have the power to change hearts and minds. Stories of those who chose life and stories of second chances are beautiful illustrations of the biblical truths and facts we hold to.

It's important to be passionately committed to the *conclusion* of the pro-life case (all life is valuable and made in the image of God), but in order to effectively dialogue, we must also be grounded in the *facts* of the pro-life case. Gregg Cunningham, director of the Center for Bio-Ethical Reform, has said that for too long, the pro-life movement has been shouting conclusions instead of establishing facts.[19] By establishing facts and being grounded in truth, we will be more prepared and equipped to engage with wisdom and clarity.

2. Expose the Culture of Death

Somehow our culture has made killing politically correct. We stare at the face of death in our society, but we don't call it that. Murdering an unborn infant has been boiled down to a choice. Discarding thousands of tiny embryos is called research. Helping an individual kill him- or herself is considered compassionate. We cover up the truth of our genocide with sugarcoated phrases and dehumanized language.

I recently read an informational article from Planned Parenthood titled "What Happens during an In-Clinic Abortion?"[20] The entire article was written in a casual, laid-back style, making it sound like having an abortion was no different from any routine procedure. Not once were the words *baby*, *infant*, or even *fetus* used. It was like they were trying to avoid the entire purpose of abortion, reducing the process to a straightforward procedure. The article said things like, "During a D&E [dilation and evacuation] abortion, the doctor or nurse will . . . use a combination of medical tools and a suction device to gently take the pregnancy tissue out."[21] In another article that asked, "What Is an Abortion?" the simple answer read, "Abortion is a medical procedure that ends a pregnancy."[22]

Abortion "ends a pregnancy." It doesn't *kill a child*. This language manipulation covers up the truth and ignores the horrendous fact that by ending a pregnancy, you're taking the life of another human being.

Assisted suicide is often referred to as "dying with dignity." "Why allow someone to suffer when a doctor could simply put them out of their pain?" people reason. But believe it or not, uncontrollable pain or terminal illness are not the sole reasons for choosing assisted suicide. In a study conducted in British Columbia, out of two hundred and fifty people who requested medically assisted death, fifty-nine people listed loss of autonomy as their reason, fifty-five loss of ability to enjoy activities, and twenty-seven fear of future suffering.[23]

No psychiatric evaluation or treatment is required before someone is eligible for an assisted suicide; the decision is left to the judgment of the physician.[24] Individuals already vulnerable enough to consider death (whether because of physical or mental distress) shouldn't have that option available to them. Instead, that's the time for family, friends, and the body of Christ to come alongside the suffering, care for them, and help them live as well as they can for as long as they can. For individuals who do experience intense pain and suffering, pain can often be managed through medication and hospice care, the goal of which is to handle symptoms to make an individual comfortable and maximize their quality of life as much as possible. Sadly, some individuals find themselves in situations where both good medical care and support from people are unavailable, so the church must be willing to step in with love, care, and compassion at every opportunity we have, proving with our actions as well as our words that every life is valuable.

Scott Klusendorf writes,

> It's time for pro-life Christians to open the casket on abortion. We should do it lovingly but truthfully. We should do it in our churches during the primary worship services, comforting those who grieve with the gospel of forgiveness. We should do it in our Christian high schools and colleges, combining visuals with a persuasive defense of the pro-life view that's translatable to non-Christians. But open the casket we must. Until we do, Americans will continue tolerating an injustice they never have to look at.[25]

How can we "open the casket"? It starts with being educated ourselves. Then sharing the truth in a spirit of love, compassion, and humility with those around us. In our daily conversations, with our peers, at our schools and college campuses, in our churches. In our individual sphere of influence, we must not remain silent about the genocides taking place but lovingly speak up for those unable to speak for themselves (Prov. 31:8).

3. Care for the Living and Prioritize the Gospel

The power, privilege, and responsibility of being made in God's image call us not only to protect life against death but to care for the living, and most importantly, to reach all with the gospel. Scripture affirms that caring for others is the definition of "pure and undefiled religion" when it challenges us to "visit orphans and widows in their trouble, and to keep oneself unspotted from the world" (James 1:27).

Have we prioritized caring for the living in our fight for life? We say we're against abortion, but do we care for the baby when it's born? Do we love the woman facing an unplanned pregnancy with tenderness and compassion? Is our goal not to just save her baby's life but to lead her to abundant life in Jesus? We say we're against assisted suicide, but are we in the trenches lifting the burden of a family nursing a terminally ill loved one or coming alongside those who have no family or friends to care for them? Are we prioritizing the gospel in our interactions so the suffering may experience not just life on earth but eternal life with Jesus in heaven?

If life matters, we must be willing to give of ourselves to prove its worth. Some common reasons women give for having an abortion are that a baby would interfere with her school or career, she's not ready to care for a child, or she can't afford to support a baby. Because we're pro-life, we say these excuses aren't valid reasons to end an innocent life. But if we're truly pro-life, we must be willing to let that baby interfere with our own lives and fight for its life not just before birth but after.

The most pro-life action a Christian can take is not to march in a rally, vote pro-life, or hold signs of protest. The most pro-life action a Christian can take is simple—to be there for the living. To help the single mom and come alongside the pregnant teenager. To comfort the family whose loved one is slipping away and support them as they grieve. To lift the burden from the caregivers' shoulders and assist the widow. To embrace the orphan as our own child, sibling, and friend. To practically support the poor and emotionally support the suffering. To bring hope to the hopeless—tell the post-abortion mother that there is forgiveness in Jesus and the suicidal teen that life is worth living. To love not just "in word or in tongue, but in deed and in truth" (1 John 3:18). And to remember that the gospel is the deepest need in each heart.

This is harder than posting our pro-life views on social media, attending a rally, signing petitions, or sitting back in silence. It means entering another person's messy situation and caring for their needs and their pain. It means sacrifice and selfless love. But it's the love Christ calls us to.

Jesus gave us each a calling to care for the least of these. The hungry, thirsty, stranger, naked, sick, imprisoned, and outcast. That's the most pro-life calling there is. With Jesus's words, "As you did it to one of the least of these My brethren, you did it to Me" (Matt. 25:40), He defined the value of human life. He equated it with His own.

The unborn baby? *The least of these.*

The woman facing an unplanned pregnancy? *The least of these.*

The elderly and terminally ill? *The least of these.*

The tiniest embryo? *The least of these.*

The suicidal, depressed, and hopeless? *The least of these.*

Ignore these and you're ignoring Him. He valued their lives when He called us to love as He does, and He sealed their value when He died on a cross for their souls and displayed before all heaven and earth how precious they are in His sight. No life was excluded, no heart exempt. Each individual was precious enough to die for, and an infinite price was paid to prove their individual worth.

In a culture that devalues life, we can cling to the hope that there is One who died to destroy the power of death. He trampled it under His feet with the words "It is finished" and the proof of an empty tomb. There may be a war on life, but we have a victor who has defeated death. And He calls our lives precious in His sight.

Going Deeper

1. In what ways have you seen or experienced culture's war on life?
2. Why are all lives valuable? What makes them valuable? Why is it wrong to intentionally take life?
3. Are you familiar with pro-life arguments? How can you learn more?
4. In what ways can you practically care for the living? Why is this important?
5. Our value in God's eyes gives us worth. How does this truth affect the way you live and treat those around you?

Further Resources

- *Life's Worth: The Case against Assisted Suicide* by Arthur J. Dyck
- *Hope Always: How to be a Force for Life in a Culture of Suicide* by Matthew Sleeth
- *Stand for Life: Answering the Call, Making the Case, Saving Lives* by Scott Klusendorf and John Ensor

- *The Case for Life: Equipping Christians to Engage the Culture* by Scott Klusendorf
- *Transforming Your Story: A Path to Healing after Abortion* by Wendy Giancola
- Care Net (this ministry has dozens of free courses, ebooks, and other resources on numerous topics regarding abortion: https://www.care-net.org/)
- Live Action (https://www.liveaction.org/)
- National Right to Life (https://www.nrlc.org/)

10

Prejudice and Injustice

(We're All Made in the Image of God)

When you hear the words *prejudice*, *discrimination*, and *racism*, what first comes to mind? What reactions fill your heart? Are they reactions of anger? Grief? Do they conjure images of slavery, civil rights activism, personal experiences, or current events? When you consider what the words *justice* and *equality* mean, where do your definitions stem from? What do you think it means to do justice and experience equality? Many of us have varied answers to these questions based on our experiences, backgrounds, and mindsets.

When it comes to these difficult and controversial (but deeply personal) topics, I believe we have at times allowed ourselves to be discipled by culture and influenced by personal opinions and biases instead of educated by the Word of God. The church is often sharply divided in its responses to injustice. On one hand, we look to current antiracist narratives and politically correct wokeness as our guide for fighting oppression. On the other hand, there's a temptation to brush injustice aside with casual indifference.

Neither response reflects the heart of God or a biblical call to justice. In a world where prejudice and discrimination attack and oppress priceless individuals who bear the image of God and acts of injustice and violence cause deep pain, grief, and brokenness, we must value true justice and search to discover what it means to do justice and love mercy (Mic. 6:8). In a culture attempting to cure the evil of oppression with unbalanced approaches that disregard God, we must seek righteousness and truth. In a society engulfed in controversies over Critical Race Theory and white supremacy, we must cut through the noise to understand God's heart for the abused and hurting and let His heart become our own.

Justice is not God's suggestion to the church. Throughout Scripture, God reveals His care and passion for the discriminated and abused, and He commands His people to care just as passionately for their suffering. We're to "mourn with those who mourn" (Rom. 12:15 NIV). We must "cease to do evil, learn to do good; seek justice, correct oppression; bring justice to the fatherless, [and] plead the widow's cause" (Isa. 1:16–17 ESV).

God's commands are clear. The topics of prejudice, discrimination, and racism—and our response to these topics—matter greatly. They matter because every person on the face of the globe bears the fingerprint of God—a God who is not simply *for* justice but is Himself the very standard and character *of* justice.

Defining Our Terms

Before we dive in, it's important to stop and clearly define what I mean by *prejudice*, *injustice*, *oppression*, and *racism*. Within society there exists two different and contrary definitions of racism and injustice. The problem is both definitions use the same language, which can make discussions about these terms incredibly confusing and cause them to be controversy-filled words.

The first definition is what I would call the old or original definition. It refers to racism that shows up within individuals through preferential and degrading thoughts, attitudes, and actions based on another person's skin color or ethnicity. Oppression and injustice in this definition are found in acts of discrimination and cruelty toward a person or people group, again based on external variables such as ethnicity, skin color, or cultural background. This definition *does* include oppression found within larger systems (i.e., it's not limited to personal, individual acts of cruelty), since groups of people who hold mindsets of oppression can come together and create systems that degrade or inflict injustice upon another people group. This definition is not limited to one particular ethnicity, skin color, or gender, but because all are sinners, people of every color, class, or sex have the ability to participate under this definition of prejudice and injustice.

The second definition has only recently emerged but has overtaken much of the conversation on injustice. This definition is *not* contingent upon racist thoughts, attitudes, and actions, but instead is found in systems of oppression or cultural norms within one group that project their ideas and standards upon another people group. This is said to create bias, power struggles, and culturally created assumptions. In other words, in the first definition, a person had to personally hold biased thoughts or enact injustice or cruelty toward another to be considered racist, while in the second definition, their skin color, gender, or status defines whether they are considered racist or an oppressor. It's more accurately described as "a system of privilege based on race"[1] instead of personal actions or evil systems backed by evil thoughts and intentions. In this definition, only those within the groups that hold power or influence can truly be racist or truly oppress others.

In the first section of this chapter, we're going to address the first definition of racism and how to counteract it with God's truth and love. In the second half, we're going to address the second definition and how and why many of the ideas within it are unhelpful and unbiblical. While those who promote the second definition have borrowed the language from the first definition of racism and oppression and redefined those terms, in my disagreement with their perspective, I do not want to push aside the fact that the original definition still exists. As long as there is sin in the world, it will bring division between God's image bearers. As long as there is division, we must seek to biblically live out unity, love, and justice.

Seeds of Division

Prejudice against and oppression of different people groups have existed in every generation. The story of humanity is a story of division, animosity, and bloodshed. Seeds of hatred were sown with Adam and Eve's first sin and displayed in Cain's unjust murder of Abel. Brother rose against brother in the first act of oppression and violence between God's image bearers. As the earth increased in population, the division widened as families rose against families, nations fought against nations, and ethnicities harbored animosity against other ethnicities. Wars broke out, slaves were taken, and arrogant hearts forgot the truth that all are made in the image of God.

Over the centuries, forms of prejudice have varied. For example, consider the division between Jews and Samaritans in the days of the New Testament. The Samaritans were descendants of the Israelite tribes of Ephraim and Manasseh, but when the Assyrians invaded Israel in 722 BC, intermarriages and idol worship emerged and the mixed people group of the Samaritans was born. Because of this, hostility between Samaritans and their full-blooded Jewish cousins grew and hardened. When Jesus came on the scene and began crossing these divides, it was both audacious and culturally inappropriate (see John 4).

Jump forward to the mid-twentieth century and you encounter the Holocaust—a horrific genocide that grew from a belief in racial superiority and hatred. Hitler claimed that the "Aryan Master Race" was superior to Jews, Slavic people, and Black individuals, among other people groups. Over six million Jews were slaughtered, and millions of other lives were taken. Hatred of the Jewish people remains one of the oldest prejudices in the world, and it's still alive and growing decades after the Holocaust.

Unjust oppression and cruel prejudice have existed in every generation and country. Throughout the history of the United States, racism has most often been directed against Blacks, Asians, and Hispanics, with anti-Semitism and discrimination against other religions also present and rising. From a young Asian woman I know who's been degraded and objectified because of her ethnicity to my Puerto Rican friend who has experienced prejudice to the stigma my Black friends experience on a regular basis, racism can rear its ugly head among many ethnicities and people groups. Unlike what culture often proclaims, no one group is always the oppressor or oppressed. Prejudice goes beyond racism and racism beyond one specific ethnicity or skin color. Shreds of hatred for others and stories of oppression by others exist within every people group and ethnicity.

Racism (and other forms of prejudice) is a human problem rooted in a sin problem. It reaches into the core of an individual to their deepest beliefs about God and humanity. It's not simply one people group pitted against another but sin deep within the heart of a person that seeks to degrade God's image bearers and elevate oneself. This knowledge brings the conversation of injustice back to the ground-level truth that all prejudice stems from sinful hearts steeped in rebellion against God. In order to fight racism, we need to call out the sin that causes it.

Gospel-Defined Unity

In calling racism sin, we acknowledge it to not just be a social problem but first and foremost a spiritual one. If the root of racism is sin, the cure can be found only in God. Yet people often push it aside as simply a social issue or turn to society for the cure. Martin Luther King Jr. wrote,

> In the midst of blatant injustices inflicted upon the Negro, I have watched white churches stand on the sideline and merely mouth pious irrelevancies and sanctimonious trivialities. In the midst of a mighty struggle to rid our nation of racial and economic injustice, I have heard so many ministers say, "Those are social issues with which the Gospel has no real concern."[2]

If the root of racism is sin, then wouldn't the gospel contain relevant truth concerning it? We may not find the word *racism* in our Bibles, but we do find much about the sins that align with racism—hatred (1 John 3:15), slander (James 4:11; Eph. 4:31), partiality (James

2:1–10), among others. God calls us to a different standard of love and unity—loving our neighbors as ourselves (Mark 12:31), walking in unity (Eph. 4:1–6), and putting off our old ways of relating to each other to embrace His new, gospel-defined way (Eph. 4:21–24). If loving our neighbor as ourselves is the second commandment Jesus gave (Matt. 22:39), how can racism not concern the gospel?

Who is our neighbor? Like the man who asked Jesus this question in Luke 10, we may want to justify ourselves through our own definition. But as Jesus told the man through the parable of the good Samaritan, there are no limits on who qualifies as our neighbor. Blacks, Asians, Hispanics, Native Americans, Caucasians, and every other ethnicity are all our neighbors. And not only neighbors but brothers and sisters. We all descend from the same family. We're all *one race* born from our first parents, Adam and Eve.

Our common ancient ancestry is not our only basis for unity in the midst of diversity. Every human from every nation bears God's image and holds equal dignity and worth. There are no racial minorities in God's eyes.

Our foundational unity, however, doesn't eliminate our distinct differences. We're vastly different people with an array of backgrounds, varied experiences, and unique cultures. Our unity doesn't minimize the value of these differences, but none of our differences add to or detract from our worth or status as image bearers of God. Instead, through our diversity, we see a grander picture of God's nature. God is multifaceted, with a depth we can't comprehend. Through the diversity of His creation, we catch a small glimpse of the depth of His character. Our differences are a profound picture of the majestic creativity of God. Diminish the difference and you diminish the creation. Find unity through the distinction and you praise the Creator.

And yet, once again, we see an attack on God's image through attacks on His image bearers. That's why racism is a spiritual problem and why the true standard of justice cannot be found within the narrative of culture, but only within the character of God. That's why the church cannot push injustice aside but instead should actively learn the truth, engage culture, and boldly seek gospel-defined unity.

Six Ways to Seek Unity and Heal Division

Our biblical principles must become bold practices. As James 1:22 says, we must "be doers of the word, and not hearers only."

While racism and injustice are large problems within the media spotlight, I want to encourage us to not overlook the opportunities for unity right in front of us. It's a temptation to open our social media accounts, toss in our opinion, and *think* we're doing justice. But if we ignore our responsibility to love our local church, seek out the overlooked within our schools and youth groups, and prioritize caring for the hurting in our communities, we're minimizing the importance of the flesh-and-blood people God has placed within our spheres of influence.

God's love and biblical justice will rarely make headlines, nor will our opportunities always look like the current politically correct version of justice dominating the media. That's why our pursuit of love and unity cannot be for the sake of popularity or cultural applause. The way God calls us to love may not be applauded by the world, but if it's done in obedience to God and in alignment with His character, we can rest assured that it will be applauded in heaven. Keeping this in mind, here are six ways we can work toward unity.

1. Study and Learn God's Narrative of Truth and Justice

Our pursuit of justice must be aligned with the heart of God. God is passionately committed to the good of His people. He feels the sting of prejudice leveled at His image bearers, and His heart is angered and grieved at the ways they are mistreated and abused. God is more fervently opposed to all forms of discrimination than we ever could be because He sees the darkness of sin fueling them. But not only does God understand the problem more than we do, He is the only One who holds the solution. He's not simply a God who promotes justice; justice is inherent within His being (Deut. 32:4).

If God Himself is the definition of justice, doesn't it follow that God knows how we should enact justice? The only true handbook for justice is the Word of God. As civil rights activist John M. Perkins states, "We have to align ourselves with his purpose, his will, his mission to let justice roll down, and bring forgiveness and love to everyone on earth. The problem of injustice is a God-sized problem. If we don't start with him first, whatever we're seeking, it ain't justice."[3]

If we love the oppressed and care about justice, we will desire to align ourselves with the One who embodies love and justice as we seek to enact His solutions.

Culture has a lot to say about how to cure injustice. Media, politicians, social media influencers, authors, and speakers all have their two cents to throw into the conversation. The desire to bring an end to oppression is admirable. But not every solution culture presents is grounded in God's wisdom. Instead, many ideas go against the foundational truths of a biblical worldview and only dig the hole of injustice deeper.

Solutions that depart from God's truth only exacerbate the problem of racism. These have at times looked like accusations of racism leveled indiscriminately toward an entire group or accusations that falsely sounded the injustice alarm before all the facts were in place. Or when people seek "wokeness" for the mere sake of being woke and politically correct. Or buying into ideas such as Critical Race Theory simply because they're the antiracist narrative of the moment. With so many ideas infiltrating the atmosphere, discernment is key. If we truly desire to bring healing to the wounds slashed deep by prejudice, we must go beyond the narratives of culture—whether they come from the political right or left—and discern how God desires His people to do justice.

Search Scripture for God's guidance on unity, division, and justice. What biblical truths can we apply to the conversation on racism? What sins does the Bible highlight that are present in every act of prejudice and discrimination? What does God's Word have to say about unity or human value or seeking truth? We must filter everything we hear through the lens of God's Word and not be afraid to reject ideas if they don't align with Scripture. It's not racist to seek to be biblically correct over politically correct. Only God's Word holds inerrant truth, and His truth is the road map that can lead us to walk out unity and love one another well.

2. Search Your Own Heart

Loving our brothers and sisters of all ethnicities and backgrounds begins within the deepest places of our hearts. We should search God's

Word not only to define our actions but also to illuminate our attitudes. We need to allow God's standard of perfect love and justice to bring conviction to areas where we've failed to reflect His heart or allowed our sin to compound the problem. Search your heart for how you've thought, spoken about, and treated people in the past. Have your thoughts reflected Christ's? Have your words and actions been filled with love? Have you been indifferent about prejudice or injustice in the past?

In an effort to simplify a complicated world, humanity has a propensity to settle for stereotypes when they think about other people. Whether those stereotypes are based on ethnicity, gender, occupation, or so on, we may tend to take the negative aspects that are often assigned to a particular group and place those assumptions on everyone who bears the same or similar attributes. Such stereotypes fuel prejudice, influence how we view people, and keep us from both living out truth and embracing biblical love.

Allow God to work in your heart to reveal any untrue assumptions or ungodly attitudes, and let Him fill you with greater humility to learn, understand, and love. As followers of Jesus, we're called to deeply love every individual, because all are infinitely precious to Him. This deep love should produce deep sorrow within our hearts for all who have suffered and been abused or discriminated against. This deep sorrow should produce deep commitment to validating the God-given value of every person and to fighting against the sin that leads to injustice and, yes, the injustice itself. But this begins with seeking the Holy Spirit to realign our hearts to God's love and truth.

3. Grow in Awareness and Seek Out the Facts

How can we fight something we don't understand? In order to do justice, we must be aware of injustices experienced. According to polls, approximately half of Americans aren't sure what anti-Semitism means.[4] Yet hatred of Jews continues to rise in various forms, such as shootings in synagogues and discrimination on college campuses.[5] The prejudice itself is a great injustice, but the oblivion people have toward it is also an injustice. The same applies for prejudice against various ethnicities.

We need to intentionally seek awareness, not only of current but also of past oppression. A disturbing trend in our culture is how little we learn from history. Instead, we scrub away the distasteful parts of our past and set ourselves on a trajectory to repeat them. A perfect example of this is our diminishing knowledge of the Holocaust. As Walter Reich, former director of the United States Holocaust Memorial Museum, wrote,

> Anti-Semitism has returned, in part, because the general public's knowledge about the Holocaust—of what exactly it was, who exactly was murdered in it, how many were killed, and how anti-Semitism spawned it—has diminished. . . . Could murderous anti-Semitism, on a large scale, resume in our time? Could "never again," vowed so solemnly and so repeatedly after the Holocaust, revert to "yet again"?[6]

The more we forget the past, the likelier it is that "never again" will become "yet again." We must grow more aware of how the past has affected the present as we seek to understand how prejudice is experienced today. By studying history, reading biblically based books on justice (recommendations at the end of this chapter), looking into the experiences of those in our own churches and communities, and listening to others firsthand, we can have a more nuanced and accurate view of the injustices around us.

We must also be committed to understanding and seeking out the facts. Post-truth thinking finds roots in conversations about race and justice by elevating emotions—someone's lived experience or personal perspective—over facts and data. While it's vital to learn from those who have experienced injustice, facts should never be subjugated by emotions. Instead, facts should enlighten emotions, helping us understand the big picture of reality.

God calls us to test all things and to seek out the truth of a matter (see 1 Thess. 5:21). If we truly care about justice and unity, we must seek to objectively understand *where* injustice is actually occurring, *to whom* it is occurring, and *by whom* it is occurring. If we don't know this critical information, how can we genuinely stand up for the oppressed? Facts matter because truth matters. And truth is the only way we can fight injustice.

Seek out facts. Look at data. Dig deeper than the news headlines. Then go to the source of injustice and fight there. If we don't seek out facts in our pursuit of justice, we're in danger of fighting the ghost of injustice instead of the actual culprit.

4. Embrace Genuine Relationships and Engage in Honest Conversations

At the same time, we cannot separate injustice from the people who experience it. Embracing friendships and intentionally engaging in honest, truth-seeking conversations can open our minds to other perspectives, our hearts to truly loving God's people, and our lives to fulfilling the calling God has given us to share the gospel. When it comes to racism specifically, friendships with people of different ethnicities can be vibrant and meaningful as we learn and grow from one another's experiences. Genuinely listening to others broadens our viewpoints and helps us grow in love, humility, and understanding. Asking questions about a friend's experience with racism and their opinion on how to walk in unity enlightens our perspectives. When we personally know and care for those who've experienced injustice, the topic moves from abstract knowledge to personal concern.

Embracing friendships can't be about tokenizing others (i.e., seeking out a friend of a different ethnicity just so you don't appear racist) or we'll miss the point. The point of building friendships with anyone is simply that—to build a friendship. Injustice won't end because of the friendship, but we'll learn and grow and experience God's gift of relationship, and that's a vital first step.

5. Care for the Hurting and Boldly Confront Injustice

Turning a blind eye is often easier than calling out injustice with love and truth. We should do so with a spirit of humility, the knowledge of our own sinful nature, and a heart that is ready to extend grace. Our job is not to weigh others on our moral scale but to point out sin where we see it and encourage repentance as we show Christ's love.

Injustice may not always appear in expected forms. Whether it's racist attitudes toward Blacks, seeds of anti-Semitism, prejudice toward someone of a different socioeconomic status, or the effects of human trafficking and sex slavery, don't let injustice slide by and harden your heart.

Instead, ask God to give you a heart of compassion that cares for the vulnerable and abused as He does, eyes to see who and where they are, and wisdom to know how to act. Philosopher Nicholas Wolterstorff says, "God's love for justice is grounded in his love for the victims of injustice. And his love for the victims of injustice belongs to his love for the little ones of the world: for the weak, the defenseless, the ones at the bottom, the excluded ones, the miscasts, the outcasts, the outsiders."[7] Caring for the oppressed and hurting means caring for those close to God's heart.

And who else is more called to do this than the church? Practically, this could look like boldly confronting an instance of sin or injustice (such as slanderous remarks, discriminatory behavior, or unbiblical mindsets), or it could look like meeting a need and bringing love, unity, and healing into the situation yourself. We're called to take a stand against evil, fight against what is wrong, and do what is right. As we have opportunity, we must bring God's love and healing into broken situations (see Isa. 58 and James 2:14–26). And while most people may not ascribe prayer as a practical way to fight injustice, we must remember that all prejudice finds its roots in the spiritual battle raging around us. The enemy of our souls has made it his mission to bring division precisely where God desires unity, confusion where God brings clarity, and hurt where God longs to heal. Illuminated with the truth of God and compelled by the love of Christ, we must seek to actively and daily live out God's truth of unity and *imago Dei* value.

6. Let the Gospel Bridge All Divides

For Christians, there is one great unifier—the gospel of Jesus Christ. Jesus made it clear that the call to share the gospel is a call to reach people of all nations and ethnicities. The Great Commission powerfully tears down hostility with these words: "Go into all the world and preach the gospel to every creature" (Mark 16:15).

No mention of "go especially to this race." No hint of "these people are more important, others don't deserve the gospel." Instead,

Jesus called us to go to *all*. Because *all* are equally in desperate need of Christ's forgiveness. None of us deserve it, but Jesus still extends it to us all. The Great Commission should eliminate all possibility of prejudice among Christians because we come together as family in Christ united by the shed blood of Jesus.

Monique Duson, cofounder of the Center for Biblical Unity, regularly emphasizes the powerful and beautiful truth that those in Christ are *family*—united in Christ, bound together by grace. She says, "The Word of God will always offer a better hope, a more unifying solution, than culture ever will."[8] The gospel offers us the transformation we need—altered lives, mindsets, and actions. It gives us the justice we seek—justice and mercy perfectly balanced and bound together through Christ's death and resurrection. It provides the identity we crave—loved and forgiven children of God. And it alone can lead to the outcome we desire—unity under one good God.

Culture-Defined Justice

Now that we've discussed a few ways to seek unity and unpacked the first definition of racism and injustice, let's dive into the second. This definition is deeply impacted by the ideas of Critical Race Theory. CRT has become a buzzword in both the church and secular culture. Is it good? Is it bad? What does it even mean? While CRT is a deeply layered and complex idea, I want to unpack a few of the foundational premises found within it. The ideas of CRT are becoming increasingly influential in media, classrooms, and even churches as the proposed solution to racism and injustice.

So first, what is CRT? It's a thought process that examines both history and our current society through the lens of *race*. It's a subset of Critical Theory, which looks at the world through the lens of *power structures*. These ideas, while they sound simple enough on the surface, have enormous consequences. Let's take a look at a few.

Cultural Lens

The foundation of CRT is the assumption that everything—not just some things—is characterized by racism. The question is not,

"*Has* this been impacted by racism?" but "*How* has this been impacted by racism?" Racism in this view is central to humanity and the normal state of society. This is possible because racism is considered to not simply be found in individuals, but in systems and structures and is believed to be deeply imbedded in every part of American society and in the minds and biases of individuals.

Group Identity

CRT views people in terms of groups. Based on your ethnicity, you're either in the *oppressed group* or the *oppressor group*. The same idea of group identity is also present in other subsets of Critical Theory, placing people in groups because of their gender, sexual orientation, economic status, or other external variables. White people are considered oppressors while Black people (and other racial minorities) are the oppressed.

This idea of oppression is different from how we typically think of the term. It's not solely that someone is oppressed through injustice or cruelty. Instead, as authors Neil Shenvi and Pat Sawyer explain, oppression in CRT should be understood as "'hegemonic power,' the ability of a particular group to impose its norms, values, and expectations on the rest of society."[9] Saying a white man is an oppressor, for instance, isn't saying that a particular man has acted cruelly or unfairly, but that simply by being a white male, he is a part of a group (white men) who have traditionally and historically held power and imposed their views on society. Racial minorities are considered unable to be racist, because their groups have, throughout history, not held power. In order to be truly racist, it's said you have to have not only prejudice but power as well.

Moral Authority

Oppression is often used to show who holds the most moral authority. John Stonestreet explains it like this:

> According to critical theory, the oppressed group automatically has moral authority, while the oppressor group does not. Someone who is a racial minority or a sexual minority of some kind is automatically a victim of oppression and has claims against oppressors.[10]

The more oppressed you are, the more moral ground you have—no matter what kind of personal morality you hold. Reality is interpreted through experience instead of facts.

Idea of Justice

Most people would agree with the statement, "We should be anti-racist." However, the perspective of anti-racism in CRT goes deeper than simply being "opposed to racism." It goes beyond being against racism and into being actively involved in dismantling the racist structures within society. If those in the oppressor group are not actively involved in surrendering their privilege and power and elevating those within the group of oppressed, they are still considered racist, even if they personally reject racist thoughts and ideas.

CRT and a Biblical Worldview

Many of the ideas in CRT are incompatible with a biblical worldview. While CRT does hold threads of truth (for example, white people have oppressed Black people, both currently and historically, and people should actively seek unity and justice), the overarching worldview contradicts the truths of Scripture and God's vision of authentic justice. The desire for justice in CRT is good, as is the call to fight injustice, but its methods are not the solution to injustice and racism. There are two important reasons why.

1. It Diminishes the Truth of the Gospel

CRT offers a vastly different view of sin, injustice, and the value of humanity than Scripture. It eliminates two biblical and universal truths: First, our identity is found in God, not in our ethnicity. Second, all are sinners in need of forgiveness. According to Scripture, people are not categorized into groups of oppressed or oppressors based on external variables. Instead, we're members of the same group—sinners in need of a Savior. The way of justification for our sins is not found in elevating the oppressed, but in receiving the forgiveness of Christ. We all have the capacity to oppress others, and no one is more bent toward sin because of their gender or ethnicity.

No one has more or less moral authority, because none are moral on their own. Christians hold a shared identity in Christ that swallows up all other sub-identities as secondary to our unity in Jesus.

2. It Destroys Unity and Fuels Partiality

CRT destroys unity by pitting people against each other simply based on their background or skin color. It seeks to view fellow image bearers through a social status and not through personal character, morality, or identity in Jesus. It feeds arrogance on the sides of both oppressor and oppressed and muddies the pursuit of true justice. Instead of exposing and destroying sinful partiality, it fuels it by identifying people according to their external characteristics. As author Allie Beth Stuckey points out, "At the heart of CRT is a love for partiality. At the heart of God is a hate for partiality."[11] (See Leviticus 19:15; Deuteronomy 16:19–20; James 2:1–13.)

I encourage you to study the ideas found in CRT through the resources at the end of this chapter and compare them with a biblical worldview. Don't shy away from engaging ideas like CRT, but think carefully, clearly, and, yes, critically on these topics. The ideas of CRT are becoming more ingrained throughout culture, and it's important to be aware of their influence. Even if something is not labeled as CRT, we need to be aware of the foundational ideas of CRT in order to point them out and counteract them with truth.

Concepts like those found in CRT have tremendous impact on how we view God, morality, and fellow image bearers. We cannot let them slip into our minds, churches, or interactions or they will turn our feet from the path of God-defined justice and destroy the unity we claim through the gospel of Jesus Christ.

A Future Hope

The beauty of unity in diversity is especially poignant for Christians. Scripture gives a glimpse of a future hope, a day when all nations will worship before God, with every division removed.

Revelation 7:9–10 paints the picture:

After these things I looked, and behold, a great multitude which no one could number, of all nations, tribes, peoples, and tongues, standing before the throne and before the Lamb, clothed with white robes, with palm branches in their hands, and crying out with a loud voice, saying, "Salvation belongs to our God who sits on the throne, and to the Lamb!"

Can you see it? People from every nation and tribe. Every language represented. Every skin color on display. Differences abound in this picture, but unity is the defining aspect. All worship *one* God.

This is our future hope. Until that day, we're called to bring this view of heaven to earth. Ephesians 4 powerfully challenges us to live out this call:

Walk worthy of the calling with which you were called, with all lowliness and gentleness, with longsuffering, bearing with one another in love, endeavoring to keep the unity of the Spirit in the bond of peace. There is one body and one Spirit, just as you were called in one hope of your calling; one Lord, one faith, one baptism; one God and Father *of all, who is above all, and through all, and in you all.* (vv. 1–6, emphasis added)

May we live out this calling and walk worthy. For the glory of God who is above, through, and in us all, may we seek to love with the barrier-breaking power of the gospel of Jesus Christ.

Going Deeper

1. Until now, what were your thoughts on racism and prejudice?
2. How does the truth that the core of racism is found in sin change your perspective on racism? Instead of making it about just one race or issue, how can this truth broaden your perspective and lead to true justice?
3. Why is justice so important to God?

4. In what practical ways can you apply the six action steps to your life today?

5. How does the gospel unify individuals? Why is that important?

Further Resources

- *Confronting Injustice without Compromising Truth: 12 Questions Christians Should Ask about Social Justice* by Thaddeus J. Williams
- *One Blood: Parting Words to the Church on Race and Love* by John M. Perkins
- *Fault Lines: The Social Justice Movement and Evangelicalism's Looming Catastrophe* by Voddie T. Baucham
- *Engaging Critical Theory & The Social Justice Movement* by Neil Shenvi and Dr. Pat Sawyer (ebook by Ratio Christi: https://ratiochristi.org/engaging-critical-theory-and-the -social-justice-movement/)
- Intro to Critical Theory: Shenvia Apologetics (https://shenvi apologetics.com/intro-to-critical-theory/)
- Center for Biblical Unity (https://centerforbiblicalunity.com/)

11

Addiction

(Finding Freedom in an Age of Bondage)

"I'm afraid I'll never be able to get sober."

Shame cloaked her, a heavy weight on her shoulders. Her voice was quiet but matter-of-fact. Amber had struggled with drug and alcohol abuse for years. She'd tried to break free before, but there she was, sitting across from me inside concrete walls wearing an orange prison uniform—again. Tears streamed down her face and caught in her voice as she poured out her struggle. It had started so slowly and went downhill so fast. In and out of jail. In and out of rehab. She was only twenty-three, but all she could see before her was a continuous pattern of addiction.

During my time in jail ministry, I encountered dozens of women like Amber. Precious women shackled by the chains of addiction. The majority of women I met inside prison walls found themselves there because of some form of substance abuse.

Addiction. It's the story no one wants but the one people find themselves a part of without even knowing how they got there. It starts with just one drink. Just one dose. Just one . . . until it isn't just one anymore.

Navigating an Addicted Culture

We are an addicted generation. Nearly twenty-one million Americans battle addiction.[1] Individuals between the ages of eighteen and twenty-five are most likely to use addictive drugs, and 90 percent of people currently struggling with addiction started to drink alcohol or use drugs before the age of eighteen.[2]

These statistics don't even include other forms of addiction, such as pornography. At Fight the New Drug, we learn,

> It may be surprising, but porn affects the brain in ways very similar to harmful substances, like tobacco. Studies have shown that porn stimulates the same areas of the brain as addictive drugs, making the brain release the same chemicals. And just like drugs, porn triggers pathways in the brain that cause craving, leading users back for more and more extreme "hits" to get high.[3]

Whether on a device or in a bottle, there are more forms of addiction than ever. And more teens are becoming enslaved to them. According to statistics, two-thirds of students have tried alcohol by twelfth grade. Approximately half of ninth through twelfth grade students report using marijuana, and a high number of teens are experimenting with vaping and e-cigarettes.[4] Porn addictions are rampant, with about 57 percent of teens searching for pornography monthly.[5]

Whether it's porn, drugs, or alcohol, the struggle of addiction is real and raw and faced by countless individuals. Fighting addiction begins with exposing lies and revealing truth.

Lie #1: _____will satisfy me and fill the emptiness inside.

Truth #1: Addictions lead to more emptiness—only God satisfies.

Fill in the blank. *Porn* will satisfy. *Alcohol* will numb the void inside. *Drugs* will distract me from my mental and emotional pain.

These lies are why many get caught in the cycle of addiction. It begins as an emotional crutch to help deal with stress, trauma, depression, or emotional pain. They think looking at porn will ease their loneliness or the numbing effect of alcohol or a high from drugs will help them handle pain or stress. And it may—for a time. But the catch of addiction is that we're not in control. Soon the addictive substance takes over and carves out deeper holes. Porn and drugs don't satisfy but instead open the door for a greater cavern of desolation to enter the human heart.

This isn't just a theory either. It's actually science. We all have what's called a reward center in our brains. The reward center floods our brain with the pleasure chemical dopamine every time we accomplish certain actions considered pleasurable or healthy, like eating, working out, or experiencing intimate physical contact. The dopamine signals to our brain "This is a good thing! Keep doing it!" to reward us for our actions, helping us develop healthy habits. It's a part of God's ingenious design for our brains. But the system can get hijacked. While good and healthy things activate the reward center, drugs, alcohol, and porn do too—and with a higher intensity.[6] Our brains become flooded with "feel-good chemicals," and soon we can't function without them and crave the dopamine high. And so an addiction is formed. We can't go without the content that triggers the reward center and experience intense withdrawal if we try. Instead of being satisfied, we're emptier than ever.

Followers of Jesus do not have to be enslaved to substances or content that leaves us empty. The emotional or mental pain that causes people to turn to drugs, alcohol, or porn can be healed and filled by God Himself. We're created to worship and live for God. When we reject Him, our hearts have a God-sized hole. Stuffing drugs, alcohol, or porn into the space where God is meant to dwell is like cramming a square peg into a round hole. But God's joy and peace transcend and surpass temporary solutions. He brings abundance to emptiness, healing to pain, and purpose to nothingness. His kind of satisfaction lasts.

Lie #2: It's not really an addiction—even if it is, it only hurts me.

Truth #2: Addictions are real and destructive.

It's not an addiction. I won't get addicted. Porn is just entertainment. Just this once. Just one more time.

These are common ways people rationalize their use of addictive substances. Maybe peer pressure makes someone try drugs. Maybe a friend exposes them to porn. Maybe they don't think just one time or watching porn occasionally will turn into an addiction. And maybe it wouldn't. Maybe someone could do drugs or watch porn only once. But why test that? The book of Proverbs warns about sexual sin: "Can a man scoop fire into his lap without his clothes being burned? Can a man walk on hot coals without his feet being scorched?" (6:27–28 NIV).

The obvious answer is, *Duh, no.* The same goes for drugs and alcohol abuse. Addictions are real, and they're so prevalent because these substances are powerful. Someone telling themselves they're strong enough to keep from becoming addicted is like picking up a hot coal and thinking it won't singe your hand.

Not only does addiction destroy self-control and overtake body and mind, it leaves a trail of destruction in its wake. The argument "It only hurts me" couldn't be further from the truth. Porn wrecks relationships, marriages, and a healthy view of sex and body image, as well as objectifies and violates those trafficked in sex slavery. Alcohol and drugs destroy families, physical health, and mental clarity. These consequences impact others. Addiction brings destruction. There is no "safe" addiction.

Lie #3: It Isn't really that bad. Everyone else seems to be doing it, why can't I?

Truth #3: What's popular is often more harmful than we realize.

In some ways, culture glamorizes addictive substances. We see ads, commercials, and billboards encouraging alcohol use. We hear about celebrities with drug addictions. With the legalization of marijuana in many states, recreational marijuana usage is growing. Some high school students are taking "porn literacy" classes that are meant *not* to help them avoid porn but to consume it "ethically."[7] Culture may speak against alcoholism and hard-core addiction, but it flirts with the fire instead of dousing the flame. This leads to confusion: Well, is it really *that* bad? If we see people engaging with a substance or activity, we may wonder, *What's the actual harm?*

Even without looking at this question through a Christian worldview, the answer is clear. Yes, drugs, alcohol abuse, and pornography are destructive. Both drug and alcohol abuse can lead to serious health problems, and porn can literally rewire and change the shape and function of your brain. Even if the consequences are downplayed or pushed aside as "no big deal," the effects are anything but glamorous.

Jesus said following Him would be a narrow road. He made it clear that His ways go against the flow. My mom has repeatedly told me, "If you see everyone going in one direction, stop and take a hard look. Often the most popular things are the most unbiblical and destructive." Many people will follow after evil. Only a few will stop, take a long, hard look, and choose to walk in the opposite direction. Just because everyone else is doing something doesn't mean it's okay. In fact, it could mean the opposite.

What Does the Bible Say about Addiction?

You probably won't find the word *addiction* in your Bible. But that doesn't mean the Bible is silent on this topic.

Most of the Scriptures dealing with substance abuse are about alcohol. Ephesians 5:18 says, "Don't be drunk with wine, because that will ruin your life. Instead, be filled with the Holy Spirit" (NLT). Proverbs 20:1 adds, "Wine is a mocker, strong drink is a brawler, and whoever is led astray by it is not wise." These passages show us that substance abuse is not wise or God-honoring, and that it could literally ruin your life. The Bible doesn't forbid all alcohol use but encourages moderation and wisdom. God leads some people to abstain from alcohol, but the Bible doesn't clearly make that command. Instead, Scripture speaks strongly about the abuse of alcohol.

Drunkenness is also listed in Galatians 5:

> When you follow the desires of your sinful nature, the results are very clear: sexual immorality, impurity, lustful pleasures, idolatry, sorcery, hostility, quarreling, jealousy, outbursts of anger, selfish ambition,

dissension, division, envy, drunkenness, wild parties, and other sins like these. Let me tell you again, as I have before, that anyone living that sort of life will not inherit the Kingdom of God. (vv. 19–21 NLT)

That's quite the list, isn't it? For substance abuse to be among sins like idolatry and sexual immorality shows what a big deal it is in our walk with God.

You might be thinking, *Here we go, the "just say no" spiel.*

"Just saying no" is important. Turning from temptation can be a difficult but critical decision. The Bible encourages us not to test our strength, but repeatedly instructs us to flee temptation. Second Timothy 2:22 is especially relevant: "Run from *anything* that stimulates youthful lusts. Instead, pursue righteous living, faithfulness, love, and peace. Enjoy the companionship of those who call on the Lord with pure hearts" (NLT, emphasis added). In other words, run *from* temptation and *toward* righteousness, and choose friends who are running in the same direction. But as important as it is to "just say no," I want to go deeper. Why does God want us to say no to drugs, alcohol abuse, and porn? Maybe it's because He wants us to say yes—to Him.

Romans 6 says,

So you also should consider yourselves to be dead to the power of sin and alive to God through Christ Jesus.

Do not let sin control the way you live; do not give in to sinful desires. Do not let any part of your body become an instrument of evil to serve sin. Instead, give yourselves completely to God, for you were dead, but now you have new life. So use your whole body as an instrument to do what is right for the glory of God. (vv. 11–13 NLT, emphasis added)

This passage isn't directly talking about addiction. But it is talking about bondage. When Jesus died to save us, His shed blood shattered the chains of sin from the lives of all who choose to accept Him. Sin can no longer be our master because Jesus purchased our freedom with His blood. But as we also see in this passage, Jesus didn't just die to set us free *from* something. He died to set us free *for* something.

He died so we could use our bodies as instruments to do what is right for His glory. We're set free for a greater purpose.

Addiction rules those who experience it. How can we use our bodies for God's glory if we're bound to a substance or glued to the impurity on a screen? We can't. First Corinthians 6 tells us, "Or do you not know that your body is the temple of the Holy Spirit who is in you, whom you have from God, and you are not your own? For you were bought at a price; therefore glorify God in your body and in your spirit, which are God's" (vv. 19–20). This passage is specifically talking about sexual sin, so it's especially relevant to porn addictions. Our bodies are temples of God, but addiction hands the key to another "little g" god. We're taking what is rightfully God's and giving ownership to a bottle or a screen.

Romans 6 also affirms this: "Do you not know that to whom you present yourselves slaves to obey, you are that one's slaves whom you obey, whether of sin leading to death, or of obedience leading to righteousness?" (v. 16). There's no edging around it—giving in to addiction is presenting ourselves as slaves to sin. The sin of sexual immorality found in porn. The sin of drunkenness, lack of self-control, or abusing our bodies (or the people around us) through drugs or alcohol. Addiction *always* requires obedience. And we cannot serve both God and drugs, alcohol, porn, or any other addiction.

God desires us to live and walk in the freedom of Jesus. To not chain ourselves to other masters but submit our lives to Him and His love. In Him is true freedom.

Do you see how God's design is bigger than just saying no? We're not saying no to something great to settle for something paltry, but saying no to something destructive to say yes to something truly satisfying. C. S. Lewis said,

> It would seem that Our Lord finds our desires not too strong, but too weak. We are half-hearted creatures, fooling about with drink and sex and ambition when infinite joy is offered us, like an ignorant child who wants to go on making mud pies in a slum because he cannot imagine what is meant by the offer of a holiday at the sea. We are far too easily pleased.[8]

Drugs, alcohol, and pornography are half-hearted "mud pies" compared to freedom in Jesus.

Walking in Freedom

Not all addictions are the same or require similar treatment. Porn addiction recovery looks different from drug abuse recovery. The points below aren't specific to one addiction but instead are five tips to help you or those you know walk in freedom.

1. Become Educated and Share with Others

Not everyone is aware of the long-term impact of recreational drugs, drinking, and porn use (or if they are aware, many ignore the facts). Educate yourself on these topics from both a scientific perspective and a Christian worldview so you can tactfully share with others and stay strong yourself.

2. Develop Healthy Relationships and Open Communication

It's proven that teens who have strong and healthy relationships with their parents or other adults are less likely to develop addictions. Teens with open communication and accountability are less likely to hide drug, alcohol, or porn use. This is hard for teens whose parents aren't invested in their lives or who don't have a strong support system. Even so, work to develop healthy relationships and open communication. If it can't be with a parent, maybe it could be with a relative, someone at church, a youth leader or worker, or another adult you know and trust. Also develop healthy peer-to-peer relationships. If you think a friend is struggling with addiction, don't be afraid to reach out.

3. Steer Clear of Situations That Might Lead to Compromise

If you know you'll be tempted to look at porn on your phone late at night, turn your phone off and leave it in another room. If you know there might be drugs or alcohol at a party you're invited to, don't go or leave as soon as you find out. Don't assume you can handle it, but get out quickly—or better yet, don't place yourself in the situation to begin with (2 Tim. 2:22).

4. Get Help If You're Struggling, and Encourage Others to as Well

If you're struggling with addiction, don't hide it or think it will go away. Reach out for help. If you know someone who's struggling, encourage them to take these steps and support them on their journey toward recovery.

- **Admit the addiction.** Sometimes admitting the issue is actually an addiction is a huge first step. Don't try to cover it up. It's hard, but worth it to break free.

- **Reach out for help.** Be honest and tell someone you trust that you're struggling—your parents, pastor, youth leader, or another trustworthy adult. You don't need to feel ashamed because of your struggle. It's incredibly courageous to be bold enough to ask for help.

- **Get treatment or counseling.** With the assistance of the person you told, the next step is to get outside help. This could be through a treatment program or a Christian counselor. There are many Christian support groups or programs such as Teen Challenge. Many churches offer programs and support as well. With someone's help, research options near you and decide what fits you best.

- **Break the cycle.** People often relapse after treatment because they return to their old lives without making changes. They hang out with the same people, go to the same places, and browse the same sites. To find long-lasting freedom, you need to break the cycle. If friends led you to your addiction, break off those friendships and find new friends who will encourage you to stay strong. If porn is your struggle, install internet filters such as those from Covenant Eyes or other sites. Don't go back to your old way of life, but intentionally set up safeguards to stop the cycle.

- **Get accountability.** Having people speak into our lives and hold us accountable is vital. Ask a trusted friend (or seek out someone at a local church) to mentor you, and ask them to check in regularly. When they do, be honest about your journey and any current roadblocks or successes you're experiencing.

5. Intentionally Grow in Your Walk with God

Freedom from addiction is only one step on the journey of living fully for Jesus. Remember, we're not just set free *from*, we're set free *for*. Nothing is more freeing than a personal relationship with Christ. People turn to addictions because they feel empty and purposeless, but Jesus overflows our hearts with His love and gives us genuine purpose. Intentionally grow in your walk with God. Spend time seeking Him in prayer and Bible study and through serving those around you. A teen firmly rooted in Jesus won't easily be shaken by addiction.

Finding True Freedom in a Bondage-Breaking Savior

The cycle can't be broken on our own. It's too strong. Only the God who broke the bondage of sin with a cry of "It is finished!" can shatter the chains of addiction. Because it's *still* finished. His power is still available to all who seek it.

When I think of the power of God to break every chain of bondage, I think of Raymond, a man at my church who was enslaved to drugs and alcohol from the age of thirteen. He spent twelve years in and out of jail and rehab, always returning to the old patterns of his life until he encountered Jesus one day in prison. After that, everything changed. He now leads a Christian-based recovery program and is a powerful witness to the mercy of Jesus. "I've been given a new life," he says. "I've been set free. I'm not 100 percent where I should be, but praise God I'm not where I used to be—it's okay, I'm on my way! Jesus did it for me. He can do it for you too."

I think of Haley, a seventeen-year-old young woman who battled porn and other sexual addictions for five years but is now walking in freedom and sharing her experiences. "Freedom is worth fighting the temptation in your life," she says. "I know freedom is worth it because I am living it."[9]

I think of the women I've met. Young women like Amber, so broken and hurting. If I could meet her again, this is what I'd say:

"You're not alone. You're struggling, but you're not hopeless. You're tired from the fight, but God can give you strength to endure. *You are not your addiction.* It's defined you for so many years, but it doesn't have to anymore. You are cherished by the God who died to show you His love—and give you His freedom.

"Yes, **freedom**.

"It's not a theory. It's reality. Even freedom from the bondage of addiction."

Going Deeper

1. Have you or someone you know battled an addiction?
2. What similarities do porn addictions have with drug or alcohol addictions? In what ways are both destructive?
3. We're not just set free *from*, we're set free *for*. Why is this important?
4. If you or someone you know battles addiction, what practical steps toward freedom can you take or encourage them to take today?
5. Even if it's not a matter of addiction, we all often look to "mud pies" for satisfaction. What "mud pies" are you looking to, and how can you look to God instead?

Further Resources

- *Freedom Starts Today: Overcoming Struggles and Addictions One Day at a Time* by John Elmore

- *Healing the Scars of Addiction: Reclaiming Your Life and Moving into a Healthy Future* by Gregory L. Jantz
- Teen Challenge (https://teenchallengeusa.org/)
- "How to (Realistically) Break Free from Sexual Addiction" by Haley Seba (https://www.therebelution.com/blog/2017/02/how-to-realistically-break-free-from-sexual-addiction/)

12

Media

(Living Transformed in a Conforming Culture)

If culture could be described as a body, media would be its heartbeat.

Media is everywhere. We carry it in our pockets on glowing rectangles commonly known as smartphones. We sit in front of it on our television screens. We listen to it through our earbuds. We scroll through it on our social media feeds. It's always at our fingertips, and it's always demanding our attention.

If I think about how much media and technology I've absorbed in the past twenty-four hours, it's staggering. My phone is in front of me on my desk as I type at my computer. Last night I watched a movie with my family. Throughout the movie, I texted my friend. This morning when I picked up my phone, I checked my email, scrolled Instagram for a few minutes, and turned on a podcast while I got ready for the day. Before I started writing, I checked my favorite blog, read a few articles, deleted junk emails, and took one more look at social media. In less than twenty-four hours, I've absorbed multiple forms of media, spent several hours in front of a screen, and, except when I was sleeping, always had my phone within reach.

Before we dive into this chapter, let's define what I mean by *media*. Google (because yes, I just googled it—one more media score for me) defines *media* as "the main means of mass communication (broadcasting, publishing, and the internet) regarded collectively."[1] Media is *mass communication*.

Social media, Netflix, video games, podcasts, music, and web surfing are all forms of media. It's a pretty broad topic, isn't it? Because it's so extensive, the examples I share may be about one specific form of media (such as social media or music), but the principles apply to other forms as well.

Now that we've defined media, let's move on from what it is to what it does to us.

Media—the Conveyor of Culture

Media is the great conveyor and creator of culture. Media conveys ideas about life, relationships, sexuality, and everything under the sun. These ideas shape culture and, in turn, shape us. Ideas make an impact. Whether true or false, they leave a mark. That's why we have to be careful about which ideas we believe and which ideas we listen to.

But that's easier said than done. Every day 350 million photos are uploaded to Facebook, 306.4 billion emails are sent,[2] and over 3.5 billion Google searches are processed.[3] In addition, YouTube fans will be glad to hear that 500 hours of videos are uploaded to the platform every *minute*[4] (set aside your fears of ever running out of new content). That's a lot of ideas, and I didn't even mention how many movies are produced and songs released each year, and how many articles are published every day. Combine it all and you have a staggering amount of noise at a decibel level ready to deafen us all.

Of course we don't process that much data ourselves, but it's available and we come across our fair share. We're swimming in an ocean of media, and the water is made up of ideas.

Maybe a song projected ideas about love and sex. Or a movie shared messages about identity or the meaning of life. Maybe you saw someone come out on social media as gay or transgender. Maybe you read an article about racism or injustice. Maybe you noticed subtle ideas about drug or alcohol use in a TV show. Then there's pornography, which is a form of media all on its own that has deeply damaged relationships, marriages, and our perspectives on sexuality, human dignity, and body image.

Hang on, Sara, it's not that big a deal. It's just entertainment, you might be saying. But that very fact makes it powerful. Nancy Pearcey explains why:

> T. S. Eliot once noted that the serious books we read do not influence us nearly as much as the books we read for fun (or the movies we watch for entertainment). Why? Because when we are relaxing, our guard is down and we engage in the "suspension of disbelief" that allows us to enter imaginatively into the story. As a result, the assumptions of the author or screenwriter may go unnoticed and seep all the more deeply into our consciousness.[5]

Not only is our guard down when we're binge-watching Netflix or jamming to our favorite songs but those who create media actually do so with the intention of conveying worldviews. If you're a *Star Wars* fan, you probably didn't think you were being educated when you watched *Return of the Jedi* or *The Force Awakens*, but according to George Lucas, producer of *Star Wars*, he's teaching viewers in every film: "I've always tried to be aware of what I say in my films, because all of us who make motion pictures are teachers—teachers with very loud voices."[6]

Consider how media pushes the LGBTQ+ agenda to make homosexual activity a culturally accepted norm. Have you ever watched a show with a character who is gay? Or seen a commercial or YouTube ad with a gay or lesbian couple? The Gay and Lesbian Alliance Against Defamation (GLAAD) has intentionally used media to highlight homosexual behavior, and they've done an excellent job. As the famous strategy paper "The Overhauling of Straight America" said, "The first order of business is desensitization of the American public concerning gays and gay rights. The visual media, film and television, are plainly the most powerful image-makers in Western civilization. . . . So far, gay Hollywood has provided our best covert weapon in the battle to desensitize the mainstream."[7] While this paper was written in the 1980s, they were right in saying their ideas were "just the beginning of a major publicity blitz by gay America" to the point that children's shows are now taking up the agenda and using their platform to educate kids on transgenderism and homosexuality. The more we let our guard down in our media choices, the more we're desensitized. Our emotions are engaged and our opinions shaped. In a phrase, it's cultural brainwashing.

These tactics of media have influenced culture and will continue to. How can we live with discernment in this ocean of ideas? Building a Christian worldview on media begins with two critical points: our *choices* and our *usage*.

Questioning Our Choices

Many of us have a split worldview when it comes to media choices. We apply God's truth to "spiritual" aspects of our lives but leave entertainment out of the equation. Let me ask you a question: If someone were to look only at the music you listen to and the shows you watch, would they see a difference between your standards and the standards of mainstream society? Would they suspect that you're a Christian?

Since worldviews are caught more than taught, what worldviews are we hanging out with? We're highly influenceable people. Several years ago, I spent a lot of time with my friend Sonya. She was extroverted and funny and had a unique personality. The more time I spent with her, the more I absorbed her attitudes, expressions, and opinions. One day I said something and realized, *I just sounded* exactly *like Sonya.* It was a wake-up call on how much she was influencing me. The same goes for our media exposure. I've had similar experiences with movies and shows. I'll say something and think, *Um, that sounded exactly like a character on such and such a show.*

We pick up on the characteristics, thoughts, and habits we're exposed to. If we're exposed to media with unbiblical worldviews and agendas, we'll pick up on those too. I would be so bold as to say it's impossible to uphold a Christian worldview in every other area of our lives if we don't live with a Christian worldview in this area. Like 2 Corinthians 6:14 says, "What fellowship has righteousness with lawlessness? And what communion has light with darkness?" You can't live a holy life if you're filling your heart with unholy things.

Much of popular media is filled with undeniable darkness. I've sensed this darkness and the presence of evil in many entertainment choices. There are often satanic forces behind mainstream media. The darker the world gets, the more the lies of Satan will creep onto our screens—if we let them.

If Satan is the god of this world and media is the heartbeat of culture, we can be sure he will use media to promote his agenda. Something doesn't have to be explicitly occult to be influenced by evil. Sometimes messages and agendas are subtle, but *subtle* doesn't mean nonexistent. Dannah Gresh, popular author and speaker to young adults, describes it like an IV drip,

> gradually pumping a foreign substance into your system. . . . Once it gets into your system, your whole body will definitely be affected! Likewise, the consequences of taking toxic media into your mind and soul may not be realized until further down the road when it's too late and the damage has been done.[8]

Drip by drip, message by subtle message. Slowly they desensitize our hearts and we become conformed by their influence. But as followers of Jesus, conforming isn't an option. As Romans 12:2 says, "Do not be conformed to this world, but be transformed by the renewing of your mind, that you may prove what is that good and acceptable and perfect will of God."

Using Discernment in Our Choices

Discernment is the key word here. English writer Samuel Johnson once described discernment as "the power to tell the good from the bad, the genuine from the counterfeit, and to prefer the good and genuine to the bad and the counterfeit."[9] For example, discernment would be the ability to identify a pair of knockoff Converse sneakers from the real deal or, in the case of media, to identify false worldviews in a film.

Developing discernment takes time, energy, and intentional thought. I've found it helpful to ask three core questions when deciding what to watch, listen to, and follow.

1. Does It Glorify and Promote Evil?

A few weeks ago, everyone was sharing their end-of-the-year Spotify Wrapped lists on Instagram. Being a music geek, I'm naturally curious (read: nosy) about the music other people enjoy. Tapping through my stories, I noticed one artist mentioned again and again. I'd heard the name but never listened to their music, so I looked up a few songs. What I found was, in a word, evil. The lyrics of several songs spoke explicitly of hell, demons, homosexuality, and sexual acts. The fact that the songs were filled with evil didn't surprise me, but the fact that my Christian friends didn't notice this evil did. Maybe that's because this kind of evil is cloaked in popularity.

Some media is clearly evil. For these, we use the 2 Timothy 2:22 model and *run*. Sadly, in a world growing darker by the day, that means a lot of running, because *evil is everywhere*. It's found in movies and shows that highlight demonic horror or sexual perversion. It's found in video games that are not only violent but filled with the darkness of Satan. It's found in music that's filled with lyrics of depravity. It's found on every porn site and in every sexually explicit magazine or app.

In case you're thinking only "really bad" things constitute evil, know that sin doesn't have to be conspicuous to be present. Evil is anything that glorifies sin. Sin-glorifying is found in many media forms that are easy to laugh off as harmless fun. But sin is never harmless. God's Word tells us to "have no fellowship with the unfruitful works of darkness, but rather expose them" (Eph. 5:11). No fellowship means *none*. Evil has no place in our media choices.

2. What Worldview Does This Communicate?

Don't you wish media came with a disclaimer? Wouldn't it be easier if we turned on a movie and the first thing that flashed across the screen said, "Worldview Alert: This film contains elements of New Age spirituality, humanism, and atheistic thinking. Viewer discretion advised." Unfortunately, media doesn't come with warning labels.

Evaluating *worldviews* is different from evaluating *content*. Choosing media with clean content is important, but it's possible for the content to be clean and the worldviews to be corrupt. It's even possible for media formats containing what could be called graphic content to have positive worldview messages, such as in the case of the film *Hacksaw Ridge*. Like I say in my book *Love Riot: A Teenage Call to Live with Relentless Abandon for Christ*,

> There's a difference between something portraying sin and something glorifying it. . . . We can learn deep truths and scripturally sound lessons through the mistakes of others and the consequences faced. The caveat is whether or not it's portrayed as wrong or whether it's lifted up as an example to follow. The former we can learn from; the latter we can be influenced by.[10]

Pay attention to underlying messages and agendas. What is this (media example) saying about the purpose of life? What is it telling me about God? What are its messages about human value? Sexuality? Marriage? Once you've identified the answers, ask: What does Scripture say about this? Do these perspectives align with the Bible? Do they affirm truth about God, the purpose of life, sexuality, identity, or marriage? Thinking through these questions strengthens our "worldview detectors." It helps us think deeply about the ideas a media form is sharing. Sometimes worldviews emerge naturally; often they're agenda-driven, such as in the case of GLAAD's goal to promote the LGBTQ+ agenda through media.

When it comes to worldviews, it takes discernment to know where to draw the line. Some messages go back to the question, "Does this promote evil?" and land automatically on our ditch list. However, it's difficult to find media that aligns 100 percent with every aspect of a Christian worldview and that's why being able to discern and evaluate worldviews is so important. The power and influence of worldview messages are found in our ignorance of them.

3. How Is It Influencing Me?

The bottom line in making media choices comes down to the question, "How is it influencing me?"

Is this actively pulling me away from God? Is it impacting my emotions? Thoughts? Attitudes? Even if it's not evil or doesn't promote secular worldviews, it still has the potential to influence us negatively if it becomes an idol that takes over our time, thoughts, and attention.

Take a hard look at the media you consume and ask yourself how it's influencing you. Ask your family how they think the media you consume impacts you. If you realize something is drawing you away from God or having negative effects on your life, make the hard choice to let it go. If it's hindering your walk with God, keeping it in your life isn't worth it.

Questioning Our Usage

"So, uh, what do you think about video games?"

I turned to my friend sitting next to me. "Video games?" I responded, startled by the abrupt change in topic.

"Yeah," he responded. "I know you probably saw my brothers playing today, and I was just wondering what you thought about it. Do you think video games are okay? Is playing them a problem?"

I thought for a second. I'm not a gamer myself. I died about a million times once playing Mario Kart. (Or at least should have died. Apparently you're indestructible in video games.) After that, I concluded it wasn't my thing. I knew many video games were incredibly violent. I knew video games could become addictive. I knew a lot of teens had a video game obsession and spent hours each day playing. But I also knew the same problems could show up in movies and music and smartphone use.

"Well, I think in and of itself, playing video games can be okay if you choose them carefully, the same as how you need to be careful about the movies you watch. I think one of the biggest things is *how* you use video games. Are they becoming an obsession? How often do you play? Can you go a day—or several days—without playing? If not, it's probably become an unhealthy preoccupation. I think it comes down to using them wisely and in moderation."

In a media-saturated world, that is a countercultural goal. We've all heard jokes about teens being glued to their phones. And it's often true. Media consumes our lives. Media consumes *us*.

Using media in a countercultural way doesn't stop with *what* we watch, listen to, play, or follow. Why, when, how, and how much matter too. Our choices can be unwise. Our usage can be abusive. Both matter.

Usage abuse can look like wasting time and becoming addicted to our devices. But usage abuse can also refer to *what* we use our devices for. Take our smartphones. We can use our phones to keep in touch with friends, take fun pictures, and find out information on the internet. These can be helpful and edifying uses. Or we can use our phones to send sexually explicit photos, look up porn, engage in cyberbullying, or play mind-numbing games that contain violence and sexual perversion. These are inappropriate and abusive uses.

It comes down to this: do we control our devices, or do our devices control us?

In many ways we've allowed our devices to become idols. We've left healthy usage behind and become consumed, addicted, and obsessed. Maybe it's an obsession with video games or social media. Or hours upon hours of binge watching. Maybe it's a constant attachment to our earbuds where we escape reality and ignore everyone around us. Maybe it's a porn addiction or frequent sexting. Whatever the obsession, we can't deny we've given media too much power. It's time to take back control and put our devices in their proper place. Let's take a look at a few of the consequences of media obsession.

Media Physically Affects Our Brains

Constant screen time and media usage can alter our brains like any other addiction. Intense media usage reroutes the neuropathways in our brains and causes us to become dependent on our screens. Studies have shown that this addiction leads to difficulty focusing on human interaction, shortened attention spans, and even acquired ADHD.[11] The time we spend on our devices is also correlated to depression and anxiety. Psychologist Jean Twenge expresses it this way:

> Adolescents who spend more time on new media . . . were more likely to report mental health issues, and adolescents who spent more time on nonscreen activities . . . were less likely. Since 2010, iGen adolescents have spent more time on new media screen activities and less time on nonscreen activities, which may account for the increases in depression and suicide.[12]

Other mental consequences include how sexting and porn change the way we view human value and can lead to body image problems and perverted forms of sexuality.

Media Influences Our Relationships with People

Media also impacts our in-person relationships and how we engage with the world. Each time we choose screen time over face-to-face communication, we miss out on precious time with the people around us.

Have you noticed at a restaurant how many people choose to stare at their screens or post the moment on their stories instead of engaging with family or friends? We've become posters instead of participators. When we see something beautiful, we don't stop in awe; we pull out our phones to snap a picture. When we're with our loved ones, we don't soak in the moments as priceless gifts; we're too busy scrolling, swiping, and tapping.

Our media obsession has shrunk our world down to the size of our screens. Dr. Jeff Myers says, "A 'selfie' isn't just a way of taking a picture. It's a cultural movement in which each person thinks the world revolves around him- or herself."[13] In this cultural movement where we create our own worlds that revolve around the god of us, we're susceptible to the invasion of post-truth thinking. Why are we more concerned about being connected to our online kingdom than embracing the real world around us? Because we've elevated ourselves—our opinions, feelings, and perspectives. Our egos have exploded faster than the rise of the iPhone, yet our lives have shrunk to the size of a snapshot.

Media Can Harm Our Relationship with God

This gets to the heart of what media obsession truly damages—our relationship with God. How often have we turned to our phones instead of looked to God? How often have we said we didn't have time to read our Bibles, but somehow found time for TikTok? How can we serve and love God when we're always glued to our screens? How can we show the world Christ's love when our worlds aren't any bigger than our devices?

First Corinthians 6:12 is applicable to media usage: "All things are lawful for me, but all things are not helpful. All things are lawful for me, but I will not be brought under the power of any."

Media might be lawful for us. We don't have to throw away our smartphones to obey God. But is the way we use it helpful? Have we been brought under the power of media? Does it control us?

Three Tips for Healthy Media Usage

If you, like me, are feeling the prick of conviction that your media usage needs some work, here are three tips to help you keep your media usage healthy and under control.

1. Set Boundaries

To take back the reins of control, we need to establish firm boundaries with our usage. Try turning off your phone every evening at a certain time, keeping it in another room at night, and having one or more days a week with reduced or no screen time. Limit the amount of time you spend playing video games or on social media (you can set a limit or download an app to block your social media apps when you've reached your limit for the day). Having screen-free days can help you remain balanced with your usage. Two ways I've done this have been by taking regular social media breaks and making Sundays screen free.

2. Have Accountability

It's easy to create boundaries but hard to stick to them. I recently set an alarm on my phone to go off every night at nine. The alarm read, "TURN OFF YOUR PHONE!!!" My hope was that the capital letters and exclamation points would intimidate me into obeying. It didn't work. After about a week, I got incredibly good at ignoring the message. The difference with the first week was that I'd told a group of friends about my decision and asked them to keep me accountable for a few days. But once I knew they would no longer be checking up on me, my good intentions started to slip.

Accountability helps us stick to our boundaries. If you set a boundary, tell someone (or better yet, come up with a list of boundaries with another person, like your parents or a youth worker) and ask them to keep you accountable.

Clear communication with your parents or a trusted adult on your media choices and usage is vital. There should be no secrets on your phone, browsing history, or watch list. If you couldn't confidently hand your phone or laptop to your parents or youth pastor without fearing what they'd find, that's probably exactly what you need to do.

3. Invest in Real Relationships and Nonscreen Activities

Even though we have hundreds or thousands of friends and followers online, many of us have little human interaction. God created us to live in community and enjoy the world He made. Put down your devices and have genuine face-to-face conversations. If you're talking to someone, don't look at your phone. If you're hanging out with friends, keep your time together screen free. Engage in nonscreen activities, like reading a book, going outside, learning a new skill, or investing in hands-on service and ministry. Most importantly, prioritize time with God without the distraction of a screen. Read your Bible before you check your phone and spend time in prayer before you spend time scrolling.

It's a Heart Thing

We can ask all the questions, set up all the boundaries, throw away all the questionable content, think through all the worldviews, and check all the boxes, but if our hearts aren't set on the goal of glorifying God, we're no better off. Legalistic rules and requirements don't make us holy or help us counter the culture. Only a heart transformed by God's grace can do that.

If our hearts aren't right, our actions won't stand a chance. Jesus's transformation invades every corner of our lives, and our media usage is not exempt from the overhaul. Let's not be conformed to the world but instead allow Jesus to transform us . . . from our hearts to our minds to our entertainment.

Going Deeper

1. How much media do you use on a regular basis? Would you call yourself addicted? How would you feel if media was suddenly taken away?

2. Think of the last two media forms you used (e.g., a song, social media post, movie). What ideas did they hold? What worldviews did they promote?

3. Using the three questions listed above, evaluate your media choices. Is there anything you need to get rid of or change? If so, how can you follow through?

4. Evaluate your media usage. Are there any areas of abuse? If so, what steps can you take to set boundaries and get accountability? Share what you learned and what steps you want to take with a friend or family member.

5. Why is your heart attitude in your media use important?

Further Resources

- *12 Ways Your Phone Is Changing You* by Tony Reinke
- *The Tech-Wise Family: Everyday Steps for Putting Technology in Its Proper Place* by Andy Crouch
- Plugged In (www.pluggedin.com)

PART THREE

generation change 101

13

Preparing for Pushback

(Staying Strong in a Compromising Culture)

One decision changed Jaelene Hinkle Daniel's life. "I'm essentially giving up the one dream little girls dream about their entire life,"[1] she said.

She made the decision to stay true to her convictions. But it didn't come easy.

Jaelene gave her life to Christ when she was twelve. She grew up in church and on the soccer field. But as a teenager, sports, popularity, and friends were higher on her priority list than a personal relationship with God.

Jaelene felt caught between two worlds. In one world she was successful and popular. She earned a full scholarship to Texas Tech University and excelled in her sport. But then there was the world of her half-hearted commitment to Christ. "On paper I was doing really well,"[2] she said. But inside the tension kept growing. Saturday night parties blended into Sunday morning church services, and she realized she couldn't fit in both worlds.

During the spring season of her junior year of college, Jaelene began having excruciating pain in her left leg. An MRI revealed an extensive blood clot. The only option was to put in a stent, but that would mean she'd never be able to play soccer again. With this news, her plans and dreams came crashing down. She'd placed her identity in her soccer career, and now it was being pulled out from under her. Instead of losing hope, Jaelene decided to pray. All through the night before the surgery, Jaelene and her family sought God's healing. At her breaking point, Jaelene told God, "If You allow me to play soccer, this is going to be for You."[3]

The next morning, her doctors discovered the blood clot was miraculously gone and there was no need for a stent. After that, Jaelene decided to go all-in. No more living in two worlds. From now on, she'd be 100 percent sold out for Jesus—on and off the soccer field.

But as her career skyrocketed, her commitment to Christ began to clash with the culture. It started in 2015 after the Supreme Court's decision to legalize same-sex marriage. That day Jaelene posted on Instagram a picture of a cross with a radical, countercultural caption: "I believe with every fiber in my body that what was written 2,000 years ago in the Bible is undoubtedly true." She wrote,

> It's not a fictional book. It's not a pick and choose what you want to believe. You either believe it, or you don't. This world may change, but Christ and His Word NEVER will. My heart is that as Christians we don't begin to throw a tantrum over what has been brought into law today, but we become that much more loving. That through our love, the lost, rejected, and abandoned find Christ.

She ended her post with the biblical meaning of the rainbow as a covenant between God and His people and said, "Love won over 2,000 years ago when the greatest sacrifice of all time was made for ALL mankind."[4]

With these words, she drew a line in the sand. No matter what stance the culture took, she would stand for God's truth. Two years later, this decision went from a post on Instagram to a choice that radically altered her soccer career.

In 2017, when she was twenty-four, Jaelene was invited to play for America in two international friendlies games. It was a dream come true and an incredible opportunity. Days before the event, it was announced that players on the American team were required to wear rainbow jerseys designed to honor the LGBTQ+ community for Pride Month. Once again, the clash of conviction, the tension between two worlds.

For three days, Jaelene prayed and sought God. Wear the jersey or not wear the jersey? I can't help but wonder if her commitment "This is going to be for You" came to mind. Maybe it did, because at the end of the three days, she pulled herself off the team roster. "I just felt so convicted in my spirit that it wasn't my job to wear this jersey,"[5] she later said.

Backlash followed. She was slammed on social media after her decision became public. She was booed on multiple occasions during games. She was called a "vocal homophobe" by sportswriters and reporters. After trying out for the Women's World Cup in 2019, she was cut from the team. Her decision to remain faithful to her convictions resulted in pushback from nearly every side.

Does she regret her choice? Not at all. "It was very disappointing," she admits. "I think that's where the peace trumped the disappointment. Because I knew in my spirit I was doing the right thing. I knew that I was being obedient. Just because you're obedient doesn't make it easy."[6]

Obedience was worth the pushback. Obedience was worth the cost to her soccer career. Obedience was worth the dream she gave up.

During this time, Jaelene's team was the North Carolina Courage. It's fitting, isn't it, that *Courage* was the name of her team, because her life looks like courage in the face of opposition for the cause of Christ. Her coach called her "one of the best defenders in the world,"[7] but I think she'll be best known for her unashamed defense of her beliefs. Soccer was a part of Jaelene's purpose, but Christ was—and is—her ultimate passion. While some may call her a hater, bigot, homophobe, or even just a fool, her commitment to Christ is one we can all be inspired by.

That's part of Jaelene's goal—to inspire Christians to live in obedience to Jesus. "I don't question His goodness," she said. "I know He's good, I know He's faithful. . . . If I never get a national team call up again . . . that's just part of His plan and that's okay. Maybe this was why [I was] meant to play soccer. Just to show other believers to be obedient."[8]

Living in a World of Opposition

As culture grows darker, more Christians are receiving pushback for living out their beliefs.

In part two, we dug into culture's perspective on numerous controversial topics and outlined God's truth. Now we need to take those truths into the world and live them out. But I'm going to be up-front: *doing so won't be easy.* It will require sacrifices. It will demand hard decisions. It will mean standing alone and making choices no one understands. It may mean giving up a dream or a friend or your reputation. In some countries, it means giving up your life. The consequences of standing for God's truth are numerous and costly.

In the United States, we haven't experienced the level of persecution Christians in other nations face every day. In countries like India and Pakistan, it's common to be imprisoned for your faith. In countries like North Korea and Saudi Arabia, it's common to be killed. Religious freedom is slipping away in America. Many Christians have faced steep consequences for affirming God's design for sexuality, gender, and marriage or sharing His truth on justice or the value of life. Some have lost jobs. Others have lost businesses. Some have been threatened, canceled, and denied free speech. The consequences of speaking God's truth on controversial, "politically correct," topics are becoming more severe and prevalent.

We have to be prepared for pushback.

Perhaps one day we'll face the same consequences our brothers and sisters in Christ have faced for centuries. Will we be ready? One thing is clear: we won't be ready to face death or imprisonment for our faith *one day* if we're not willing to be mocked, fired from our jobs, or called intolerant for the sake of God's truth *today.*

Standing strong starts now.

Standing strong *needs* to start now. Jesus told us opposition would come. He spoke of His followers being beaten, imprisoned, betrayed, and killed for the gospel and ended His warning with these words: "And you will be hated by all for My name's sake. But he who endures to the end shall be saved" (Mark 13:13).

When the stakes increase, the temptation is to live a privatized faith. To push our Christianity into one corner and not allow Christ to impact our daily choices and nitty-gritty beliefs. But an authentic relationship with Jesus can never be secluded or compartmentalized. The way of Christ doesn't keep itself neatly packaged in one or two areas of our lives but overtakes and overhauls every nook and cranny. In a culture growing increasingly anti-Christ, this transformed life-style spells danger and discomfort for all who choose it. David Platt once said, "The danger of our lives increases according to the depth of our identification with Jesus. If you want a safe, carefree life, don't become like Jesus."[9]

With so much at stake we might wonder, *Is it really worth it?* Brian Jones, founding pastor of Christ's Church of the Valley, understands: "The reality is that I want to live like religion doesn't matter too; I want to live like what I actually believe isn't that important. I like being liked. I don't like making waves. I don't like making people feel awkward. But I can't back down from what I know to be true."[10]

A safe life isn't worth the sacrifice of our relationship with God. In the same way, our relationship with God is well worth the sacrifice of a safe life—even if obedience to God requires disobedience to the ways of the world, to authorities asking us to sin, or to an evil government. Even if our humble audacity leads to unimagined consequences.

How do we practically prepare for pushback and stay strong under pressure? Here are five steps.

1. Count the Cost and Be Prepared to Stand Alone

Peter gives us a loaded statement in 1 Peter 4:12: "Do not be surprised at the fiery trial when it comes upon you to test you, as though something strange were happening to you" (ESV).

Why are we surprised when we face opposition? The Bible tells us we'll face trials and persecution for Jesus. The first step in standing strong is preparing for opposition. If we've already counted the cost, we won't have to decide if obeying God is worth the price in a moment of pressure. We'll already know.

When you're verbally attacked for your faith, you won't be surprised. When you're passed by for a job or position because of your stance on God's design for sexuality, it won't blindside you. When you have an opportunity to speak up about your beliefs, you won't have to debate if it's worth it. When your biblical convictions go against popular opinion, you'll be prepared to stand firm. Don't be surprised. Instead, be prepared and stand strong.

2. Know Your Why

Saeed Abedini, a man persecuted for Christ in Iran, once wrote, "People die and suffer for their Christian faith all over the world, and some may wonder why. But you should know the answer of WHY is WHO. It is for Jesus. He is worth the price."[11]

The foundation of our *why* is Jesus. Our commitment to Christ requires commitment to His ways and His words. We obey Him because we consider Him worth our obedience and because the "love of Christ compels us" (2 Cor. 5:14). He is glorified in our obedience as we strengthen our relationship with Him. Our commitment *to* Christ is only as strong as our relationship *with* Christ.

3. Grow in Biblical Literacy

God's Word is the number one tool in our cultural tool kit. Biblical literacy equips us to stay strong under pressure. The Word of God does not bend and change with the culture, but sheds light beyond the culture by sharing unwavering truths about God's character, our purpose, and how to worship and follow Jesus Christ. These unchanging truths enable us to live beyond our cultural moment because we're rooted to a firm foundation of biblical truth.

Bible teacher Jen Wilkin says, "Biblical literacy matters because it protects us from falling into error. Both the false teacher and the secular humanist rely on biblical ignorance for their messages to take root, and the modern church has proven fertile ground for those messages. Because we do not know our Bibles, we crumble at the most basic challenges to our worldview."[12]

We need to read God's Word, absorb the truth within its pages, and build our lives upon His words. Biblical ignorance is a shaky foundation, one that can't weather the storms of cultural pressure or unbiblical worldviews. But when we're grounded in the Word, we have a sure and solid foundation that can last through the winds and rain of an anti-Christian culture (Matt. 7:24–27).

4. Seek Christian Community and Support

It's hard to go it alone. The support of Christian family members and friends helps us survive pushback. They can speak truth to us when we're discouraged and help us think through hard issues and choices. They can point us in the right direction, encourage us to be faithful, and pray for us in the middle of the struggle. "Two are better than one," Ecclesiastes says, "for if they fall, one will lift up his companion. . . . Though one may be overpowered by another, two can withstand him. And a threefold cord is not quickly broken" (4:9–10, 12). That's one reason God designed the church—to suffer and rejoice together and support one another through life's struggles (see 1 Cor. 12:26).

If your own family members aren't strong Christians, be intentional to seek support from people at your church or other Christians you know. The influence of those you hang out with will directly impact your strength in the middle of pushback.

Remaining faithful to Jesus is a lonely road, but walking with others along the journey can bring encouragement and strength. While we may be required to stand alone at times, we also need faithful Christians uplifting us along the way.

5. Know What You Believe and Why You Believe It

We know *what* we believe, but do we know *why*? Many teenagers walk away from God because they can't handle the pushback they receive. Sadly, this is often because the foundation of their beliefs was too unsteady to weather the storm of opposition unleashed on their faith. With opposition only increasing, we need a stronger foundation. We need to equip ourselves with truth so we can "always be prepared to give an answer to everyone who asks you to give the reason for the hope that you have" (1 Pet. 3:15 NIV). We need to know what we believe, but we also need to know *why*.

For example, why is marriage designed by God to be between one man and one woman? Why is abortion morally wrong? Why is evolution not a solid theory for the creation of the world? Why does sex belong only in the context of marriage? Why do we believe that the Bible is our source of truth? The questions are endless. If these ideas are challenged (and in our society, they will be), do we have the knowledge to back them up? If we don't, it's likely we'll begin to doubt. Because we've never learned the why, we may start to think our ideas *have no why*. But it's not actually the fault of the belief—it's the fault of our lack of understanding and knowledge.

Colossians 2:6–8 encourages us,

> So then, just as you received Christ Jesus as Lord, continue to live your lives in him, rooted and built up in him, strengthened in the faith as you were taught, and overflowing with thankfulness.
> *See to it that no one takes you captive through hollow and deceptive philosophy*, which depends on human tradition and the elemental spiritual forces of this world rather than on Christ. (NIV, emphasis added)

There are many hollow and deceptive philosophies. Not only will our beliefs be attacked but other philosophies will be taught as truth (see 2 Pet. 1:16–3:9; 1 Tim. 4:1–5). Satan, the father of lies, will do anything he can to get us to wander from the path of God's truth. The Bible warns us against false ideas that sound good on the surface, but underneath are nothing but empty promises that go against God. Again, biblical literacy is a vital tool to help us root out false messages, but we also need several other key tools:

- **Solid apologetics.** Apologetics can be defined simply as "the defense of the Christian faith."[13] It's basically the study of *why*. Knowing the basics of apologetics can help us become better equipped to answer hard questions with clarity and truth.
- **Solid theology.** If apologetics is the study of our faith, theology is the study of God. A strong foundation of

theology, combined with biblical literacy, arms us with the truth of God's character and why believing in His existence is not only possible but actually the most reasonable conclusion. We may be tempted to think secular theories hold more weight, but that's simply because we've never learned the powerful and logical arguments in favor of God. Solid theology arms us with confidence to face the attacks against our beliefs with clarity and truth.

- **Critical thinking.** Critical thinking means considering an idea and evaluating it from every angle instead of blindly accepting it. Just because an idea claims to be true doesn't mean it's rooted in biblical truth—even if it's promoted as such. Asking questions and filtering ideas through Scripture can help us think critically and thoroughly, instead of being "tossed back and forth by the waves, and blown here and there by every wind of teaching and by the cunning and craftiness of people in their deceitful scheming" (Eph. 4:14 NIV). We need to both *recognize* and *test* ideas. Test every opinion, theory, worldview, and argument against the truth of God's Word. Even teaching *about* God's Word can be false since Scripture can be twisted to fit an agenda (see 2 Pet. 3:16). Put ideas to the test and think critically so you won't be blown away by false teaching.

It comes down to the words in 2 Timothy 2:15–17: "Be diligent to present yourself approved to God, a worker who does not need to be ashamed, rightly dividing the word of truth. But shun profane and idle babblings, for they will increase to more ungodliness. And their message will spread like cancer." It's hard work and requires diligence to know what we believe and why we believe it. But it's worth the effort.

What Choice Will You Make?

If you were Jaelene, what choice would you have made?

Maybe you've already faced a choice like hers. What decision did you make then? Whether or not you've ever been forced to take a stand for your beliefs, the day is coming when you will. If you live for Christ and with a biblical worldview, you won't be able to stay on the sidelines forever. What choice will you make then? What choice will you make today?

Will you accommodate the culture and let its opinions mold you? Or will you stand firm on God's truth?

Will you retreat during pushback? Or will you dig in your heels with holy defiance and refuse to budge on what you know to be true?

Will you be lazy with your beliefs? Or will you do the hard work of knowing what you believe and why you believe it?

Will you compromise and give in, little by little? Or will you refuse to make concessions to an ungodly culture?

It comes down to this question: will you be faithful to God . . . no matter the cost?

Going Deeper

1. What stood out to you about Jaelene's story? What choice would you have made?
2. Have you experienced pushback for your faith?
3. How often do you read and study Scripture? What's one way you can grow in biblical literacy?
4. Do you know the *why* of your beliefs? If not, what practical step can you take to grow in a deeper understanding of them?
5. Why is critical thinking important?

Further Resources

- *Understanding the Faith: A Survey of Christian Apologetics* by Dr. Jeff Myers
- *The Reason for God: Belief in an Age of Skepticism* by Timothy Keller

- *Mere Christianity* by C. S. Lewis
- *The Case for Christ: A Journalist's Personal Investigation of the Evidence for Jesus* by Lee Strobel
- *Confident Faith: Building a Firm Foundation for Your Beliefs* by Mark Mittelberg
- *Cold-Case Christianity: A Homicide Detective Investigates the Claims of the Gospels* by J. Warner Wallace
- *Transformed by Truth: Why and How to Study the Bible for Yourself as a Teen* by Katherine Forster

14

Taking Your Worldview into the World

(Sharing Truth with Grace and Love)

You're in the classroom and your teacher says, "The Bible is just a book of stories and fables. It can't be trusted." You squirm in your seat and feel like speaking up, but what can you say?

You're hanging out with a group of friends and someone mentions their brother just came out as gay. Everyone says how great that is, but you're not sure what to say. Eventually they turn to you and ask what you think. How do you reply?

You're in a conversation and someone says, "I would never have an abortion, but I believe women should have a choice. That's why abortion should be legal." What should your response be?

Your stomach flips, your heart rate speeds up, your palms get sweaty, and your knees start to shake. I've been there, and I know the hot seat is not a fun place to be.

As we live out a biblical worldview, we're bound to encounter tough conversations. Not only will our lifestyle generate questions but we're also called to share the truth. To take our worldview into the world and proclaim Christ's love. Jesus commanded, "Go therefore and make disciples of all the nations . . . teaching them to observe all things that I have commanded you" (Matt. 28:19–20).

One of our most important callings as Christians is to share the gospel. But did you notice the second part of Jesus's words? "Teaching them to observe all things that I have commanded you." That gets into the nitty-gritty. Sharing the entirety of the Christian message—the commands of Christ and ways of God—comes along with our presentation of the gospel. We're called to be ambassadors of God's truth, including the gospel and extending from the gospel.

But doing so is *not* popular. If you share God's truth, brace yourself to make some waves. If you're quiet or shy, the very thought of engaging in tough conversations might be terrifying. Even if you're outspoken, maybe the consequences seem too great or you're afraid you'll get in over your head. The temptation is to shy away from controversial topics. But as Dr. Jeff Myers reminds us,

> Rather than hide away from culture, we're called to advance. That we live in evil times is no excuse for doing otherwise. Ephesians 5:15–16 says, "Look carefully then how you walk, not as unwise but as wise, making the best use of the time, because the days are evil." Evil days are a given. The only variable is whether we'll make the most of them. Engaging in a culture that could hurt us requires strong convictions and an unshakeable trust in God. It's a call to speak the truth with thoughtful, well-formed arguments presented persuasively through loving dialogue.[1]

Evil days are a given. So are hard conversations.

Five Conversation Tactics

Colossians 4:6 encourages us to "let [our] speech always be with grace, seasoned with salt, that [we] may know how [we] ought to answer each one." Second Timothy adds another challenge: "Preach the word! Be ready in season and out of season. Convince, rebuke, exhort, with all longsuffering and teaching" (4:2).

Apologist Greg Koukl's book *Tactics: A Game Plan for Discussing Your Christian Convictions* equips Christians to engage in conversations on their convictions. In it, he shares that being Christ's ambassador requires three basic skills: *knowledge* necessary for the task, *wisdom* to make the message clear and persuasive, and *character* that can make or break our mission.[2] Focusing on these three qualities, let's dive into five conversation tactics to help us confidently engage our friends, family members, and community with God's truth.

1. Do Your Homework

Successful and effective conversations start long before you open your mouth. As in sports, there's a lot of hard work, practice, study, and strengthening that take place before the game begins. It's the same with good conversations.

Our first skill is *knowledge*. It sounds rudimentary, but—spoiler alert—we can't talk about what we don't know. Yet that's exactly what many Christians try to do. They hear the conclusion of a matter—such as that God created the world or that abortion is wrong—and run with it. But when their conversation partner raises objections or asks questions, they don't know how to respond because they never delved deeper than the bottom line of their argument.

Our first line of defense is coming prepared with the knowledge we need. That doesn't mean we have to be experts on every topic or can't evangelize if we don't have a PhD. We'll never know everything, and if we wait until we do, we'll never talk to anyone. But if we're complacent in our ignorance, we'll do more harm than good. As we do the behind-the-scenes work and engage with others throughout our learning process, we'll gain both on-the-field skills and off-the-field strength.

This removes the intimidation in striking up conversations and answering questions. If we know our topic, we're in the driver's seat, prepared to answer objections or clarify points. If we're familiar with an opposing view (such as an argument in favor of abortion or evolution), we won't be taken off guard when someone uses it.

Research topics and think through opposing views. Look at issues from different angles, try to understand varying viewpoints, and ask yourself if the claim contradicts itself in any way. You can't be an expert on every topic, but do your homework on ideas you're interested in or ones you think you'll encounter. If you have a conversation on an idea you're less familiar with, research it afterward so you can be better equipped next time.

2. Ask Good Questions

"Never make a statement . . . when a question will do the job."[3]

The point of our conversations is to share God's truth. But our goal is not to simply blurt out our point and shove it in someone's face. Instead, we want to help the other person understand and simultaneously learn more ourselves. Questions are often more effective than statements because they inspire deeper thinking and help expose the weaknesses in a viewpoint.

What kinds of questions should we ask? First, what's the goal of the question? Is it to introduce a new concept? Expose a flaw in a viewpoint? Glean new information? Clarify a point? Our questions must be pointed and purposeful.

Consider these:

- **What's your view on _____?** This is a great opening question to kick off dialogue on a hard topic. Notice I said "dialogue," not "debate." If you begin a conversation about a controversial topic, genuinely listen to the other person's opinion. Ask questions to understand their view. Don't interrupt or interject, but let them share and seek to learn. After they're finished (and if you don't agree with their opinion), say something like, "Hey, thanks for sharing your thoughts! I appreciate it, and I enjoyed listening to your opinion. Do you mind if I take a few minutes to share what I think about _____?" and then do so in a loving and truth-filled way.

- **What do you mean by that?** A request for clarification forces the other person to take another look at their view and evaluate it. For example, if someone says, "All religions are basically the same," ask them, "What do you mean by that? Why do you think all religions are basically the same? What about them do you believe is the same?" Many people hold views they've never examined, and a simple "What do you mean?" could lead them to reevaluate what they actually do mean.

- **How did you come to that conclusion? What proof do you have? What are your reasons for believing** _____? When someone shares a viewpoint on a topic that contains objective truth (such as religion, creation, morality, and so on), it's their job to back up their view with evidence. Koukl says, "The burden of proof is the responsibility someone has to defend or give evidence for his view. . . . It's not your duty to prove him wrong. It's his duty to prove his view."[4] Once someone has made a claim, ask for solid reasons, not just personal opinions.

General questions like these can be handy tools in your back pocket. But the power of good questions can be more specific as well. When you're in a hard conversation, think of specific, to-the-point questions to uncover the other person's view and clarify your own. For example, in a conversation about abortion, when someone says, "I believe women should have a choice," you could respond with, "What choice exactly do you believe women should have?" or "Why do you believe women should have the choice of having an abortion when the baby's opinion is not taken into account? What about the baby's choice?" These questions expose what is truly at stake within the word *choice*. In this conversation, you could also use the "Trotting out the toddler"[5] technique and ask, "If women should have the choice to kill their unborn children, should they also have the choice to kill their toddlers? Should their freedom extend to the children they've already given birth to?" If they answer yes (which would be the only answer logically consistent with abortion), they've just approved murder. If they answer no, ask what the difference is between a baby before it's born and after. Why is killing an infant okay while they're in the womb but become murder the second they leave the womb? Do you see how these questions require the other person to think about the topic more than if you simply stated your views?

3. Analyze the Argument

Some arguments aren't arguments at all. They're just assertions. Here's the difference. Koukl says, "An assertion simply states a point. An argument gives supporting reasons why the point should be taken seriously. . . . Opinions by themselves are not proof. Intelligent belief requires reasons."[6]

Too often we're bowled over by simple assertions without realizing their lack of logic or supporting reasons. For example, would you be intimidated if someone said, "It's impossible to know if God exists. There's no proof"? That's quite a strong statement, isn't it? It's strong enough that many of us would back away, intimidated by what we thought was an argument against God's existence.

In reality, it's just an assertion of opinion. The statement "There is no proof of God's existence" holds no proof that there is no proof of God's existence. (Read that sentence again.) Don't be intimidated by assertions. Ask yourself, "Is this an argument (a view with supporting, unbiased reasons) or a personal opinion?" If it's just an assertion or personal opinion, point that out with a question like, "What are your reasons for believing that?" or "What proof do you have to back up that view?" and pay close attention if the answer is another assertion.

4. Don't Try to Win the Argument

Winning arguments is not our goal. Sharing truth and making people think is.

If we go into conversations already on the defense, we do two things: First, we lose our own ability to listen and learn. Second, we miss the point of conversation altogether. It's to *converse*, not *coerce*. If we forget this, we'll turn our conversation partner into the enemy and become discouraged when they stick to their own views instead of accepting the truth we share.

If winning arguments isn't our goal, what is? Simply this: *put a stone in their shoe.*[7] When someone brings up an argument in favor of abortion or same-sex marriage, don't make it your goal to prove them wrong in one conversation. Instead, present the truth in such a way that it makes them think about (and hopefully reconsider) their own view. Our job is to plant seeds of truth in every conversation and leave the results to God. Truth is God's battleground. He alone can alter a perspective and change a heart. "We are not in this alone," Koukl says. "Each of us has an important role to play, but all the pressure is on the Lord. Sharing the gospel is our task, but it's God's problem. . . . I focus on being faithful, but I trust God to be effective."[8]

It's not your job to win the argument. Just put a stone in their shoe.

5. Stay Humble throughout the Conversation

What's the identifying mark of a follower of Jesus? "By this all will know that you are My disciples, if you have love for one another" (John 13:35). In our hard conversations, our behavior should be distinctly different from that of unbelievers. Our dialogue should be filled with love and humility. This is the third skill of Christ's ambassadors: *character*.

We resolutely stand behind truth and boldly share our beliefs, but no one should be able to accuse our attitude and methods of being offensive. Jesus told us when we venture into the world with the message of truth, we're like sheep among wolves. His advice isn't to become wolves ourselves or to play by the rules of the world but to "be wise as serpents and harmless as doves" (Matt. 10:16). Wisdom is our message, and love is our method.

Our attitude can build or destroy our credibility. Let's say we're talking about God's design for marriage. We're sharing that homosexuality is a sin but God offers grace and forgiveness. We get defensive and angry as we counter the other person's objections. How will they believe our message of love and forgiveness if our attitude is one of anger? Humility and love are especially needed when we're discussing these topics with people who experience them personally. Our conversation methods will be different with someone who personally experiences same-sex attraction or gender dysphoria than with someone who simply supports LGBTQ+ views. The topic extends from abstract beliefs to personal experience, and we must be sensitive to the real person, emotions, and experiences in front of us.

In our conversations, we need to infuse our words with uncompromising truth shared in uncompromising love, compassion, grace, and humility. We're not dealing with abstract arguments, opinions, and theories. We're dealing with real, broken, often hurting individuals who are cherished by their Creator. As we engage those with whom we don't agree, we don't have to validate their opinions as truth, but we do need to validate their worth as people. Even if their opinions are biblically incorrect, the individual still deserves to be treated with respect.

Humility also includes realizing that we are prone to error. We don't know everything. Our views could be refined by challenges from an unbeliever or corrected by someone with a different opinion. We need to be committed to truth first and foremost—not simply our own feelings about a topic.

Your attitude speaks as loudly as your message. Keep both in line with love and truth.

This Is Your Moment

The time for truth-telling is *now*.

Culture is drowning in a sea of lies. The world needs bold truth-tellers who will strip back the lies, point to the truth, and be ambassadors of Christ's love no matter the cost.

It's up to us in this generation to proclaim and share truth with the world around us. The truth about God. The truth about grace, forgiveness, and salvation. The truth about His ways and His design for our lives.

Opportunities are everywhere. But the question is, will we be ready? First Peter 3:15 tells us to "always be prepared to give an answer to everyone who asks you to give the reason for the hope that you have" (NIV). When we're asked, will we be prepared? Will we have an answer and the conversational skills to effectively communicate?

We are Christ's ambassadors entrusted with His message. Sharing it won't be easy. There will be backlash. You may not see results. You may often feel at the end of a conversation that you failed or you didn't know how to counter the objections you received. If this happens, don't give in to discouragement, think it was your fault, or succumb to doubts about your beliefs. Instead, dive back into learning and growing so you can be better equipped for the next conversation. You will never be a perfect communicator—but that can't stop you from communicating.

Fellow truth-teller, this is your mission. Know the truth. Study the Word of God. Research the hard topics. Be prepared to give an answer. Then boldly go out and take your worldview into the world through the power of Christ.

Going Deeper

1. Have you encountered a tough or awkward conversation about your beliefs? How did you handle it?

2. Why is it necessary to have hard conversations on important topics? What do these conversations accomplish?

3. Pick one topic from this book. Think of a question you may receive or argument you wouldn't know how to counter on that topic. Research the topic and write out your conversation game plan.

4. Why are questions so effective? What makes them more powerful than statements?

5. What's your biggest fear about having hard conversations? What truth in God's Word combats that fear?

Further Resources

- *Tactics: A Game Plan for Discussing Your Christian Convictions* by Gregory Koukl
- *Challenging Conversations: A Practical Guide to Discuss Controversial Topics in the Church* by Jason Jimenez
- *What Would You Say?* (video series: https://whatwouldyousay.org/)

15

Culture Changers Then and Now

(Learning from Heroes Past and Present)

Who are your heroes?

I'm not talking about superheroes like Wonder Woman or Iron Man or anyone you'd find in a Marvel movie. The heroes I have in mind don't have superpowers, can't leap tall buildings in a single bound, and have probably never even owned a cape. But they're heroes just the same.

I'm talking about everyday individuals who leave their mark on the world and on the people who know them or hear their stories. Individuals like our parents. Our pastors. The missionaries who speak at our churches. Or the people we read about in history books who never would have considered themselves anything but ordinary, but whose extraordinary lives left an indelible imprint upon history that hasn't faded with time.

As you consider what it means to live counterculturally, you may find yourself asking, "Who actually lives like this? What does it *really* look like to engage culture with the gospel, stand firm under pressure, and impact society? How can my life make a difference?"

In this chapter, I want to introduce you to a few of my heroes. These are ordinary people who made—and are making—an extraordinary difference in the world. Superheroes? Not really. More like everyday men and women with passionate convictions, deep commitment, audacious courage, and a supernatural God.

We Will Not Be Silent: The Students of the White Rose

Munich, Germany. 1942. World War II had been raging for three years. Countless cities had been bombed, homes destroyed, and lives stolen. Thousands of soldiers were on the lists of casualties coming from the front lines. Millions of Jewish people had been rounded up into ghettos, sent to concentration camps, and murdered in gas chambers or by mass shootings.

Most Germans turned a blind eye. Many bought into Hitler's ideological brainwashing that called Jews subhuman and elevated Germany above all else. Some saw the desecration of their country, the murder of the innocent, and turned away in fear of the consequences of speaking out. Few saw the horror unfurling around them and decided to act, no matter the cost. Among those few were five college students.

Their names were Hans and Sophie Scholl, Alexander Schmorell, Christoph Probst, and Willi Graf. All under the age of twenty-five, they attended Ludwig Maximilian University in Munich. The five friends were originally drawn together by a shared love of music, nature, and literature. But a deeper bond soon united them—their convictions on the injustice of the Nazi regime and the horrors enacted by their country. Their free-thinking natures and intelligent minds chafed against the brainwashed conformity, and their deep faith and commitment to God refused to allow them to turn a blind eye and silence their consciences. As crucifixes in churches were removed and replaced with swastikas, and the anthem of Germany became a roar of *Sieg Heil*, the hearts of these five students burned with a love for truth and a passion to resist the evil enshrouding their country.

The seeds of resistance were planted in them each early on. As a teenager, Willi Graf resolutely refused to participate in the Hitler

Youth. He made a list of all his friends, and those who joined the Hitler Youth he crossed off the list and never associated with again. Hans and Sophie were once actively involved in the Hitler Youth, but the longer they participated, the more their eyes were opened to the mind-numbing indoctrination, and they became disillusioned with the regime. By the time war broke out in 1939, they were ardently opposed to National Socialism and disgusted by the unjust deaths of so many innocents. In 1941, their desire to resist turned from passion to possibility when Hans received a copy of a sermon by Bishop Clemens von Galen protesting the *Aktion T4* euthanasia program, in which the mentally ill, physically handicapped, and others considered "undesirable" were killed. Thrilled by the truth-filled words, Hans turned to his family and exclaimed, "Finally someone has the courage to speak!" and then added, "And all you need is a duplicating machine."[1] In that moment, a spark of resistance was lit, and an idea was born.

At the same time Hans was contemplating resistance, the desire to speak out was growing in the others. Upon hearing of *Aktion T4*, Christoph Probst shared his anger and disgust with his sister. "It [is] not given to any human being, in any circumstance, to make judgments that are reserved to God alone. No one can know what goes on in the soul of a mentally afflicted person. No one . . . can know what secret inner ripening can come from suffering and sorrow. Every individual's life is priceless. We are all dear to God."[2]

By 1942, the five students were deeply grounded in their desire to resist. The only question was how? And would it be worth the sacrifice? They knew the cost of resistance. Those who dared speak out were imprisoned or executed. They knew it would be easier, simpler, safer to turn their backs. While wrestling with this question, Hans wrote, "Where does the truth lie? Should one go off and build a little house with flowers outside the windows and a garden outside the door and extol and thank God and turn one's back on the world and its filth? Isn't seclusion a form of treachery—of desertion? . . . I'm weak and puny, but I want to do what is right."[3]

Despite the danger, they knew they had to act. The students formed a resistance group that became known as the White Rose. In June, the first anti-Nazi leaflet appeared in the mailboxes of the people of Munich. Titled "Leaflets of the White Rose," it was an eloquent plea for resistance and truth aimed at the millions of Germans who shut their eyes to the brutalities enacted by their dictator.

A second leaflet soon followed, highlighting the mass killings of the Jewish people, which they called "a crime that has no counterpart in human history."[4] A third and fourth came in quick succession, landing in mailboxes, phone booths, and other public places. Each pamphlet was a cry for resistance, and the students used Scripture and the writings of prominent thinkers to make their case. Their fourth leaflet ended with the haunting words, "We will not be silent. We are your bad conscience. The White Rose will not leave you in peace!"[5]

The Gestapo soon became aware of the leaflets and began to hunt for the mysterious members of the White Rose. The students knew they were marked but continued their work. Later Alex looked back and said, "I counted on the possibility of losing my life should I be found out. I simply disregarded all of that, because my inner obligation to act against the National Socialist regime prevailed."[6]

To these five college students and the others who joined them, the risk was worth taking. Freedom and truth were more priceless than safety. While they knew it could cost them their lives, they also knew the weight on their conscience if they remained silent would be a greater price to pay. "It is high time that Christians made up their minds to do something," Hans said. "What are we going to have to show in the way of resistance . . . when this terror is over? We will be standing there empty handed. We will have no answer when we are asked: 'What did you do about it?'"[7]

As the months went by, their resistance grew bolder and riskier. They expanded their leaflet operation, increasing distribution from several hundred copies to thousands and mailing them from various cities across Germany to give the impression of a larger network. They took to the streets at night, leaving a trail of leaflets behind them— along with messages of resistance smeared in tar-based paint across the sides of buildings—*Freedom! Down with Hitler!* But the bolder they became, the more the stakes increased. In February 1943, eight months and six leaflets after their first call for resistance, everything collapsed.

On a leaflet distribution mission at the university on February 18, Hans and Sophie were spotted by a janitor and arrested on the spot.

Four long days and nights of interrogation followed. The net widened as Christoph Probst was also arrested and brought in for interrogation. At first Hans and Sophie denied all charges, but as more evidence was found, they confessed. Each sought to take sole responsibility to spare the other members, and they refused to compromise on their convictions even in the face of certain death. Impressed by her courage, Sophie's interrogator tried to convince her to renounce her beliefs and claim she had been swayed by her brother. "This would have been in fact," he said, "the only way to save her life."[8] Sophie refused. "You're wrong," she replied. "I would do it all over again—because I'm not wrong. *You* have the wrong worldview."[9]

On Monday, February 22, Hans, Sophie, and Christoph were brought before the infamous People's Court. In her trial, Sophie spoke: "Somebody, after all, had to make a start. What we wrote and said is also believed by many others. They just don't dare to express themselves as we did."[10]

After the trial, the verdict was read.

Guilty.

All three were sentenced to death. As Hans and Sophie were led away, their younger brother, Werner, pushed his way toward them in the crowd. For a brief moment, they grasped hands and Hans spoke his last words to his brother: "Stay strong, no compromises."[11]

They were immediately transferred to Stadelheim Prison to be executed by guillotine. At 5:00 p.m., Sophie was led to the execution chamber. Hans and Christoph followed. With his last breath, Hans cried out a final act of resistance, "Long live freedom!"[12]

In the months that followed, more individuals connected to the White Rose were imprisoned, and on April 19, another trial was held. Alex Schmorell, Willi Graf, and the students' professor Kurt Huber, who authored their sixth and final leaflet, were all sentenced to death. Alex and Professor Huber were executed on July 13. In a final letter to his parents, Alex wrote, "I leave this life with the knowledge that I have served my deepest conviction and the truth."[13] Willi, the last to be executed, died on October 12, 1943.

To some, their deaths might seem like a waste. The lives of these five college students and their professor ended too soon. But their passion and commitment to God and truth made an indelible mark on the world they left behind. As Sophie told her parents in their last meeting before her death, "What we did will cause waves."[14] And it did.

After their deaths, others took up the baton of resistance, spreading truth across the darkness of war-torn Germany. Their sixth leaflet was distributed once again, this time with the heading "Despite everything, their spirit lives on!"[15] The Royal Air Force dropped millions of copies over the cities of Germany, and the impact of the White Rose spread farther than ever before.

How could these students stand strong in the face of danger and death? Simply this: they were committed to something greater than themselves. James 1:22 spurred Sophie on: "Be doers of the word, and not hearers only."[16] They sought to live and speak truth in every aspect of their lives. As Sophie once wrote, "How then can we expect fate to make a righteous cause prevail when there is hardly anyone who unequivocally gives himself up to a righteous cause?"[17]

In a post-truth culture of darkness and immorality, the bold faith of the White Rose students shines like a beacon, challenging us each to "give ourselves up to a righteous cause." No matter the cost, no matter the consequences, at the end of our lives, may we be able to say along with Hans, Sophie, Alex, Christoph, and Willi that *we were not silent.*

Undercover for the Unborn: Lila Rose

With a video camera hidden in her backpack, twenty-year-old Lila Rose walked into a Planned Parenthood clinic in Bloomington, Indiana. But she wasn't there to get an abortion. She was there to expose the truth about abortion.

A nurse met her at the front desk and handed over a stack of paperwork. With the stroke of a pen, Lila Rose became Brianna—thirteen years old and pregnant by her thirty-one-year-old boyfriend. The goal? To record and expose the complicity of America's largest abortion provider in covering up sexual abuse. Since it's a felony in

Indiana for a thirteen-year-old to be sexually active with an adult, the test was to see if Planned Parenthood would follow the laws of the state—or conceal the evidence of sexual abuse. They decided to cover it up, encouraged "Brianna" to have an abortion, and told her to lie about her boyfriend's age. The video footage went viral.[18]

This was only one of Lila Rose's undercover missions. She first went undercover when she was eighteen, visiting a Planned Parenthood facility posing as a pregnant fifteen-year-old. Since that first video, she and other friends conducted stings at dozens of Planned Parenthood clinics, videotaping and exposing their illegal and suspicious actions. They posed as pregnant teens and sex traffickers, revealing how Planned Parenthood staff protected and aided traffickers, lied to girls about the safety of abortion, advised underage girls to lie to their parents, and covered up obvious sexual abuse. Each video opened the eyes of the public to the underhanded activities of a supposedly "trusted healthcare facility." But for Lila Rose, the goal wasn't just to expose Planned Parenthood. It was to protect the lives of the unborn.

When Lila was nine, she saw a picture of an aborted baby and discovered the truth about abortion. It struck her heart. *How could anyone do this to a baby?* she wondered. In the following years, as she learned more, she realized she "couldn't think of a greater injustice" in the world.[19]

In her parents' living room, with a group of friends, she founded Live Action—a pro-life organization dedicated to educating the public about the humanity of the unborn and the violence of abortion. Later, Lila looked back and said, "When we say 'yes' to [God's] will, it will take us on an adventure that we could have never imagined."[20] For this passionate fifteen-year-old, that couldn't have been truer. Her adventure was just beginning.

Three years later, Lila was a freshman at UCLA. While on campus, she noticed there were no resources for pregnant women, and she wondered why. With this question in mind, she embarked on her first undercover investigation, posing as newly pregnant to see what the university health clinic would offer. During her appointment, she realized why there wasn't need of resources for pregnant women—because the only "help" offered was encouragement to have an abortion. Lila was infuriated and wrote about her experience in a campus magazine she'd founded called *The Advocate*. After that, she went from Planned Parenthood clinic to Planned Parenthood clinic, exposing the truth through her hidden video camera. The viral videos propelled Lila into the spotlight, giving her a platform to share her passion for the unborn.

By the time Lila graduated from college, Live Action was one of the most influential pro-life organizations in the United States. Since then, it's only continued to grow. Lila Rose and Live Action are fighting on the front lines against abortion, changing hearts and minds with their educational content and investigational work. "Hearts and minds do change,"[21] Lila often says. The impact of Live Action is proof of that. With millions of followers on social media and hundreds of millions of views on their video content, babies' lives are being saved and people are becoming aware of the truth. The fight is far from over, but Lila is more committed than ever. "There's much work left to be done, but I am completely determined to end abortion in this country and beyond—soon—both abolishing it legally and making it culturally unacceptable."[22]

What makes Lila so passionate about saving the lives of the unborn? "Ultimately, I'm pro-life because I'm Christian," she explains. "But I think that, even if I weren't Christian, I would still see the facts. Abortion literally tears apart a human being . . . who deserves the right to life."[23]

It's this unshakable conviction that led Lila to devote her life to this cause. Her success is not due to anything special in herself but grounded in her faith in God and passion to make a difference. "We're not meant to be passive people of faith," she said. "We're meant to use our gifts for God."[24] For Lila, using her gifts for God meant founding an organization at fifteen years old in her parents' living room. For each of us, it means rejecting the temptation of passivity and stepping out as God leads.

When asked what she would say to a teen attending the annual March for Life in Washington, DC, Lila responded,

> Don't just make it one day a year. . . . We need you tomorrow; we need you the next day; we need you on Sundays at your church; we

need you at your schools standing up for life; we need you voting for life; we need you encouraging and working with your friends to make sure they're not having abortions; helping them stand up for chastity; helping them stand up for sexual integrity, understanding of their own sexuality; standing up for holy purity. We need you speaking out the truth whenever you have an opportunity—activism on your campus; passing out [literature]; doing displays or having speakers come or hosting debates—anything. There's so many ways to get involved. We need you every day, not just today.[25]

For the sake of the unborn, may we join Lila in the fight against the holocaust of our generation and "speak up for those who cannot speak for themselves" (Prov. 31:8 NIV). May we stand up, speak out, and fall to our knees in our fight for the unborn, knowing that their lives are precious in God's sight.

After all, the fight for the unborn is God's battle, and He will see it won. As Lila encouraged us, "We all know that we are very, very weak, but with God, who is all powerful and all strong, anything is possible."[26]

Beyond Bell Ringers: William and Catherine Booth

We're all familiar with the sight and sound of Salvation Army bell ringers at Christmas. But most of us don't know the story of the man and woman behind one of the most well-known ministries in the world. It all began with a fifteen-year-old boy who had the courage to pray a simple prayer and dedicate his life to God: "God shall have all there is of William Booth."[27]

God stirred up a passion in William's heart to draw people to Christ and alleviate the suffering of the poor. The first time he shared the gospel was on the street corners of his town soon after he became a Christian. Both bricks and insults were thrown at the teenage boy, but William wasn't discouraged. He kept preaching in the streets, reaching out to the poor in the slums, and visiting the sick and dying.

At the same time God was working in William's heart, He was also at work in the life of a young woman named Catherine Mumford.

Quiet and serious, Catherine was as devoted to God as William. It's said she read the Bible straight through eight times before the age of twelve. Despite battling chronic illness, she was actively involved in local charities and had a deep passion for the gospel. William and Catherine met in 1852 and were married four years later. Both individually committed to serving God; together they were a dynamic powerhouse of passion for Christ.

Years passed as William traveled as an evangelist, but both William and Catherine longed for those considered "undesirable" by their society—prostitutes, prisoners, and those living in London's poverty-stricken neighborhoods—to hear the gospel. William's and Catherine's hearts beat with a passion for the impossible and a desire to reach all with the good news of Jesus—especially those who would be turned away at most church doors.

In 1865, they embarked upon what would become their life's work: setting up a tent in the slums of London's East End and holding nightly meetings where William preached. Hundreds poured into the tent every night until they had to relocate to a large unused warehouse. But the work of the East London Christian Mission went beyond preaching. The Booths passionately believed in caring not only for the spiritual needs but also for the physical needs of those they encountered. They opened soup kitchens called Food for the Million and cared for the impoverished in London's East End. "Faith and works should travel side by side, step answering to step, like the legs of men walking," William explained. "First faith, and then works; and then faith again, and then works again—until they can scarcely distinguish which is the one and which is the other."[28]

The East London Christian Mission became the Salvation Army as we know it in 1878. By 1879, it had grown to 81 stations, 127 full-time evangelists, and thousands of evangelism services per year.[29] The Army circled the globe as workers traveled to the United States, France, India, Australia, and numerous other countries, taking the message of the gospel and the passion of the Booths to "do the most good" to everyone they could.

Twenty-five years after the first tent meeting in the slums of London, Catherine, the much-loved, fiery, and determined "Mother of the Army," died from cancer in 1890. The people of London mourned and filled the streets during her funeral procession. Grieving the loss of his wife and helpmate, William nonetheless continued the work they began together, his desire to reach as many people as possible never wavering. He continued traveling, preaching, and serving until his death in 1912. Forty thousand people attended his funeral to pay their respects to the man who'd spent his life reaching out to them with the good news of Jesus.

Today the Salvation Army operates in over 130 countries and has reached millions with the love of Christ. They've cared for countless individuals through their charity programs and opened hundreds of health facilities, addiction recovery programs, homeless shelters, and other community service programs.[30]

When William and Catherine Booth began their ministry in the London slums, did they have any idea of the world-changing impact that would follow? Their desire wasn't fame or fortune but simple obedience to Jesus. When asked the secret of their success, William replied,

> I will tell you the secret. God has had all there was of me. There have been men with greater brains than I, men with greater opportunities. But from the day I got the poor of London on my heart and caught a vision of all Jesus Christ could do with them, on that day I made up my mind that God would have all of William Booth there was. And if there is anything of power in the Salvation Army today, it is because God has had all the adoration of my heart, all the power of my will, and all the influence of my life.[31]

The Booths heard the call of Jesus to "go and make disciples" and decided to start with the poorest and neediest outside their front door. God took their obedience and made it grow until it impacted millions and touched the earth in places William and Catherine never walked themselves.

The same urgent needs surround us today—for food, clothes, hope, and the gospel. The call of Jesus remains. The question is, Will we answer it? The work isn't finished yet. May our hearts be moved by the needs of "the least of these" as we declare along with William,

While women weep, as they do now, I'll fight; while children go hungry, as they do now, I'll fight; while men go to prison, in and out, in and out, as they do now, I'll fight; while there is a poor lost girl upon the streets, while there remains one dark soul without the light of God, I'll fight, I'll fight to the very end![32]

Walking in Their Footsteps

These three stories, while different, share one common thread: a desire to obey God and remain faithful to Him no matter the cost. Whether that looks like opposing an evil regime, fighting for the unborn, or sharing the gospel in the slums, faithfulness and obedience always make an impact.

Your life has the same potential as the students of the White Rose, Lila Rose, and William and Catherine Booth. Not because of you but because of the power of God *in* you. Faithfulness to God will look different for you than it did for these individuals, but God always uses a heart and life set apart and dedicated to Him.

So what about you? Jesus is calling. The needs are everywhere. What are you waiting for?

Your story is yet to be told.

Going Deeper

1. Who are your heroes? Why are they heroes to you?
2. Which story stood out to you the most? What main points did you take away from each?
3. The commitment "God shall have all there is of William Booth" propelled William to his radical, gospel-focused lifestyle. What would happen in your life if you gave God "all there is" of you?
4. Lila Rose founded Live Action as a teenager. Have you ever felt hindered by your age? How does her story encourage you that you're never too young to make a difference?

5. Hans Scholl wrote, "I'm weak and puny, but I want to do what is right." We all feel weak when we look at the problems of the world, but why is it important to take steps to "do what is right"? What stirs your heart? How can you "do what is right" today?

Further Resources

- *Sophie Scholl and the White Rose* by Annette Dumbach and Jud Newborn
- *At the Heart of the White Rose: Letters and Diaries of Hans and Sophie Scholl* edited by Inge Jens
- *Sophie Scholl: The Final Days* (movie)
- *Fighting for Life: Becoming a Force for Change in a Wounded World* by Lila Rose
- *The Life & Ministry of William Booth: Founder of The Salvation Army* by Roger Green
- *Do Hard Things: A Teenage Rebellion against Low Expectations* by Alex and Brett Harris

Conclusion

What Culture Really Needs
(Changing the World One Life at a Time)

I was fifteen when God lit a fuse that led to an explosion in my soul. It started on an ordinary Sunday in late August.

"We must live with intentionality," my youth pastor said from the stage. "Life is too short to waste a chance. We cannot be so busy and self-centered that we shut our eyes to the world around us."

I'd heard sermons like this before. I mean, I'd practically grown up sitting in church. But the tugging on my heart that morning was something new. *Yes*, I thought. *That's how I want to live. I don't want to waste my life. I don't want to waste a single chance.*

"God is calling us to give our lives fully to Him. We give our lives." He paused for a moment. "Because *God will not settle for mediocre.*"

His words hit me hard. That Sunday I decided I was done with mediocre Christianity. Six years later, I look back on that day as a pivotal turning point in my life, a moment when God lit a passion in my heart for the gospel.

In the church today, we often have a diluted understanding of the gospel and a compromised commitment to it. This word *gospel* that we stick in our church names and hear preached about on Sundays is the most culture-changing, life-altering news the world has ever known—the mind-blowing truth of a bloodstained cross, an empty tomb, and a Savior whose love goes beyond comprehension. But we've lost our passion for it.

In many ways, we've settled for mediocre. We've looked at the culture with its confusion, pain, and immorality and called it too broken, too far gone, too hard, while we retreated into the corner with the one thing that has the power to transform it all. We've compromised our commitment to truth and weakened the power of the gospel we proclaim. As a result, our lives have begun to look more like the world and less like Christ.

It's time to revive the dying spark of the gospel in the church and breathe our commitment back to life. Culture has suffered because of our apathy. Immorality has flourished because the people of God have abandoned their responsibility. Culture can be transformed only by the power of the gospel of Jesus Christ. It's time we stepped back into our role as conveyors and ambassadors of this good news.

We've settled for mediocre too long. It's not enough to just know truth. We have to put truth into action.

Culture-Changing Gospel Power

The gospel has the power to impact entire cities, cultures, countries, and communities. It's been making waves ever since Jesus gave His church the Great Commission to "go into all the world and preach the gospel to every creature" (Mark 16:15).

Christians have long been serving on the front lines and impacting society. From building hospitals to founding universities, from fighting against slavery to caring for the poor, from opening schools and churches in remote villages to providing clean water for those same villages, Christians have grasped the baton of the gospel and made a mark through both their message and their service.

The effect has been unmistakable. Even nonbelievers can see the difference. Matthew Parris, a devoted atheist, admits in an article he wrote titled, "As an Atheist, I Truly Believe Africa Needs God," that the impact Christians have made upon his homeland is not only needed but obvious. He writes,

It confounds my ideological beliefs, stubbornly refuses to fit my world view, and has embarrassed my growing belief that there is no God. Now a confirmed atheist, I've become convinced of the enormous contribution that Christian evangelism makes in Africa: sharply distinct from the work of secular NGOs, government projects and international aid efforts. These alone will not do. Education and training alone will not do. In Africa Christianity changes people's hearts. It brings a spiritual transformation. *The rebirth is real. The change is good.*[1]

Change and rebirth arise from Christ followers who are faithful with the message and sacrificial with their love. The real culture-changing work doesn't begin on a community- or citywide scale. Instead, communities and cultures are impacted person by person, family by family, friend by friend. The gospel repaints the big picture as individuals encounter the love of Jesus and are transformed by its power.

People need this gospel-led transformation. Yet my heart aches as I see so many Christ followers rejecting their commission. I'm struck with conviction as I realize my own tendency toward apathy. Culture-changing begins with realigning our lives to the mission of God's heart. With renewing our commitment to take up the cross, follow Jesus, and faithfully live out the message He's entrusted to us.

Four Crucial Questions

As I think about what this kind of gospel-led life looks like, I want to ask four radical questions that will have a defining impact on how we engage the world.

1. Will We Sacrifice Our Foremost Calling for Secondary Substitutes?

How often do we forget our main calling in a distracted pursuit of secondary things? It's easy to offer excuses when Jesus says, "Follow Me."

"*Lord, I'll follow You, but first . . .*"

"*Lord, I'll follow You, but hang on a second . . .*"

"Share the gospel? Reach out and share Jesus's love? Fulfill the Great Commission? Sure, no problem. But first . . ."

I so often get distracted by petty, temporal things. I let fear overtake my heart. I shut my eyes to the problems in the world and say, "Somebody else will do something."

The gospel is our foremost calling as followers of Jesus because God's glory is our ultimate purpose. Nothing else matters so much as sharing Christ's love. As David Platt writes, "Jesus has not given us a commission to consider; he has given us a command to obey."[2] Will we obey?

The mission of the gospel is a call to selflessly love. To desire that others encounter the power of the God who's transformed our own lives. If the Word of God is true and every person who doesn't know Christ is destined for eternal separation from Him in hell, then shouldn't we love each person enough to share the key to life with them? Platt challenges us with these words: "We who know the gospel have been given the greatest gift in all the world. We have good news of a glorious God who has come to deliver men, women, and children from all sin and all suffering for all time. Therefore, we cannot—we must not—stay silent with this gospel. Gospel possession requires gospel proclamation."[3]

We need to reject the idea that gospel proclamation is someone else's job. No, it's our job. It's our commission. If we don't fulfill it, who will? As followers of Jesus, this command still stands. Our moment to impact this generation is now.

I love how Nate Saint, a missionary in Ecuador who lost his life proclaiming the gospel to the Huaorani people, described it:

> If God would grant us the vision, the word sacrifice would disappear from our lips and thoughts; we would hate the things that seem now so dear to us; our lives would suddenly be too short, we would despise time-robbing distractions and charge the enemy with all our energies in the name of Christ.[4]

Don't sacrifice your foremost calling for secondary pursuits. Popularity, possessions, prestige . . . these will one day fade away. Only the impact we make for the kingdom of God will last forever. May the words of Nate Saint's fellow missionary Ed McCully become the anthem of our hearts: "I have one desire now—to live a life of reckless abandon for the Lord, putting all my energy and strength into it."[5]

2. Will We Be His Hands and Feet or Will We Lock Up Our Love?

There's a whole lot of hurting hearts in the world. There's a whole lot of need across the face of the globe. From the brokenhearted girl in your classroom to the orphan in Nepal to the drug-addicted teen in the inner city, brokenness and need abound.

Our calling to impact culture is intrinsically bound together with our calling to care for people. Caring for spiritual and for physical needs go hand in hand. The gospel is our priority, but if we ignore physical needs, our message falls flat. In the same way, if we simply care for physical needs, our care ends too soon because "a cup of cold water" (Matt. 10:42) is quickly drained, but the living water of the gospel lasts forever (John 4:14).

The calling of the gospel is to love as Christ loves and lay down our lives in service to others because He laid down His life to save us all. The gospel and service are fused together so strongly that the book of James tells us faith without works is dead. "What does it profit," he writes,

> if someone says he has faith but does not have works? Can faith save him? If a brother or sister is naked and destitute of daily food, and one of you says to them, "Depart in peace, be warmed and filled," but you do not give them the things which are needed for the body, what does it profit? Thus also faith by itself, if it does not have works, is dead. (2:14–17)

If we truly believe the gospel and desire to show Christ's love to the world, we will accept our calling to care and let our hearts be moved by compassion. Compassion *always* requires action and demonstration. This call to compassion is one that looks at the wrongs, injustice, confusion, and pain in the world and stands up and says, "I will do something about that." I will fight to free the enslaved. I will work to feed the hungry. I will give of myself to care for the widow and orphan. I will sacrifice and serve to bring the gospel to every person on earth. Because the girl bound in sex trafficking matters to Jesus. Because the starving orphan matters to Jesus. Because the man experiencing homelessness in my city matters to Jesus. Because the drug-addicted teen matters to Jesus. Because the woman who regrets her abortion matters to Jesus. Because the unborn baby matters to Jesus. Because every person on the face of this earth and every need they have *matters to Jesus*. So we give them the gospel as we care for their needs and care for their needs as we point to the One who cares for them most.

One of the best descriptions of this calling comes from the author Paul Lee Tan: "A Christian is a mind through which Christ thinks, a heart through which Christ loves, a mouth through which Christ speaks, a hand through which Christ helps."[6]

Will we be the hand through which Christ helps? Will we dedicate *our* hands and feet to being *His* hands and feet?

3. Will We Faithfully Live Out the Message or Will We Compromise Our Standards?

Sharing the gospel and being Christ's hands and feet come with a heavy responsibility. As we proclaim Christ and serve in His name, the world is watching. They're learning who God is and what the Bible teaches as they observe our lives.

Our personal walk with God matters deeply in our cultural mission. If we proclaim a gospel we don't live or bend the truth on unpopular topics, we dilute our impact and the entire message. Paul encourages us in Philippians 1:27 to "let [our] conduct be worthy of the gospel of Christ." Is our conduct worthy of the gospel? Are we committed to both *proclaiming* and *living* the message every day?

Let me get practical. If we proclaim the gospel but compromise on God's standards for marriage and sexuality, our proclamation falls flat. If we serve those around us but never dig into God's Word ourselves, our service is no different from an unbeliever's. If we talk about Jesus but never share His standards of morality, we're not sharing the full message. If we embrace God's grace but shun the commands in His Word or twist them to serve our own purposes, we're rejecting the heart of God. If we preach the gospel but live a gospel-less life, our words carry no weight. If we preach a diluted gospel and live a compromised life, our message is more repellent to God than silence would be because we're misrepresenting His Son.

We're all flawed representations of Christ. We're not called to be perfect but are called to strive to be faithful and earnestly seek God for grace and strength to live out His message. May our lives reflect the message and the message be a pure reflection of God's truth.

4. Will We Love Comfort or Christ?

Faithfulness to the gospel demands the sacrifice of our comfort zones. Like Jesus told the man in Luke 9, "Foxes have holes and birds of the air have nests, but the Son of Man has nowhere to lay His head" (v. 58).

To be honest, this is something I struggle with deeply. It's one thing to say you value the gospel in the safety of your own home. It's another to act like you value the gospel when you're confronted with an uncomfortable opportunity. As I've wrestled with the question "Will I love comfort or Christ?" I've missed opportunities and let fear take over, but I've also found the joy and peace that comes when I'm bold enough to take the first hard step. Despite the fear and discomfort, I can say with certainty, the gospel is worth it. Jesus is worth it.

The gospel is worth the demolition of our comfort zones. The gospel is worth that awkward moment. The gospel is worth the risk of reaching out. You know why? Because it's the message of how Jesus called *us* worth it—worth the suffering of the cross, the rejection and agony, the abandonment by God. He called us worth the grief He bore on earth. Despite what it cost Him, He considered our salvation worth it all. That's a message that can revolutionize lives. Is a transformed life worth the cost of discomfort? Jesus said it was. How can we say anything else?

As the world grows darker, it will become more antagonistic to the message of Christ. Those who are of the world hate the gospel because of the light of truth it shines on their lives. Jesus told us, "Everyone practicing evil hates the light and does not come to the light, lest his deeds should be exposed" (John 3:20). The gospel is the light shining in the darkness of a broken world. As its messengers, we are the city on a hill shining for the world to see (Matt. 5:14). The more we share the gospel, the more we'll stand out. The less we're like the world, the more the world will hate us. We can stand strong only if we love Christ more than we love our own comfort. Only if we boldly proclaim along with Paul, "I am not ashamed of the gospel of Christ, for it is the power of God to salvation for everyone who believes" (Rom. 1:16).

The gospel is worth it. For the hope it breathes into hopeless hearts, for the culture-changing power it holds, for the life-altering truth it gives, the gospel is worth every bit of discomfort.

A Culture-Changing Savior

The world is crying out for hope. When we're sinking under the weight of the sin and immorality permeating our culture, only one thing can pull us out—our culture-changing Savior.

The greatest need in the world is not for social justice. It's not for political change. It's not for a better economy. It's for Jesus Christ. The baton of the gospel is in our hands. The truth of Jesus Christ is alive in our hearts.

The only question is, What will we do with it?

Jesus once told His disciples, "The harvest truly is plentiful, but the laborers are few. Therefore pray the Lord of the harvest to send out laborers into His harvest" (Matt. 9:37–38). As I look at the world, I see a plentiful harvest. But the laborers are few. The individuals whose hearts beat with a passion to see the gospel transform people's lives, and yes, the very foundations of society, are few and far between.

Will you be one of them? It's time to stand up and stand strong, because this world needs a revolution of truth. God has placed us in this moment in history for a divine purpose. We have the mission field of the twenty-first century before us. It's the commission of our generation to boldly proclaim the mercy-filled, hope-drenched, life-transforming, sin-erasing, world-shattering good news of Jesus Christ with confidence that He is the One who redeems broken cultures for the glory of His name.

Don't fall for the lie that God has given up on the world. Don't settle for complacency or allow fear to call you too weak, too inadequate, or too imperfect. Don't believe that the big things, the hard things, the out-of-this-world, only-by-the-power-of-God things are impossible. With the power of God, a passion in your heart, and a commitment to keep going no matter how tough it is, you can be a light in this world of darkness.

So, stand up and live with the unshakeable conviction that God's Word is inerrant, His salvation complete, and His ways good. Stand strong upon the rock-solid foundation of His righteousness, and let His truth transform your life from the inside out, no matter the cost or consequences. Live boldly and bravely for the cause of Christ, pouring all your energy and strength into the abounding joy of expending your life for our glorious Savior.

You are alive at this moment for a reason beyond yourself. Jesus Christ has saved you for a purpose in the unfurling of a greater story. Will you accept His invitation to step out from the sidelines and join in His radical story of redemption? Because that's what culture really needs. That's what once turned this world upside down and what is, even now, two millennia later, still changing the world.

One heart, one soul, one life at a time.

Going Deeper

1. Why have we lost our passion for the gospel? How can we revive that passion?

2. Why does the gospel make such a positive impact on communities? What does the gospel offer that secular humanitarian aid doesn't?

3. Which question was most convicting to you? How did you answer the four questions?

4. Why is Jesus worth the cost of discomfort? How can you live like He's worthy of any and all sacrifices you may have to make?

5. What was your main takeaway from this book? Which chapter was your favorite? How are you going to "step out from the sidelines" and impact the world around you?

Further Resources

- *Love Riot: A Teenage Call to Live with Relentless Abandon for Christ* by Sara Barratt
- *Radical: Taking Back Your Faith from the American Dream* by David Platt

Acknowledgments

I wrote this book in a season of brokenness. When I sat down one warm July day to type the opening words of the first chapter, "Jesus turned the patterns of the world upside down," I had no idea *my* world was about to be turned upside down. Typing those words, I was excited, more than a little intimidated, and absolutely stunned God would allow me the privilege of writing another book. A soul-deep passion for His truth and a desire to share it with others spurred me on, but I didn't realize then how impeccable God's timing would be— He knew, more than I, how deeply my heart would need to be pointed to the One who is the way, the truth, and the life in the months that followed. Studying and examining God's truth on the topics within this book reminded me that the God who holds total truth on every one of those hard issues is also the God whose truth I can trust to lead and guide my life. A roundabout way to point me to Jesus? Maybe. But writing this book breathed life into my soul when I needed it most, and I pray with all my heart reading it does the same for you.

I am indebted to so many who came alongside me and poured their time, energy, and insight into these pages.

To my mom—I can't say thank you enough for all you've given me. Your passion for God's truth and for changing the culture birthed the same passion within me. This book wouldn't exist without you. You are a true culture-changer and one of my heroes.

Dad, thank you for always asking, "How is the book coming?" and for your continual support! I couldn't do this without you! Thank you for reading my books even though I have yet to include even one action scene or airplane. (I'll do that one day!) I love you!

Amanda, my sister, confidant, brainstorming partner, and best friend—thank you for reading the manuscript numerous times, even when on your own deadline, and for always being there for me. You are a blessing to me in so many ways, and I'm beyond grateful God gave me a sister like you!

Much thanks to my sweet friend Tabitha. Your prayers and encouragement brought so much healing to my heart and helped pull me through. Thanks for always pointing me to Jesus . . . and for always having a song to send. You know how to speak my language, and both I and my music playlist thank you.

A huge thank you to Matthew, Isabelle, Katelynn, Tabby, Gabrielle, and Joshua who read early drafts and offered so much helpful insight. This book is stronger and more grace-filled because of your wisdom.

Thank you to Rebekah Guzman for all your kind and generous support and guidance! Thank you for giving me the opportunity to share this message. You play such an integral role in every book you champion, and I'm so thankful I get to work with you!

Huge round of applause to my fantastic editor Jamie Chavez! Thank you for your spot-on insights and your word-cutting superpowers. This wordy writer appreciates both more than you know!

Many thanks to Robin Turici for once again being such an incredible editor and for helping hone this message to be the best it can be. I love working with you!

To the entire Baker Books team—from cover design to editing to marketing, you consistently blow me away with the time, energy, and genius you pour into each book. Thank you for your hard work in bringing this one to life!

Heartfelt thanks to my amazing agent, Steve Laube. I'm so grateful for all your advice, encouragement, and guidance. It's a true privilege and joy to work with you!

Thank you to Brett Harris and the Rebelution team and community. Brett, thank you for supporting my writing and for continually offering such wise counsel and insight. You have impacted me and my writing in countless ways. Thanks also to my fantabulous team members at the Rebelution and to our beautiful community of "rebelutionaries"—I always write with you in mind!

Thanks to the Devine family for lending me your internet connection and turning your upstairs bedroom into a "podcast studio." Y'all are the definition of generosity and hospitality, and I'm pretty sure I've got the best neighbors on the planet. (See? I told you I'd put you in the acknowledgments.)

I'm so grateful for the prayer warriors behind me—"Grandma" Westheim, Betty, Tabitha, Angela, Jenn, Annette, Jocelyn, Carol, and Marla. Thank you for your faithfulness to pray for me. Each of the prayers lifted up on behalf of this book is a true gift for which I am thankful!

Finally, my deepest thanks to YOU—the person on the other side of the page. I'm humbled at the thought of you reading these words. I pray this book has deepened your love for God's truth and strengthened your commitment to His Word. May you always stand strong upon the unshakable Rock of Ages and find hope and fullness of joy within His words of life.

And lastly, but most of all, thank you to my precious Jesus. Tears fill my eyes and gratitude floods my heart when I think of Your immeasurable goodness to me. Your love holds me close through every storm, and Your truth is the anchor of my soul. If there is anything worthwhile or true within these pages, it is solely the result of Your mercy. May Your name be lifted high in every word I write and every breath I breathe. All for Your glory.

Notes

Introduction

1. *Merriam-Webster*, s.v. "culture," accessed June 7, 2021, https://www.merriam-webster.com/dictionary/culture.

Chapter 1 One Man Flipped the World

1. "Manhattan Declaration: A Call of Christian Conscience," November 20, 2009, https://www.manhattandeclaration.org/.

Chapter 2 What on Earth Is Worldview?

1. W. Gary Phillips, William E. Brown, and John Stonestreet, *Making Sense of Your World: A Biblical Worldview*, 2nd ed. (Salem, WI: Sheffield, 2008), 86.

2. Phillip E. Johnson, foreword to Nancy Pearcey, *Total Truth: Liberating Christianity from Its Cultural Captivity* (Wheaton: Crossway, 2004), 11.

3. Jeff Myers and David A. Noebel, *Understanding the Times: A Survey of Competing Worldviews* (Colorado Springs: David C Cook, 2016), 6.

4. Jonathan Morrow, "Only 4 Percent of Gen Z Have a Biblical Worldview," Impact 360 Institute, https://www.impact360institute.org/articles/4-percent-gen-z-biblical-worldview/.

5. Chuck Colson as quoted in Christopher Brooks, "Christopher Brooks' Summit Adult Conference 2014 Address," Summit Ministries, February 24, 2015, https://www.summit.org/resources/articles/christopher-brooks-summit-adult-conference-2014-address/.

6. Unlike what many people assume, the Islamic God is not named Allah. Rather, *Allah* is an Arabic word for God, the same as we call God . . . *God*. Christians who speak Arabic also refer to the Christian God (Yahweh) as Allah.

7. Myers and Noebel, *Understanding the Times*, 62.

8. Myers and Noebel, *Understanding the Times*, 13.

9. Peter Singer, "Sanctity of Life or Quality of Life?," *Pediatrics* 72, no. 1 (July 1983): 128–29.

10. Gary Zukav, *Seat of the Soul* (New York: Simon & Schuster, 1999), 85.

11. Abdu Murray, *Saving Truth: Finding Meaning and Clarity in a Post-Truth World* (Grand Rapids: Zondervan, 2018), 207.

12. Barna Group, "Competing Worldviews Influence Today's Christians," Barna, May 9, 2017, https://www.barna.com/research/competing-worldviews-influence-to days-christians/.

Chapter 3 The Battle Surrounding You

1. "Why Did Nebuchadnezzar Change Daniel's Name to Belteshazzar?," Got Questions, accessed October 7, 2021, https://www.gotquestions.org/Daniel-Belteshazzar .html; Strong's Concordance 2608, Biblehub.com, accessed October 7, 2021, https:// biblehub.com/hebrew/2608.htm.

2. It's unknown why Daniel wasn't included in this story. Some suppose he was exempt because of his high position or that his enemies were afraid to accuse him to the king. No matter why Daniel isn't mentioned, it's clear that his choice would have been the same as his friends'.

3. Pearcey, *Total Truth*, 44.

Chapter 4 Don't Buy the Lies

1. Oxford Languages, "Word of the Year 2016," accessed June 8, 2021, https:// languages.oup.com/word-of-the-year/2016/.

2. Murray, *Saving Truth*, 23–24.

3. Francis Schaeffer, *How Should We Then Live? The Rise and Decline of Western Thought and Culture* (Old Tappan, NJ: Revell, 1976), 145.

4. For a more in-depth look at these requirements for tolerance, check out J. Warner Wallace's article, "Is Christianity Intolerant?," Cold-Case Christianity, March 16, 2015, https://coldcasechristianity.com/writings/is-christianity-intolerant/.

5. Dallas Willard as quoted in Brad Stetson and Joseph G. Conti, *The Truth About Tolerance: Pluralism, Diversity, and the Culture Wars* (Downers Grove, IL: IVP Academic, 2005), 139.

6. David Platt, *Counter Culture: Following Christ in an Anti-Christian Age* (Wheaton: Tyndale, 2017), 249.

7. *Merriam-Webster*, s.v. "marriage," accessed September 5, 2020, https://www .merriam-webster.com/dictionary/marriage.

8. "Marriage," *Psychology Today*, accessed September 30, 2021, https://www .psychologytoday.com/us/basics/marriage.

9. *American Dictionary of the English Language*, s.v. "marriage," accessed September 5, 2020, http://webstersdictionary1828.com/Dictionary/marriage.

10. John M. Perkins, foreword to Thaddeus J. Williams, *Confronting Injustice without Compromising Truth: 12 Questions Christians Should Ask about Social Justice* (Grand Rapids: Zondervan, 2020), xvi.

11. C. S. Lewis, *Mere Christianity* (San Francisco: HarperSanFranciso, 2001), 32.

12. Murray, *Saving Truth*, 31.

13. Murray, *Saving Truth*, 35.

Chapter 5 Identity

1. John Stonestreet as quoted in, "Sex, Race & Identity—How Does the Gospel Answer the Critical Questions of Today?" YouTube video, 24:36, posted by Colson Center, September 18, 2021, https://www.youtube.com/watch?v=8xzZfBfkULI.

2. If this is your struggle, we're going to dive more deeply into identity and sexuality in the upcoming chapters.

3. C. S. Lewis, *A Grief Observed* (New York: HarperCollins, 2001), 65, 67.

4. Gerald Sittser, *A Grace Disguised* (Grand Rapids: Zondervan, 1996), 78–79.

Chapter 6 Sex, Purity, and Relationships

1. Kaleigh Fasanella, "How to Decide If You're Ready for Sex," *Teen Vogue*, October 26, 2016, https://www.teenvogue.com/story/how-to-know-if-you-are-ready-to-have-sex.

2. Jeff Diamant, "Half of U.S. Christians Say Casual Sex between Consenting Adults Is Sometimes or Always Acceptable," Pew Research Center, August 31, 2020, https://www.pewresearch.org/fact-tank/2020/08/31/half-of-u-s-christians-say-casual-sex-between-consenting-adults-is-sometimes-or-always-acceptable/.

3. David J. Ayers, "Cohabitation among Evangelicals: A New Norm?," Institute for Family Studies, April 19, 2021, https://ifstudies.org/blog/cohabitation-among-evangelicals-a-new-norm.

4. Buddy T, "Does Sex and Drug Use Increase Teen Suicide Risk?," Very Well Mind, September 27, 2021, https://www.verywellmind.com/sex-drug-use-increase-teen-suicide-risk-69465; also see Joseph J. Stabia, "Does Early Adolescent Sex Cause Depressive Symptoms?," *Journal of Policy Analysis and Management* 25, no. 4 (Fall 2006): 803–25, https://www.jstor.org/stable/30162763.

5. Dr. Juli Slattery, *Rethinking Sexuality: God's Design and Why It Matters* (Colorado Springs: Multnomah, 2018), 20.

6. Slattery, *Rethinking Sexuality*, 20.

7. Slattery, *Rethinking Sexuality*, 39.

8. Yadaʿ, Bible Study Tools, accessed October 9, 2021, https://www.biblestudytools.com/lexicons/hebrew/kjv/yada.html.

9. Alex Morris, "Tales from the Millennials' Sexual Revolution," *Rolling Stone*, March 31, 2014, https://www.rollingstone.com/interactive/feature-millennial-sexual-revolution-relationships-marriage/.

10. Morris, "Tales from the Millennials' Sexual Revolution."

11. "Why Is Oxytocin Known as the 'Love Hormone'? and 11 Other FAQs," Healthline, accessed October 9, 2021, https://www.healthline.com/health/love-hormone.

12. John Stonestreet and Brett Kunkle, *A Practical Guide to Culture: Helping the Next Generation Navigate Today's World* (Colorado Springs: David C Cook, 2017), 174–75.

13. Dannah Gresh, *What Are You Waiting For? The One Thing No One Ever Tells You About Sex* (Colorado Springs: WaterBrook, 2011), 42.

14. Megan Hull, ed., "Pornography Facts and Statistics," The Recovery Village, accessed March 5, 2021, https://www.therecoveryvillage.com/process-addiction/porn-addiction/related/pornography-statistics/.

15. Timothy C. Morgan, "Porn's Stranglehold," *Christianity Today*, March 7, 2008, www.christianitytoday.com/ct/2008/march/20.7.html.

16. "Pornography Statistics," Covenant Eyes, accessed March 5, 2021, https://www.covenanteyes.com/pornstats/.

17. Kristen Clark and Bethany Beal, *Sex, Purity, and the Longings of a Girl's Heart: Discovering the Beauty and Freedom of God-Defined Sexuality* (Grand Rapids: Baker Books, 2019), 144.

18. "What Should I Teach My High School–Aged Teen about Sex and Sexuality?," Planned Parenthood, accessed March 5, 2021, https://www.plannedparenthood.org/learn/parents/high-school/what-should-i-teach-my-high-school-aged-teen-about-sex-and-sexua.

19. Jonathan Pokluda, *Outdated: Find Love That Lasts When Dating Has Changed* (Grand Rapids: Baker Books, 2021), 149–50.

20. Clark and Beal, *Sex, Purity, and the Longings of a Girl's Heart*, 154.

Chapter 7 Sexual Orientation

1. Jeffrey M. Jones, "LGBT Identification Rises to 5.6% in Latest U.S. Estimate," Gallup, February 24, 2021, https://news.gallup.com/poll/329708/lgbt-identification-rises-latest-estimate.aspx.

2. David Kinnaman and Gabe Lyons, *unChristian: What a New Generation Really Thinks about Christianity . . . and Why It Matters* (Grand Rapids: Baker Books, 2012), 93.

3. Kinnaman and Lyons, *unChristian*, 92.

4. This description was shared in a video from McLean Bible Church called "What Is the Christian Way to Think about Same-Sex Attraction?," YouTube video, 27:52, McLean Bible Church, February 13, 2021, https://www.youtube.com/watch?v=o26mlMRNZnk.

5. Platt, *Counter Culture*, 156.

6. Sam Allberry, *Is God Anti-Gay? And Other Questions about Homosexuality, the Bible, and Same-Sex Attraction* (Surrey, UK: Good Book, 2013), 17.

7. Jackie Hill Perry, *Gay Girl, Good God: The Story of Who I Was, and Who God Has Always Been* (Nashville: B&H, 2018), 180.

8. Nancy Pearcey, *Love Thy Body: Answering Hard Questions about Life and Sexuality* (Grand Rapids: Baker Books, 2018), 169.

9. Perry, *Gay Girl, Good God*, 148.

10. Jackie Hill Perry, "Love Letter to a Lesbian," Desiring God, July 20, 2013, https://www.desiringgod.org/articles/love-letter-to-a-lesbian.

11. Christopher Yuan and Angela Yuan, *Out of a Far Country: A Gay Son's Journey to God. A Broken Mother's Search for Hope* (Colorado Springs: WaterBrook, 2011), 187.

12. Matt Moore, "I Begged God to Make Me Straight and He Never Answered. Here's Why," To Save A Life, accessed September 29, 2021, https://tosavealife.com/faith/identity/i-prayed-for-god-to-make-me-straight-why-didnt-he-answer-me/.

13. Moore, "I Begged God to Make Me Straight."

14. Moore, "I Begged God to Make Me Straight."

15. Moore, "I Begged God to Make Me Straight."

16. Jocelyn Kaiser, "Genetics May Explain up to 25% of Same-Sex Behavior, Giant Analysis Reveals," Science Mag, August 29, 2019, https://www.sciencemag.org/news/2019/08/genetics-may-explain-25-same-sex-behavior-giant-analysis-reveals.

17. Perry, *Gay Girl, Good God*, 173.

18. Allberry, *Is God Anti-Gay?*, 74.

Chapter 8 Gender

1. "Gender Identity: Can a 5′9″, White Guy Be a 6′5″, Chinese Woman?," YouTube video, 4:13, posted by Family Policy Institute of Washington, April 13, 2016, https://www.youtube.com/watch?v=xfO1veFs6Ho.

2. John Stonestreet and Shane Morris, "The Experts Challenging Treatment of Gender Dysphoria," Breakpoint, October 11, 2021, https://breakpoint.org/experts-are-challenging-the-transgender-craze/.

3. "Boy or Girl?," YouTube video, 1:40, posted by BBC The Social, October 24, 2016, https://www.youtube.com/watch?v=udI-Go8KK2Q.

4. SIECUS, "Time for Change: Sex Education and the Texas Health Curriculum Standards," September 2019, https://siecus.org/wp-content/uploads/2019/09/TX_Time _for_Change_FINAL_9.19.2019.pdf, 17.

5. SIECUS, "Time for Change," 17.

6. As quoted in Pearcey, *Love Thy Body*, 196.

7. Leonard Sax, *Why Gender Matters: What Parents and Teachers Need to Know about the Emerging Science of Sex Differences* (New York: Broadway Books, 2005), 14.

8. Sax, *Why Gender Matters*, 30.

9. Sax, *Why Gender Matters*, 17.

10. Sax, *Why Gender Matters*, 30.

11. Walt Heyer, "Transgender Characters May Win Emmys, but Transgender People Hurt Themselves," *The Federalist*, September 22, 2015, https://thefederalist .com/2015/09/22/transgender-characters-may-win-emmys-but-transgender-people -hurt-themselves/.

12. Richard P. Fitzgibbons, "Transsexual Attractions and Sexual Reassignment Surgery: Risks and Potential Risks," *The Linacre Quarterly* 82, no. 4 (2015): 337–50, published online by Taylor and Francis Online, February 26, 2016, https://www .tandfonline.com/doi/full/10.1080/00243639.2015.1125574.

13. Cecilia Dhejne et al., "Long-Term Follow-Up of Transsexual Persons Undergoing Sex Reassignment Surgery: Cohort Study in Sweden," *PLoS One* 6, no. 2 (2011): e16885, https://www.ncbi.nlm.nih.gov/pmc/articles/PMC3043071/.

14. Paul Dirks, "Transition as Treatment: The Best Studies Show the Worst Outcomes," *Public Discourse*, February 16, 2020, https://www.thepublicdiscourse.com /2020/02/60143/.

15. Paul McHugh, "Transgenderism: A Pathogenic Meme," *Public Discourse*, June 10, 2015, https://www.thepublicdiscourse.com/2015/06/15145/.

16. Pearcey, *Love Thy Body*, 223.

17. Sam Allberry, "What Christianity Alone Offers Transgender Persons," The Gospel Coalition, January 10, 2017, https://www.thegospelcoalition.org/article/what -christianity-alone-offers-transgender-persons/.

18. For further reading on the various perspectives of this issue, check out the following articles from Got Questions: "Should Christians Use Preferred Pronouns?," https:// advocatesfortruth.com/blog/should-christians-use-preferred-pronouns; "Should Christians Use the Preferred Pronouns of Transgender Individuals When Referring to Them?," https://www.gotquestions.org/transgender-pronouns.html; "On the Use of Preferred Pronouns," https://seanmcdowell.org/blog/on-the-use-of-preferred-pronouns; and "The Problem of Pronouns," https://www.breakpoint.org/point-problem-pronouns-2/.

19. Caleb Park, "College Student Kicked out of Class for Telling Professor There Are Only Two Genders," Fox News, March 12, 2018, https://www.foxnews.com/us/college-student-kicked-out-of-class-for-telling-professor-there-are-only-two-genders.

20. Murray, *Saving Truth*, 128.

21. Elinor Burkett, "What Makes a Woman?," *New York Times*, June 6, 2015, https://www.nytimes.com/2015/06/07/opinion/sunday/what-makes-a-woman.html.

22. Pearcey, *Love Thy Body*, 224.

23. Pearcey, *Love Thy Body*, 224.

Chapter 9 Life

1. For more information on 40 Days for Life, check out https://www.40daysforlife.com/en/.

2. Maanvi Singh, "'It's Dehumanizing': Texas Valedictorian Goes Off Script to Attack Abortion Ban," *The Guardian*, June 3, 2021, https://www.theguardian.com/us-news/2021/jun/02/texas-valedictorian-graduation-speech-abortion-ban.

3. Shout Your Abortion, accessed October 29, 2021, https://shoutyourabortion.com/.

4. "94% of Belgian Doctors Surveyed Support 'After-Birth Abortion' for Babies with Disabilities," *Right to Life News*, August 10, 2020, https://righttolife.org.uk/news/94-of-belgian-doctors-surveyed-support-after-birth-abortion-for-babies-with-disabilities/.

5. Alberto Giubilini and Francesca Minerva, "After-Birth Abortion: Why Should the Baby Live?," *Journal of Medical Ethics* 39, no. 5 (May 2013), accessed March 8, 2021, https://jme.bmj.com/content/39/5/261.

6. "94% of Belgian Doctors Surveyed Support 'After-Birth Abortion.'"

7. Jeff Myers, *Understanding the Culture: A Survey of Social Engagement* (Colorado Springs: David C Cook, 2017), 209.

8. Ellen Wiebe, "Reasons for Requesting Medical Assistance in Dying," *Canadian Family Physician* 64, no. 9 (September 2018): 674–79, https://www.ncbi.nlm.nih.gov/pmc/articles/PMC6135145/.

9. "State of Oregon Sees 28% Increase in Assisted Suicides in One Year," *Right to Life News*, March 5, 2021, https://righttolife.org.uk/news/state-of-oregon-sees-28-increase-in-assisted-suicides-in-one-year.

10. John Stonestreet, "BreakPoint: Assisted Suicide and Manipulating the Vulnerable," BreakPoint, November 26, 2018, https://www.breakpoint.org/breakpoint-assisted-suicide-and-manipulating-the-vulnerable/.

11. Bradford Richardson, "Assisted-Suicide Law Prompts Insurance Company to Deny Coverage to Terminally Ill California Woman," *The Washington Times*, October 20, 2016, https://www.washingtontimes.com/news/2016/oct/20/assisted-suicide-law-prompts-insurance-company-den/.

12. Jojo Moyes, *Me Before You* (New York: Penguin Books, 2013), 194.

13. Check out more reasons why *Me Before You* contains a dangerous message: Stephanie Gray, "You Before Me Is Better Than Me Before You," *Love Unleashes Life* (blog), May 30, 2016, https://loveunleasheslife.com/blog/2016/5/30/you-before-me-is-better-than-me-before-you-by-stephanie-gray.

14. Michael Berenbaum, "T4 Program, Nazi Policy," *Britannica*, accessed October 19, 2021, https://www.britannica.com/event/T4-Program.

15. Sabrina Tavernise, "U.S. Suicide Rate Surges to a 30-Year High," *New York Times*, April 22, 2016, https://www.nytimes.com/2016/04/22/health/us-suicide-rate-surges-to-a-30-year-high.html.

16. National Institute of Mental Health, accessed November 17, 2020, https://www.nimh.nih.gov/health/statistics/suicide.shtml.

17. National Institute of Mental Health, "Release of '13 Reasons Why' Associated with Increase in Youth Suicide Rates," April 29, 2019, https://www.nimh.nih.gov/news/science-news/2019/release-of-13-reasons-why-associated-with-increase-in-youth-suicide-rates.shtml.

18. Scott Klusendorf, *The Case for Life: Equipping Christians to Engage the Culture* (Wheaton: Crossway, 2009), 24.

19. Gregg Cunningham, the executive director of the Center for Bio-Ethical Reform, has said this in various public presentations: www.abortionno.org.

20. "What Happens during an In-Clinic Abortion?," Planned Parenthood, accessed March 8, 2021, https://www.plannedparenthood.org/learn/abortion/in-clinic-abortion-procedures/what-happens-during-an-in-clinic-abortion.

21. "What Happens during an In-Clinic Abortion?"

22. "In-Clinic Abortion," Planned Parenthood, accessed March 8, 2021, https://www.plannedparenthood.org/learn/abortion/in-clinic-abortion-procedures.

23. Wiebe, "Reasons for Requesting Medical Assistance in Dying."

24. Secretariat of Pro-Life Activities, "Top Reasons to Oppose Assisted Suicide," United States Conference of Catholic Bishops, July 12, 2017, https://www.usccb.org/issues-and-action/human-life-and-dignity/assisted-suicide/to-live-each-day/upload/Top%20Reasons%20to%20Oppose%20Assisted%20Suicide-071217.pdf.

25. Klusendorf, *The Case for Life*, 243.

Chapter 10 Prejudice and Injustice

1. David Wellman as quoted in Beverly Daniel Tatum, *Why Are All the Black Kids Sitting Together in the Cafeteria?: And Other Conversations About Race* (New York: Basic Books, 2017), 87.

2. Martin Luther King Jr., "Letter from Birmingham City Jail," April 16, 1963, https://swap.stanford.edu/20141218230016/http://mlk-kpp01.stanford.edu/kingweb/popular_requests/frequentdocs/birmingham.pdf.

3. Perkins, foreword to Williams, *Confronting Injustice*, xv.

4. Ben Sales, "Almost All American Jews Say Anti-Semitism Is a Problem, According to a New Poll. Half of Americans Don't Know What It Means," *Jewish Telegraphic Agency*, October 26, 2020, https://www.jta.org/2020/10/26/united-states/almost-all-american-jews-say-anti-semitism-is-a-problem-according-to-a-new-poll-half-of-americans-dont-know-what-it-means.

5. Blake Flayton, "On the Frontlines of Progressive Anti-Semitism," *New York Times*, November 14, 2019, https://www.nytimes.com/2019/11/14/opinion/college-israel-anti-semitism.html.

6. Walter Reich, "Seventy-Five Years After Auschwitz, Anti-Semitism Is on the Rise," *The Atlantic*, January 27, 2020, https://www.theatlantic.com/ideas/archive/2020/01/seventy-five-years-after-auschwitz-anti-semitism-is-on-the-rise/605452/.

7. Nicholas Wolterstorff, "Why Care About Justice?" *The Reformed Journal* 36:8 (August 1986): 9.

8. Monique Duson as quoted in, "Sex, Race & Identity—How Does the Gospel Answer the Critical Questions of Today?," YouTube video, 1:50:31, posted by Colson Center, September 18, 2021, https://www.youtube.com/watch?v=8xzZfBfkULI.

9. Neil Shenvi and Pat Sawyer, *Engaging Critical Theory and the Social Justice Movement* (ebook, Ratio Christi), 4, file:///C:/Users/Owner/Downloads/E-Book -Engaging-Critical-Theory-and-the-Social-Justice-Movement.pdf.

10. John Stonestreet and Shane Morris, "What Do We Do with Critical Theory?: Racism, White Privilege, and Christianity," BreakPoint, June 17, 2020, https://break point.org/what-do-we-do-with-critical-theory-racism-white-privilege-and-christianity/.

11. Allie Beth Stuckey, "Episode 451: On CRT, the Right Is Winning," July 8, 2021, in *Relatable with Allie Beth Stuckey* (podcast), 30:36, https://podcasts.apple.com/us /podcast/ep-451-on-crt-the-right-is-winning/id1359249098?i=1000528280119.

Chapter 11 Addiction

1. Nathan Yerby, "Statistics on Addiction in America," Addiction Center, accessed March 9, 2021, https://www.addictioncenter.com/addiction/addiction-statistics/.

2. Yerby, "Statistics on Addiction in America."

3. "How Porn Can Affect the Brain Like a Drug," Fight the New Drug, August 23, 2017, https://fightthenewdrug.org/how-porn-can-affect-the-brain-like-a-drug/.

4. "Teen Substance Abuse and Risk," CDC, accessed October 11, 2021, https:// www.cdc.gov/ncbddd/fasd/features/teen-substance-use.html; "The Rise of Teen Vaping," The Recovery Village, October 11, 2021, https://www.therecoveryvillage.com /teen-addiction/drug/teen-vaping/.

5. "Pornography Statistics."

6. For more info on the reward center and how porn can trigger it, check out "How Porn Can Affect the Brain Like a Drug," Fight the New Drug, https://fightthenewdrug .org/how-porn-can-affect-the-brain-like-a-drug/.

7. Valeriya Safronova, "A Private-School Sex Educator Defends Her Methods," *New York Times*, July 7, 2021, https://www.nytimes.com/2021/07/07/style/sex-educator -methods-defense.html.

8. C. S. Lewis, *The Weight of Glory* (San Francisco: HarperOne, 2001), 27.

9. Haley Seba, "How to (Realistically) Break Free From Sexual Addiction," The Rebelution, February 15, 2017, https://www.therebelution.com/blog/2017/02/how-to -realistically-break-free-from-sexual-addiction/.

Chapter 12 Media

1. Google search, s.v. "media," https://www.google.com/search?q=media.

2. Dhruba Karki, "Can You Guess How Much Data Is Generated Every Day?," Takeo, November 9, 2020, https://www.takeo.ai/can-you-guess-how-much-data-is -generated-every-day/.

3. Jacquelyn Bulao, "How Much Data Is Created Every Day in 2020?," *Tech Jury* (blog), September 9, 2021, https://techjury.net/blog/how-much-data-is-created-every-day/.

4. Maryam Mohsin as quoted in, "10 YouTube Stats Every Marketer Should Know in 2021," *Oberlo* (blog), January 25, 2021, https://www.oberlo.com/blog/youtube -statistics.

5. Nancy Pearcey, *Saving Leonardo: A Call to Resist the Secular Assault on Mind, Morals, and Meaning* (Nashville: B&H, 2010), 253–54.

6. "George Lucas: Heroes, Myths, and Magic; About George Lucas," *American Masters*, January 13, 2004, www.pbs.org/wnet/americanmasters/database/lucas _g.html.

7. Marshall Kirk and Erastes Pill, "The Overhauling of Straight America," Gay homeland.org, accessed June 16, 2021, http://library.gayhomeland.org/0018/EN/EN _Overhauling_Straight.htm.

8. Dannah Gresh, *Lies Young Women Believe: And the Truth That Sets Them Free* (Chicago: Moody, 2018), 160.

9. Samuel Johnson as quoted in James Boswell, *Boswell's Life of Johnson*, ed. Charles Grosvenor Osgood (New York: Charles Scribner and Sons, 1917), xviii.

10. Sara Barratt, *Love Riot: A Teenage Call to Live with Relentless Abandon for Christ* (Grand Rapids: Baker Books, 2020), 153.

11. See chapter 1 in Thomas Kersting, *Disconnected: How to Reconnect Our Digitally Distracted Kids* (Grand Rapids: Baker Books, 2020).

12. Jean M. Twenge, Thomas E. Joiner, and Megan L. Rogers, "Increases in Depressive Symptoms, Suicide-Related Outcomes, and Suicide Rates among U.S. Adolescents after 2010 and Links to Increased New Media Screen Time," *Clinical Psychological Science Journal* 6, no. 1 (November 14, 2017): 3–17, https://journals.sagepub.com/doi /abs/10.1177/2167702617723376?journalCode=cpxa.

13. Myers, *Understanding the Culture*, 158.

Chapter 13 Preparing for Pushback

1. Jaelene Daniels, "Controversial Decision Threatens Budding Soccer Career," *The 700 Club* news interview, CBN, accessed March 9, 2021, https://www1.cbn.com/video /SPR65v3/controversial-decision-threatens-budding-soccer-career.

2. Daniels, "Controversial Decision Threatens Budding Soccer Career."

3. Daniels, "Controversial Decision Threatens Budding Soccer Career."

4. Jaelene Daniels, Instagram post, June 26, 2015, https://www.instagram.com /p/4aCLOlD9sx/.

5. Valerie Richardson, "U.S. Women's Team Snub of Christian Player Roils Soccer," *Washington Times*, July 10, 2019, https://www.washingtontimes.com/news/2019/jul /10/jaelene-hinkles-world-cup-snub-sparks-debate/.

6. Daniels, "Controversial Decision Threatens Budding Soccer Career."

7. "Former Tech Great Jaelene Daniels Announces Retirement," TexasTech.com, November 4, 2020, https://texastech.com/news/2020/11/4/womens-soccer-former-tech -great-jaelene-daniels-announces-retirement.aspx.

8. Daniels, "Controversial Decision Threatens Budding Soccer Career."

9. David Platt, "God, Government, and the Gospel: Session Four—Biblical Truths Part 2," Secret Church 2020, June 23, 2020, as transcribed by the author, https://radical .net/?session=session-4-biblical-truths-part-2.

10. Brian Jones, *Hell Is Real: But I Hate to Admit It* (Colorado Springs: David C Cook, 2011), 141.

11. As quoted in Jeff Myers, "An Amazing Story of Hope," *Summit Journal* 15, no. 3 (April 2015): 2, https://www.summit.org/archives/journal/Summit_Journal_-_April _2015.pdf.

12. Jen Wilkin, *Women of the Word: How to Study the Bible with Both Our Hearts and Our Minds* (Wheaton: Crossway, 2019), 47.

13. "What Is Apologetics?," Bible.org, accessed October 15, 2021, https://bible.org /seriespage/1-what-apologetics.

Chapter 14 Taking Your Worldview into the World

1. Myers, *Understanding the Culture*, 117.
2. Gregory Koukl, *Tactics: A Game Plan for Discussing Your Christian Convictions* (Grand Rapids: Zondervan, 2009), 24–25.
3. Koukl, *Tactics*, 47.
4. Koukl, *Tactics*, 59.
5. Thanks to Scott Klusendorf for sharing this in his book *The Case for Life* (Wheaton: Crossway, 2009), 25.
6. Koukl, *Tactics*, 60.
7. Koukl, *Tactics*, 38.
8. Koukl, *Tactics*, 37.

Chapter 15 Culture Changers Then and Now

1. Annette Dumbach and Jud Newborn, *Sophie Scholl and the White Rose* (London: Oneworld Publications, 2006), 68.
2. Richard Hanser, *A Noble Treason: The Story of Sophie Scholl and the White Rose Revolt against Hitler* (San Francisco: Ignatius Press, 2012), 117–18.
3. Inge Jens, ed., *At the Heart of the White Rose: Letters and Diaries of Hans and Sophie Scholl* (Walden, NY: Plough Publishing House, 2017), 123.
4. Dumbach and Newborn, *Sophie Scholl and the White Rose*, 191.
5. Dumbach and Newborn, *Sophie Scholl and the White Rose*, 198.
6. Elena Perekrestov, *Alexander Schmorell: Saint of the German Resistance* (Jordanville, NY: Printshop of St Job of Pochaev, 2017), 80.
7. Hanser, *A Noble Treason*, 103.
8. Dumbach and Newborn, *Sophie Scholl and the White Rose*, 151.
9. Dumbach and Newborn, *Sophie Scholl and the White Rose*, 151.
10. Hanser, *A Noble Treason*, 251.
11. Dumbach and Newborn, *Sophie Scholl and the White Rose*, 159.
12. Hanser, *A Noble Treason*, 260.
13. Perekrestov, *Alexander Schmorell*, 132.
14. Hanser, *A Noble Treason*, 255.
15. Perekrestov, *Alexander Schmorell*, 139.
16. Hermann Vinke, *The Short Life of Sophie Scholl* (New York: Harper & Row, 1984), 112.
17. Vinke, *The Short Life of Sophie Scholl*, 72.
18. "Sexual Abuse Cover Up," Live Action, accessed June 18, 2021, https://www.liveaction.org/what-we-do/investigations/sexual-abuse-cover-up/.
19. Adelaide Darling, "Lila Rose Highlights Role of Faith in Fighting Abortion," Catholic News Agency, accessed March 10, 2021, https://www.catholicnewsagency.com/news/26403/lila-rose-highlights-role-of-faith-in-fighting-abortion.
20. Darling, "Lila Rose."
21. Mary Rose Short, "Lila Rose of Live Action: 'The Pro-Life Movement Is Growing,'" *National Catholic Register*, January 18, 2020, https://www.ncregister.com/interview/lila-rose-of-live-action-the-pro-life-movement-is-growing.
22. Short, "Lila Rose of Live Action."
23. Katy Carl, "Undercover and Over Obstacles—All for the Unborn," *National Catholic Register*, February 13, 2007, https://www.ncregister.com/features/undercover-and-over-obstacles-all-for-the-unborn.

24. Darling, "Lila Rose."

25. Justin Bell, "How Lila Rose Became Pro-Life . . . and Catholic," *National Catholic Register*, February 3, 2012, https://www.ncregister.com/news/how-lila-rose-became-pro-life-and-catholic-5pi856vs.

26. Darling, "Lila Rose."

27. Jessica Brain, "William Booth and the Salvation Army," Historic UK, accessed October 28, 2021, https://www.historic-uk.com/CultureUK/William-Booth-Salvation-Army/.

28. William Booth as quoted in "The Founder's Messages to Soldiers," *Christianity Today*, October 5, 1992, 48.

29. The Gospel Truth, "William Bramwell Booth," https://www.gospeltruth.net/booth/boothbioshort.htm.

30. The Salvation Army International, "Countries Where The Salvation Army Is Officially at Work," accessed October 15, 2021, https://www.salvationarmy.org/ihq/statistics.

31. The Gospel Truth, "William Bramwell Booth."

32. "'I'll Fight': 100 Years Since Booth's Final Address," The Salvation Army, accessed March 10, 2021, https://www.salvationarmy.org/nhqblog/news/2012-05-09-ill-fight-100-years-since-booths-final-address.

Conclusion

1. Matthew Parris, "As an Atheist, I Truly Believe Africa Needs God," *The Times*, December 27, 2008, https://www.thetimes.co.uk/article/as-an-atheist-i-truly-believe-africa-needs-god-3xj9bm80h8m (emphasis added).

2. Platt, *Counter Culture*, 272.

3. Platt, *Counter Culture*, 268–69.

4. Elisabeth Elliot, *Through Gates of Splendor* (New York: Harper & Brothers, 1957), 176.

5. Elliot, *Through Gates of Splendor*, 50–51.

6. Paul Lee Tan as quoted in Abdu Murray, *Saving Truth: Finding Meaning and Clarity in a Post-Truth World* (Grand Rapids: Zondervan, 2018), 44.

Sara Barratt is an author, speaker, and editor-in-chief for TheRebelution.com. Her passion is challenging and encouraging teens to live sold out and set apart for Jesus. When she's not writing or dreaming up a new book idea, she loves spending time with family and friends, taking long walks, drinking copious amounts of tea, and scribbling down random thoughts that eventually get lost in her purse. Come hang out with her on Facebook, on Instagram, and at her website, SaraBarratt.com.

Connect with
SARA

SARABARRATT.COM

 @SaraBarrattAuthor

BE BOLD AND
SHATTER EXPECTATIONS

Not content with safe religion that demands nothing of us,
Sara Barratt is calling you to stop giving in to the status quo and
devote yourself fully to Christ, following Him no matter what your
friends do or the culture around you promotes.

theReb

rebelling against low expectations

Imagine if teens woke up in the morning energized and ready to get out of bed because they knew they had a **purpose** and were **needed** in the world.

Here's the deal though:
**It's not just a fantasy we're imagining.
It's already happening.**

WELCOME TO THE REBELUTION.
TheRebelution.com

LIKE THIS
BOOK?
Consider sharing
it with others!

- Share or mention the book on your social media platforms. Use the hashtag **#StandUpStandStrong**

- Write a book review on your blog or on a retailer site.

- Pick up a copy for friends, family, or anyone who you think would enjoy and be challenged by its message!

- Share this message on Twitter, Facebook, or Instagram: **I loved #StandUpStandStrong by @SaraBarrattAuthor // @ReadBakerBooks**

- Recommend this book for your church, workplace, book club, or class.

- Follow Baker Books on social media and tell us what you like.

 ReadBakerBooks

 ReadBakerBooks

 ReadBakerBooks